THE
OUTSIDE

Public Cultures of the Middle East and North Africa

Paul A. Silverstein, Susan Slyomovics, and Ted Swedenburg, editors

THE
OUTSIDE

Migration as
Life in Morocco

ALICE ELLIOT

INDIANA UNIVERSITY PRESS

This book is a publication of

Indiana University Press
Office of Scholarly Publishing
Herman B Wells Library 350
1320 East 10th Street
Bloomington, Indiana 47405 USA

iupress.org

Manufactured in the United States of
America

First printing 2021

Library of Congress Cataloging-in-
Publication Data

Names: Elliot, Alice (Social
anthropologist), author.
Title: The outside : migration as life in
Morocco / Alice Elliot.
Other titles: Public cultures of the Middle
East and North Africa.
Description: Bloomington, Indiana :
Indiana University Press, 2021. |
Series: Public cultures of the Middle East
and North Africa | Includes
bibliographical references and index.
Identifiers: LCCN 2020048946 (print) |
LCCN 2020048947 (ebook) | ISBN
9780253054739 (hardback) | ISBN
9780253054746 (paperback) | ISBN
9780253054753 (ebook)
Subjects: LCSH: Immigrant families—
Morocco—Social conditions. | Emigrant
remittances—Morocco. | Morocco—
Emigration and immigration—Social
aspects.
Classification: LCC JV8978 .E54 2021
(print) | LCC JV8978 (ebook) | DDC
304.809664—dc23
LC record available at https://lccn.loc.
gov/2020048946
LC ebook record available at https://lccn.
loc.gov/2020048947

CONTENTS

Acknowledgments

This book would not exist without the kindness, trust, and intellectual generosity of Moroccan friends, neighbors, acquaintances, chance *grand taxi* travel companions on both sides of the Mediterranean Sea. Most are, following discussion and mutual agreement, anonymized in the book—but you know who you are. I am especially grateful to all the people I have met over the years in the Tadla, for the shared thinking and shared life at the heart of this book, for the unquestioning hospitality and teasing warmth, and for the lasting friendships. I want to thank, in particular, the families who opened their doors and lives to me during my doctoral fieldwork as well as my Tadla roommates for taking care of me when I first arrived and for being there ever since. I remain indebted to my language teacher Hassan Eddahabi, who taught me Moroccan Arabic with incomparable expertise, patience, and wit.

It has taken a long time to write this book, and it would have been impossible without the support of many people. Sara Randall has been there from the very beginning, supervising my undergraduate, master's, and PhD work, supporting me professionally and personally, opening her Shropshire home to me, and above all trusting me. I am deeply grateful to my anthropology companions for their vital friendship, thinking, and solidarity over the years and across countries: Karin Ahlberg, Ana Carolina Balthazar, Igor Cherstich, Alexandra D'Onofrio, Tobia Farnetti, Martin Fotta, Paolo Gaibazzi, Ashraf Hoque, Dimitra Kofti, Hege Høyer Leivestad, Laura Menin, Camilla Morelli, Carl Rommel, Julia Sauma, Nico Tassi, Cătălina Tesăr, Francesco Vacchiano, Antonia Walford, and the PrecAnthro collective. Alison Macdonald has been a colleague and a sister from the start, and I cannot thank her enough.

The UCL Department of Anthropology, the University of Bristol Department of Anthropology and Archaeology, and the Goldsmiths

Department of Anthropology have provided me with safe harbors for writing, teaching, and thinking over the years. Students and colleagues at Goldsmiths Anthropology, my anthropology home, have been a real strength and inspiration in good times and bad, as have Goldsmiths Justice for Cleaners/Justice for Workers comrades. Thank you to the KU Leuven Interculturalism, Migration and Minorities Research Centre, and especially to Noel B. Salazar for his continued support; Michael Stasik and the Bayreuth Academy of Advanced African Studies for a visiting fellowship at a crucial time in the writing; and All Souls College Oxford for an Evans-Pritchard Lectureship that provided me with feedback and confidence to finish the book—special thanks to David Gellner for the perfect hosting and to Marthe Achtnich and Ina Zharkevich for the instant solidarity.

Loubna Akhrif, Morgan Clarke, David Crawford, Robert Elliot, Lucia Enia, Michael Herzfeld, Martin Holbraad, Hasna Khatibi, Samuli Schielke, and Paul Silverstein have read the book at different stages of its evolution and have provided priceless feedback that has made it simply better. Michael Herzfeld has supported me over the years well beyond the call of duty of a PhD examiner—he believed in my work from the start and it has made all the difference. Samuli Schielke has become a precious mentor and a precious friend.

Research for the book was made possible by a UK Economic and Social Research Council studentship, a Research Foundation Flanders (FWO) Pegasus Marie Skłodowska-Curie Fellowship, and a Leverhulme Early Career Fellowship. Sections of chapter 3 first appeared in *Time & Society* (2016) 25(1), and a version of chapter 4 was first published in *American Ethnologist* (2016) 43(3). Thank you to everyone at Indiana University Press for transforming my writing into a book, and to Jennifer Crane for shepherding its production; to Paul Silverstein, Susan Slymovics, and Ted Swedenburg for welcoming my work to the PCMENA series and supporting the project from the start; and to Omar Oualili for helping me standardize my unruly Darija.

Finally, this book would not have been possible without family. My deepest thanks to my lifelong friends who have been there through thick and thin: Aziza Bouchnaoui, Alessandra Checchinato, Jihane Choukri, Diletta Diazzi, Hayat Eddine, Rose Hackman, Giacomo Lo Giusto, Alison Macdonald, Serena Matarese, Ania Obolewicz, Caterina Palli, Diego Rinaldi, Yeni Rizzuti, Eugenio Sorrentino, David Štefan, Joshua Surtees. Thank you to my Peverati, Elliot, Carli, and Ma family for their love. Thank you to my brother, Colin, and my parents, Carola and Rob, for being my safety and my inspiration. And thank you to Martin and Lila for everything.

Note on Transliteration

Moroccan Arabic, or Moroccan dialectal Arabic (Darija), does not have a standardized written form and varies significantly across regions as well as along gender, generational, and many other lines. In my rendering of the language, I have standardized the transliteration, which unavoidably compromises some of Darija's vibrant variations and regional specificity but hopefully helps with consistency and clarity across the book. I have mostly followed the transliteration method of the *Georgetown Classics in Arabic Language and Linguistics* volumes on Moroccan Arabic (Harrell and Sobelman 2015; Harrell 2004). I have, however, simplified diacritics to make the text more widely accessible—for example, the letter *s* is used to transcribe both س and ص (respectively, s and ṣ in standard transliteration) and the letter *h* for both ه and ح (respectively, h and ḥ in standard transliteration)— and consonants not found in English are rendered as follows:

غ *gh* (pronounced as a French *r*)
خ *kh* (as the last consonant in *Bach*)
ع ' (a voiced pharyngeal fricative)
ء ' (a glottal stop)

Hyphens are used to indicate a definite article, which is generally determined by the first sound of the word to which it is prefixed: *l-brra* (the outside), *d-dar* (the house), *le-bnat* (the girls). When quoting other authors and sources, I maintain the original transliteration—for example, *el ghorba* (state of feeling out of place, loneliness, homesickness) instead of *l-ghorba* when quoting Abdelmalek Sayad. I have left names of known figures and places as they are commonly recognized in English (hammam, souk, Casablanca).

THE
OUTSIDE

INTRODUCTION

"The outside is everywhere," Saliha murmurs as she looks down at her village from a hill of the Moroccan Middle Atlas. She extends her arms, gesturing to what stands below us, taking in the clustered village houses of varied shapes and heights, the paved and unpaved streets, the shops, the hammam, the mosques, the three buses rattling toward the village, the bustling market. From afar, with striking precision, she recites the transnational ties of each building, providing me with a visual census of her village's migratory trajectories: "Italy, Italy, Spain, Italy, America, Italy, France then Italy. . . ." Two of the mosques, she tells me, were built with *l-flus dyal brra* (the money of [the] outside). The bright sign advertising the hammam was shipped from France. We look down at the miniature people walking through the narrow alleyways, sitting at the cafés, shuffling through the market lanes. "*Kollhom f l-brra*" (they are all in the outside), Saliha says. "You see them here now, but they are also somewhere else: Italy, Spain, America, Saudi Arabia. There's even someone in Russia, I've heard. . . ." She pauses and then adds, "Anyway, if they are not in the outside, the outside is inside them" (*l-brra kayn fihom*).

The Mediterranean Atlas

This book is about the striking place migration has come to occupy in people's lives in contemporary Morocco, one of the major emigration countries in the world, with more than 10 percent of its total population living abroad. The book is about migration in its most intimate and dramatic guise, when it becomes the very foundation upon which forms of social and individual life are built. The book deliberately focuses on people, like Saliha, who have not yet migrated but who still reckon on a daily basis with the powerful reverberations of such a pervasive phenomenon, which, as an exemplary total social fact, brings into play the economic, religious, and aesthetic aspects of collective and intimate life. I show how migration acquires distinctive characteristics and properties when observed from the standpoint of so-called sending communities such as the Moroccan ones of this book. While grounded in ideas of past, present, and future movement, migration in Morocco goes beyond questions of movement, becoming an abiding force in the intimacy of everyday life—an imposing imaginative horizon toward which young graduates and young field laborers alike orient future expectations, a temporal rhythm that regulates encounters between kin, a nebulous bureaucratic machinery that administers hope and despair, and even a recognizable physical attribute marking returning spouses, who are said to be indelibly different because of "the outside" on their skin. Delving into Morocco's intimate experience of migration, my hope is to show how the very outlines of the socioeconomic construct of migration come to be recast when observed through the unusual lens of the places from which migration originates.

The book draws on my ethnographic research in a rural area of Morocco that has in recent decades become the epitome of the country's pervasive migratory inclinations. A mixture of agricultural and mountainous land, the Tadla is a rural region in central Morocco, at the foot of the Middle Atlas Mountains, where migration to Europe—particularly to Southern Europe—is ubiquitous and, in a sense, inescapable. Although migration from the Tadla gained momentum in the 1980s, later than in other regions of Morocco such as the northeastern Rif, today it is one of the regions with the highest levels of migration in the country. Indeed, movement to Italy and Spain has become one of its defining characteristics, to the point that I have heard people in Rabat, Morocco's capital, refer to the Tadla as *le-ʿrubiya dyal talyan*, which can mean both Italy's countryside and, disparagingly, Italy's peasants. The region is also sometimes referred to as *le triangle de la mort* (the triangle of death [French]), a chilling reminder of the ceaseless deaths in the Mediterranean Sea of young *harraga* (clandestine crossers, from the verb *haraqa*, to burn) from the area produced by European migration regimes, and a chilling testimony to the role migration has assumed in the administering of life, and death, in the region.

I first visited the Tadla in 2009, following in reverse the trajectories of Moroccan family friends and research interlocutors who had migrated to my northern Italian hometown in the early 1980s and thereafter. Reflecting major migration patterns linking rural central Morocco to northern Italian cities, most of my Moroccan acquaintances in Italy come from (in)famous "sending" towns and villages of the Tadla such as Béni Mellal, Khouribga, Fquih Ben Salah, and Ouled Youssef.[1] Others, although they migrated from working-class neighborhoods in the sprawling outskirts of major urban centers like Casablanca, have deep family ties within these rural central regions, from which either they or their parents moved not long before their migration to Europe.

My idea before leaving for the rural Tadla was to engage with families that had relatives abroad, and, with the relatives' help, begin to understand the effects of enormous out-migration. Once in Morocco, however, my focus kept slipping away from people who were directly involved with migration and toward everyone I met along the way: migration was "there" wherever I turned. Rather than narrowing down and becoming more focused over time, my field-site seemed to be constantly expanding, as if spilling out in different directions to include everything I observed, experienced, and encountered. As Saliha warned me from the top of the hill overlooking her village, I soon realized that migration, in the Tadla, is "everywhere."

In the Tadla, everyone seems to have at least one relative (if not a whole kinship group) living abroad, everyone seems to have planned to leave at some point in their life, and everyone's future plans seem to include references to *l-brra* (the outside). Migration slips into and often dominates everyday conversations and political debates, daydreams and nightmares, and wedding arrangements and religious consultations. Signs of migration can be seen everywhere in the Tadla's landscape. Carcasses of unfinished houses built by returning migrants dot the countryside in complex patterns, brash Spanish and Italian number-plated cars regularly roam the towns, and neon *Bar Italia* or *Café Paris* signs illuminate the streets, heralding the owners' successful or imagined migration projects. Migration and its geography are also part of the local soundscape, as I realized very early on in my fieldwork. The windows of the first room I rented in Zafiah, the Tadla migrant town at the heart of this book, overlooked a small square known in the neighborhood as *qisariya Milano* (Milan market), where men sell *le-hwayej dyal brra* (clothes/things of [the] outside). Their cries of "Bologna! Bologna! Bologna!"—the declared origin of the secondhand clothes and also my own area of origin—regularly woke me up in the morning.

During my first weeks in the Tadla, I was confronted with a realization I found myself grappling with throughout my fieldwork—and what has become, ultimately, the subject of this book. Migration is a fundamental ingredient of local life in the Tadla, something that goes beyond, not only in its actualization but also in its conceptualization, the movement of people from one country to another. The closer one looks at migration in Morocco, the more one realizes the depth of its involvement in the most intimate aspects of life. One of the aims of this book, then, is to show how migration comes to bear on the very principles, categories, imaginings, and practices around which local life unfolds and the ways in which it inflects the experiences of temporality, the nurturing of social relations, and the formation of personhood.

Crucially, however, rather than conceptualizing migration as a predetermined force—let alone one that is abstractly deterministic—a core theoretical aim of this book is to unpack the very notion of migration as a socioeconomic construct, making my interlocutors' conceptualizations and experiences of migration my analytical guide as well as my ethnographic point of departure. In other words, in the process of tracing how migration operates in the life of the Tadla, my aim in this book is to understand what it is as an ethnographically contingent object of study. The premise of this book is that to undertake a study of migration, one needs first of all—perhaps above all—to put the idea itself under ethnographic scrutiny. Because of its political and economic resonance, migration has become a high-profile, thorny topic, not only in local and international politics but also in academia and the social sciences. However, despite the unfaltering attention migration continues to receive in public and scholarly debates, limited attention has been devoted to understanding what migration actually is and is imagined to be for those involved in the national and transnational movements that shape it. Indeed, when analyses of migration consider migration's causes and effects, they often assume that the researcher, the researched, and the reader share an understanding of what migration means, experientially and conceptually, in the first place.

Eduardo Viveiros de Castro's (2003) plea for an anthropology that might be able to imagine each society as positing its own distinct problems, rather than as embodiments of a specific solution to a generic problem that is already known, is particularly salient and urgent in the study of migration. Economistic push-of-poverty-pull-of-wealth frameworks and the assumptions they inform, still so predominant in the social sciences as well as in broader public debate, persist in postulating the varied and socially specific forms that migration takes as variable solutions to what is assumed to be a generic problem—namely, a form of socioeconomic disadvantage. But what if this way of approaching the matter forecloses more basic questions about the many and varied things migration might be imagined to be in the first place and the ethnographically specific and specified problems it can be conceived as addressing?

In putting the question in this way, I do not wish to suggest that migration is not necessarily about socioeconomic disadvantages in Morocco. Throughout the book, we will see the many ways in which it is. Rather, as does Michael Scott (2000), I want to urge caution in focusing on isolated phenomena such as socioeconomic disadvantage per se without also asking "how these phenomena are manifestations of root assumptions about the nature of things and the relationship within total cosmological schemes" (57). My sense is that to begin to understand migration in Morocco or anywhere else, one needs to trace how it is part of what could be termed a complex and specific cosmology—a term that I use here in an uncomplicated sense, to refer to the ways in which people imagine the world and their existence within it (Humphrey 2014). Following in the steps of classic anthropological works about the cosmological underpinnings of pragmatic and imaginative reckonings with geopolitical "outsides" (MacGaffey 1968, 1972; Sahlins 1985) and works about the complex intersection of local cosmologies and migratory movement (Chu 2010; Malkki 1995; Newell 2012; Pandolfo 2007; Piot 1999), my sense is that close attention to local cosmologies and their specific ethnographic textures is crucial in the field of migration studies, where so often people's understandings of the elements that are involved in migration—conceptualizations of personhood, movement, and success, to take three indicative examples—are excluded from knowledge-making processes.

My point about the cosmological and ethnographic textures of migration is fundamentally methodological. It is, in other words, about the questions migration prompts us to ask, the location of our ethnographic and analytic thinking, and the ways in which knowledge about it is constructed. With important exceptions that have become my close travel companions in this book, my impression on navigating the extensive body of literature on migration is that too often critical questions are left unasked, resulting in analysis that is impervious to the conceptualizations and experiences of the people it claims to analyze. Much migration literature, for example, posits migration is about socioeconomic disadvantage but leaves unexamined not only the neoclassical macroeconomic foundations of this analytic model but also what "disadvantage," "the social," and "the economic" may be for the people involved. Some anthropologists of migration have framed this problem in the mainstream literature as a failure to take into account the existential dimension of transnational movement (e.g., Graw and Schielke 2012; Jackson 2013; Lucht 2012). My suggestion here is that the problem lies also in the fact that the rationale that guides the formulation of the analytical questions posed when talking about migration has remained largely unchallenged. As I see it, the challenge for contemporary migration scholarship is not only to acknowledge migration's varied cultural, social, and existential dimensions but also to expand the anthropological understanding of what migration might be in light of them—a matter not, in the first instance, of explaining or accounting for migration but rather of conceptualizing what might count as migration in the first place.

In this book, then, I start from the beginning, so to speak, by asking what migration may be, mean, and do for my interlocutors and attempt to ethnographically redraw migration's very texture and proportion in light of this. To do this, I suggest that it is important to begin from an ethnographic exploration of how migration is conceptualized, experienced, and reckoned with in those areas where it originates. This methodological and conceptual step is inspired primarily by the work of the late Algerian sociologist Abdelmalek Sayad (1999), one of the pioneering proponents of observing where migration begins rather than solely where migrants arrive. For Sayad, the sociology of migration must "imperatively start, not from the concerns and cleavages of the receiving society, but from the sending communities, their history, structure, and contradictions" (Bourdieu and Wacquant 2000, 174). With notable exceptions (e.g., Brettell 1986; Cohen 2004; Gardner 1995; McMurray 2001; Persichetti 2003), migration studies have traditionally focused on the phenomenon of immigration rather than emigration.[2] Although in recent years the focus has shifted at times, particularly in anthropology, to the study of "sending communities" (e.g., Atekmangoh 2017; Bellagamba 2011; Chu 2010; Ennaji and Sadiqi 2008; Gaibazzi 2015; Pedersen 2013; Piot 2019), the bulk of the literature remains firmly anchored in the study of "receiving countries." In this book, I have developed an analytical frame that has migration include not only the people who travel from one country to another or from village to city but also the myriad different elements that are implicated in this movement or, indeed, its imagination, starting from people who are not actually "on the move." By grounding my study in a so-called sending area, I have stretched the social phenomenon of migration to make it include its origins, so to speak. My suggestion is that by stretching migration geographically, by shifting ethnographic thinking from the places where migrants arrive to those from which they depart, it also becomes possible to stretch migration conceptually, opening a space for its ethnographic reimagination.

"The Outside" as Intimate Theory

At the heart of the book's geographical and conceptual "stretching" of migration lies the Moroccan notion of *l-brra*. Literally "the outside" in Moroccan Arabic, *l-brra* is the term used in the Tadla for the aim of migratory endeavors, referring mostly to Europe or "the West." Powerful force and shrewd metaphor, hopeful horizon and tragic bureaucratic machinery, *l-brra* is an exceptionally difficult concept/place/power to pin down, both ethnographically and theoretically.

At its most basic level, *brra* means outside, external, outdoors. *Brra* indicates exteriority (Bennani-Chraïbi 1994, 62): the exterior of a house, an open-air space, and, more traditionally, the country in contrast to the city. On a summer evening in the Tadla, people will say, "*yallah ngelsu brra*" (come on, let's sit outside). Plastic chairs or cushions are placed in the narrow street by the front door, and neighbors will sit chatting and watching people go by. *Brra*, in this context, simply means outdoors and can denote the intimate outdoors of the neighborhood, where people walk to the corner shop without needing to cover their indoor pajamas with a jellaba, the hooded robe worn by women and men. *Brra* can also denote a less familiar outdoors. If a Moroccan friend tells me "*lebsi le-hwayej dyal brra*" (wear the outside clothes/the clothes of [the] outside), it implies that we are going for an evening promenade in the medina, the lively old town center—or even perhaps that a coach journey to the urban metropolis of Casablanca has been planned.

In the context of migration, *brra*—often accompanied by the definite article *l*, making it *l-brra*, *the* outside—has acquired new and complex connotations in Morocco.[3] A synonym of *l-kharij* (outside, abroad, overseas), which comes from the verb *kharaja* (to exit, to leave a place), *l-brra* is a peculiar concept that means, simultaneously, a geopolitical space and an "imaginary elsewhere" (Yurchak 2005), a metaphor for technological and human advancement and a bureaucratic system erratically regulating the comings and goings of loved ones, a space of hope and possibility and an entity that can affect people's well-being and sanity. In other words, *l-brra* has properties that go well beyond its mere geographical positioning in fundamental ways.

My claim, then, is that in order to begin to understand what migration is and does in the Tadla, one needs to start through and with the complex local concept of *l-brra*. In the Tadla, migration is mainly about *l-brra*, and *l-brra* is mainly about desired, imagined, or actual migration toward it. *Hijra*, the Arabic word for migration, is rarely used in conversation, and I would tentatively say that, taken on its own, it doesn't mean much in local life. *Hijra* is not used when referring to one's own migrant son or daughter, nor when speaking of a leaving plan, nor when things linked to migration are discussed—foreign money, a neighbor's new car, visa applications, strange illnesses. *Hijra* is a rather abstract term used on TV and in newspapers, accompanying footage of overcrowded boats and menacing graphs, and not necessarily applicable to, say, one's migrant lover. It is *l-brra* that is referred to constantly and with familiarity when speaking of a migrant relative (*kayn f l-brra* or *huwa 'la brra* [he is/lives (in the) outside]), intentions (*gha nemshi l l-brra* [I am going to the outside]), or even a beautiful girl (*bhal shi brrania* [(she is) like an outsider]). The ubiquitous use of *l-brra* indicates more than just a local appropriation of the general, descriptive term *migration*. Rather, my sense is that it indicates that what is of significance about migration in the Tadla is *l-brra*, which both defines and shapes its nature.

Three main arguments about *l-brra* guide this book. The first is that *l-brra* is the constitutive feature of an entire cosmology and cartography in the Tadla, a "cultural geography of value" (Newell 2012, 207) within and through which not only migration but also crucial aspects of life are imagined, evaluated, and experienced. I use the term *imagination* here to refer to the creative ways in which my interlocutors speak of realities, relations, and futures that go beyond their immediate and tangible surroundings. Its use intends to evoke the anthropological/philosophical notions of "social imaginaries" (Comaroff and Comaroff 1999; Taylor 2004) and "imaginative horizons" (Crapanzano 2004) and thus to invoke the ways in which migration becomes part and parcel of the horizon within which people conceive of their lives and, in the same way, part of what Henrik Vigh (2009, 100), writing about Guinea Bissau migration, describes as the "imagined unfolding of social life which orients our movement and positions in the present." But rather than considering this migratory imaginary as a holistic and homogeneous cosmological background for action (see Strauss 2006), the book develops it as an active ingredient in people's lives that changes in close relationship with their tangible experience of *l-brra*.

Indeed, the second main argument of this book is that *l-brra* is not only part of the horizon within which people imagine the unfolding of their lives and their migratory trajectories. *L-brra* is also a concept/place/power that implicates itself in the practical progression of life in very concrete ways, manifesting itself at particular times like an entity or force in the intimacy of everyday life. *L-brra* is about filling in visa application forms, visiting a *fqih* (Muslim local cleric) for divine protection on an imminent Mediterranean crossing, dealing with the consequences of a migrant husband's absence, and restlessly waiting for the arrival of remittances. But *l-brra* can manifest itself also on more intimate, less conspicuous scales—in a recurrent nightmare, in a tender gesture between spouses, in a long pause during a conversation, in a murmured prayer. The question of scale becomes fundamental when attending ethnographically to *l-brra*. What should an anthropological engagement with something that is, as Saliha describes it, *everywhere* look like? Should a study of "the outside" be located in colonial history or in bodily practices? In migration data or in everyday domestic tensions? In geopolitical relations of value and power or in the silent tears for a migrant brother lost at sea?

While these contrastive questions are evocative, the issue of scale cannot, in reality, be addressed through an either/or framework when it comes to Moroccan migration—the whole point about *l-brra*, I would argue, is that it intersects radically different scales at once, defying any simple description, let alone, as I explore in chapter 6, theorization. Moving beyond what Anna Tsing (2005, 58) coins the dichotomy "between the global blob and local detail," my interest here is to trace the complex interpenetration of different orders of magnitude in my interlocutors' lives that takes place in the presence of migration: the scale, for example, of transnational migration and the scale of a woman's womb (chap. 3), the scale of geopolitical bureaucracy and that of divine and romantic hope (chap. 4). My choice has been to trace such "scalar work" in intimate details—observing the presence of *l-brra* in gendered bodies, for example (chap. 5), or tracing the constitutive role of migration in daily kinship relations (chap. 1). The book is, in this sense, an intimate ethnography of the everyday textures of *l-brra*—an "ethnography of the particular," in Lila Abu-Lughod's (1991) sense. Following in the steps of Abu-Lughod, my hope, however, is not to simply deliver quaint ethnographic details about a global political phenomenon that is already known. Rather, my ambition is to make such intimate details theoretically productive, key agents in the kind of anthropological stretching, expanding, and recasting of migration described above. Attention to migration's intimate textures at its origins—not only its feel, consistency, quality, and touch but also its operation, work, intrusion, and extrusion in the very emergence and progression of local life—has the power to reveal a different kind of object altogether and perhaps even redefine what migration as an object of study may be. The book is dedicated to this project of intimate redefinition—what Michael Herzfeld (2015, 18) defines as the anthropological art of finding "alternative realities in detail."

This project of intimate redefinition of migration is deeply linked with the specific historical as well as ethnographic landscapes from which it emerges. The third argument guiding this book, then, is that *l-brra* is a fundamentally contingent concept/place/power, its very shape and texture defined by the specific life circumstances through which it emerges and on which it operates—that is to say, the specific bodies, words, gestures, and households we will encounter in the book that actualize *l-brra* and are actualized through it. This means that this book is itself a constitutively contingent project, reflective of the specific time, place, and ethnographic relationships from which it has emerged. In the following two sections I outline some of the key contingencies that shape this book: from the long, varied, and ever-evolving history of migration in Morocco to the ethnographic, methodological, and relational landscape of my own engagement with *l-brra* in the Tadla. The fact that the book is mostly a synchronic rather than a diachronic study of *l-brra*—focusing on the manners in which *l-brra* was experienced and conceptualized during my ethnographic fieldwork rather than providing a broader historical account of its development—is an explicit attempt to capture the workings of such contingency in its everyday detail. But my synchronic focus on the intimate operations of *l-brra* is not meant to suggest that "the outside" is somehow static or ahistorical—as I argue in the conclusion, *l-brra*'s contingency makes it a fundamentally transforming concept/place/power (cf. Clancy-Smith 2012; Silverstein 2015). As we shall see, it also makes the need for a conceptual reimagination of *l-brra*—and of migration as an anthropological concern more broadly—a constant and humbling possibility.

Migrant Morocco

Morocco occupies a special place in the anthropological imagination (Rachik 2012). Particularly up to the late 1980s, the country was a crucial setting for the production of anthropological knowledge—segmentary models of political and social organisation were energetically debated in the High Atlas Mountains (Berque 1978; Gellner 1969; Hammoudi 1980), symbolic and interpretative anthropology was refined in the study of urban Morocco

(Geertz, Geertz, and Rosen 1979), and experimental engagements with so-called Moroccan Islam, ranging from psychoanalysis to theories of divine and social power, were to have lasting effects on the discipline (Crapanzano 1973; Eickelman 1981; Rabinow 1975). Today, Morocco imposes a new kind of ethnographic and theoretical thinking ground to anthropology. With a global diaspora estimated between three and four million, today Morocco is one of the world's main emigration countries, and Moroccan migration has become a social and economic force to be reckoned with on both sides of the Mediterranean and beyond.

While migration has always had important traction and power in Morocco—from different forms of internal migration (nomadic movement, seasonal transhumance, rural-urban exoduses) to transnational voyages like those of the iconic Moroccan medieval adventurer Ibn Battuta—the first consistent and substantial movement beyond the Moroccan border coincided with the French colonization of Algeria in the 1830s. Demand for laborers initiated a cycle of seasonal migrations between Algeria and, mainly, the eastern part of the Moroccan Rif Mountains (de Haas 2007b; Fadloullah et al. 2000). The establishment of a French protectorate in Morocco in 1912 (with the northern Rif and the deep south allotted to Spain) and the subsequent forty-four years of French "indirect rule" inflected the migratory destiny of the country in fundamental ways.

First and foremost, French colonialism dramatically increased rural-urban migration toward major cities like Casablanca. This internal migration was produced by new urbanization projects that offered, or promised to offer, work opportunities and by the transformation of a number of rural areas into large agricultural estates through the purchase or appropriation of land by French *colons* and associated local notables and protégés. Scholars of Morocco argue that the colonial appropriation of rural areas resulted in a de facto expropriation of fertile land that much of the local population used for cultivation or animal herding—which in turn produced a movement toward urban centers, particularly those along the Atlantic coast (Abu-Lughod 1980; Laroui 1970; Swearingen 1988; Vacchiano 2007). The area at the heart of this book, the Tadla, was directly implicated in this process as part of what the French labeled *le Maroc utile* (useful Morocco)—regions of the country identified as agriculturally rich and economically exploitable, drawing colonial settlement and investment. Indeed, a major colonial irrigation project was implemented in the Tadla plain from the mid-1930s (Préfol 1986), which both attracted labor to the area and triggered an out-migration of peasants toward Casablanca.

Colonialism also played a part in the shaping of Moroccan international movements. During World War I, France recruited Moroccan men, mainly from the southwestern regions, for its industries, mines, and army, and men were also recruited during World War II and for the subsequent wars in Korea and French Indochina (see Maghraoui 1998, 2004). Labor migration continued in peacetime, and Moroccan migration to France slowly gained momentum. Hein de Haas (2007b), scholar of Moroccan migration, suggests that France strategically selected laborers in an attempt to curb political unrest, often recruiting workers from the Tamazight-speaking internal regions—what colonial ethnographers and government officials called the "land of dissidence" (*blad s-siba*) (see Burke 2014)—where there was major resistance to colonial power and more generally to urban state authorities. This strategy, de Haas argues, was then appropriated by the *makhzen* (government) itself following independence through the selective issuing of Moroccan passports.[4]

The end of the French Protectorate (1956) did not end migration flows, neither internal nor international. Whereas until the 1950s Moroccan migrants were mainly seasonal workers in Algeria and France, migration in the 1960s began to take a longer-term character and head toward new destinations. An increasing demand in Europe for "guest workers" led to the signing of work recruitment agreements between Morocco and former West Germany, France, Belgium, and the Netherlands. However, migration was also beginning to take place independently of formal agreements between states, and by the late 1960s Moroccans were moving to Europe through family connections with already settled migrants, informal work recruitment, tourist visas, and other legally sanctioned and unsanctioned migration routes. De Haas positions the Moroccan "migration boom" in this historical period: Moroccan nationals in Europe increased from about thirty thousand in 1965 to over four hundred thousand a decade later.[5]

The sudden severe restrictions on legal entry to France, Belgium, and Holland in 1973–74, directly linked to the 1973 oil crisis and the ensuing period of economic stagnation and industrial restructuring, brought about a change in the structure and composition of Moroccan migration. First, the increasingly restrictive migration policies, rather than triggering mass returns, led to the permanent residency of migrants in Europe, interrupting, in this way, "the traditional, circular character of Moroccan migration" (de Haas 2007b, 46). Second, family reunifications and reformations became one of the only ways to enter France, Belgium, and Holland legally, and around this period there began to be a rise in Moroccan migrant women moving to Europe (Salih 2003). Third, and crucially for the setting of this book, the closing of the borders of countries of traditional Moroccan migration resulted in a new movement toward Italy and Spain, countries just on the other side of the Mediterranean that had not yet developed a comprehensive system of migration control and had a high demand for migrant labor in agriculture, construction, care, and other services (Berriane et al. 2015; Persichetti 2003). Initially, migration to southern Europe had a circular and seasonal character, and Moroccans could travel freely back and forth (see Alzetta 2006)—as we shall see, however, just as with the guest worker generation, migration restrictions and border controls would soon interrupt this circular flow.

It was in this historical period, when the borders of countries traditionally involved in Moroccan migration were closing, and southern European countries like Italy and Spain were moving from being emigration countries to immigration ones, that migration from the central Moroccan rural areas of the Tadla gained momentum that would transform the region, in just over two decades, into one of the main emigrant areas of the country.[6] The Tadla had always been marked by intense internal migration, with people moving either to coastal cities like Casablanca or within the area itself, mainly from more rural and mountainous villages to medium-size urban centers such as the phosphate town of Khouribga.[7] From the 1970s, internal and international migration began to converge. Today, Khouribga, for example, is one of the three apexes of the "triangle of death" I mention above: together with Fquih Ben Salah and Béni Mellal, other core emigrant towns of the Tadla, Khouribga marks out the central Moroccan area characterized by imposing migration toward Italy.

The pioneers of the Tadla migration are often identified as the Ouled Meskin, an Arabic-speaking kin group of livestock breeders and farmers whose traditional territory spans the Tadla area (Capello 2008, 105). The Ouled Meskin were some of the first to leave for Italy in the late 1970s and profoundly influenced the development of migration from the region in the years to follow. Originally living off impoverished, drought-stricken land, the Ouled Meskin, in a period when Italy's borders were still open and transnational movement was significantly easier than today, were able, through their seasonal work in Italy, to buy fertile land in the Tadla Plain, move their families to more urban centers, and build new, imposing houses (Capello 2008, 105). The Ouled Meskin set up a migration network between the Tadla and Italy that has sustained transnational movement up to the present day. The origins of this migration movement are distinctly rural—the image of Tadla migration as one of *'rubiyin/'rubiya* (peasants, a term that, in certain contexts, has scornful connotations) is still dominant in contemporary Morocco, affecting, as we shall see, the presentation and self-presentation of people of the area. However, shortly after its inception, Tadla migration quickly came to involve different sections of the population, from lower class peasants to lower-middle-class urban dwellers to middle-class university-educated families, and remains to this day a deeply cross-sectional reality.

The Moroccan population in Italy has increased exponentially since the first Ouled Meskin travels of the 1970s—the figure of 136 Moroccan citizens officially residing in Italy in 1970 (Salih 2003) had risen to more than 400,000 in 2019 (ISTAT 2019)—and Tadla migration has transformed substantially over the years, as is the case for Moroccan migration more generally. In 1990–91, Italy and Spain introduced visa requirements to comply with Schengen agreements, with drastic consequences, as we shall see, on the routes and patterns of Tadla migration; the Mediterranean passage has become increasingly and purposely deadly, actively transformed by European migration policies into a space of migrant death and part of what Ruben Andersson (2014) describes as a multimillion "illegality industry";[8] as with France and other traditional "receiving" countries of Moroccan migration in the early 1970s, family reunification visas have become one of the only ways to enter Italy and Spain legally, contributing further to the gender and generational diversification of migrants; and most Moroccans in Italy today are no longer seasonal migrants like their Ouled Meskin predecessors but are instead living in the country long-term. Such permanency is often linked to the formation of families and reflects a major shift from Moroccans being a marginal all-male presence to an integral multigenerational component of Italy's social fabric. But permanency is also linked, as we shall see in the case of many of the protagonists of this book, to what Nicholas De Genova (2002) calls sociopolitical processes of "illegalization" across Europe, which produce and reproduce migrant "illegality," a status that invariably truncates transnational movement—and consequently interrupts, I will be arguing, the lives and ties linked to these movements on both sides of the Mediterranean.

Finally, although it has not involved the Tadla in a major way, one last meaningful development in the Moroccan migratory landscape needs to be mentioned. While remaining a "sending country" par excellence, Morocco has also evolved, since the mid-1990s, into a destination country for migrants from sub-Saharan Africa, Europe, and elsewhere. Morocco has increasingly become not only a place of transit but also a destination for a variety of people, with tens of thousands of migrants settling in major cities like Casablanca, Fez, and Rabat, bringing to the surface questions of economic and political rights, religious pluralism and national identity, collective memory and future belonging (Bachelet 2019; Berriane et al. 2015; Khrouz and Lanza 2015). How these multiple and multidirectional human movements will affect the future of Morocco is difficult to predict, but it may well be that a new chapter in the country's migration biography has opened.

Field and Method

This book is the result of a longstanding multiscalar and multilayered encounter with Morocco, an encounter that started in my Italian hometown with stories about *le-blad* ([one's] country/land/home) of Moroccan family friends, acquired ethnographic substance when I moved to live in the Tadla region for a year and a half for my doctoral fieldwork, and continues to develop, surprise, and keep me on my anthropological toes through regular visits to Morocco and Italy, and through old friendships and new encounters with Moroccans living on both sides of the Mediterranean Sea.

The main bulk of the book's ethnography comes from the seventeen months of fieldwork I conducted in the Tadla region between March 2009 and July 2010. Rather than an administrative region, *the Tadla* or *the Tadla region* refers to the mostly Arabic-speaking area of central Morocco that includes the fertile Tadla plains at the foot of the Middle Atlas Mountains and its surrounding rural territories that extend toward the Atlantic coast. Mostly contained within the administrative boundaries of the Béni Mellal-Khénifra region, where the major "sending hubs" of migration toward Southern Europe are located (Béni Mellal, Khouribga, Fquih Ben Salah, Ouled Youssef), fieldwork often crossed regional and provincial boundaries to follow interlocutors' movements and their family ties. In this sense, fieldwork in Morocco was, and continues to be whenever I return, of a distinctly mobile nature, with its barycenter in one of the Tadla's main emigrant towns, which I have named Zafiah,[9] but characterized also by movement between different emigrant households scattered across the Tadla region and beyond.

The rural town of Zafiah became my base mainly by coincidence and by virtue of the kind of disarming hospitality that has always shaped my stays in Morocco, which I discuss below. When Amal, a young woman I met in

Rabat through mutual acquaintances, heard about my plan to do research in the Tadla, she took me with her on one of her visits home in the outskirts of Zafiah and told me I could (indeed, should) stay for as long as I wished with her family. Amal's family welcomed me immediately into their home and took it upon themselves to introduce me to le-'rubiya (the countryside). When I first met them in 2009, the Ghzaouli family was made up of two children (Amal's niece and nephew), their mother, their two (paternal) uncles, and their (paternal) grandmother. The children's father, Amal's eldest brother, was (and remains to this day) a migrant in Italy—we will learn more about his migratory story in chapter 5, where I describe one of his complex visits home from l-brra. The Ghzaouli family quickly became my safe harbor in the first stages of my fieldwork, offering me not only a place to stay but also real welcoming warmth, affection, and protection. My early months in Zafiah were spent following the daily routines of the Ghzaouli family, getting to know their neighbors and relatives, and visiting other emigrant families in both Zafiah and its surrounding rural areas.

These early months were also spent learning to communicate in Darija, a variety of colloquial Arabic and the most widely spoken language in Morocco.[10] I had studied Modern Standard Arabic, or Fusha, before moving to Morocco, and I attended Darija classes in Rabat before starting my Tadla fieldwork. But when I first arrived in Zafiah, my language skills were, to put it generously, limited: Darija is an unwritten language, distinct from other strands of Arabic, and generally learned by full immersion in Moroccan social life rather than solely through academic study. Learning Darija quickly became an integral part of my research and a powerful way of creating and developing new bonds, as people would actively involve themselves in my progress, teaching me new expressions, explaining the origins and roots of words, providing me with Tamazight translations, and so on. In fact, Darija remains one of the most challenging and rewarding dimensions of my ongoing engagement with Morocco, mainly because of the intrinsic dynamism, shrewdness, and nonconformity of this language, which makes it impossible to ever feel entirely comfortable or settled with one's knowledge—a feeling that epitomizes almost perfectly, for me, the more general experience of doing research in Morocco.

As my first summer in the Tadla approached, fieldwork became an intense series of movements between the Ghzaouli household and different towns and villages of the Tadla, as Moroccan friends and acquaintances living in Italy returned for their summer holidays and invited me to their family homes. Although quite intense—delicately balancing multiple offers of hospitality and constant travelling on buses, coaches, taxis, and carts across the Tadla countryside and beyond—these summer months gave me a real perspective on the complexities and joys of "coming home" for long-term migrants as well as satisfying updates on life back in my Italian hometown. After a summer of intense traveling, I returned to Zafiah. My return coincided with the beginning of the academic year—Zafiah, home to one of the few universities in the Tadla, was being repopulated by students who had gone home for the summer break. Though I continued spending a lot of time at the Ghzaouli household, I rented a room in the center of town with a group of students who had come down from their Atlas Mountain villages for the term. While I was still sharing living and sleeping spaces with roommates and flatmates, renting a room in Zafiah was an enjoyable change after many months spent as a guest (*difa*) in other people's homes. The new living arrangement also allowed me to spend time with young, unmarried women away (at least partially so) from the gaze of their own kin, a specific kind of social and ethnographic setting I explore in chapter 4. Like the Ghzaouli family, my roommates, whom we will meet properly in chapter 4, quickly became and remain a key point of reference for my thinking and living in the Tadla. Perhaps because we were exactly the same age, or because we shared, among the many differences, the fact of being young students away from home, or because, as one of my very first roommates still puts it, "*kan mektab*" (it was destiny), a strong bond that I can call only friendship quickly formed between us and remains to this day.

Although I was now renting a room in Zafiah and developing close ties with the town, my movements between different households in the Tadla continued throughout the rest of my fieldwork, as I followed up the relationships formed during the summer months. Someone would call me, for example, to invite me to the wedding of a relative or to the circumcision ceremony of a sister's son: "so you can see our tradition(s) (*taqalidna*)," they would say over the phone in a gently mocking but always warmly welcoming tone. Over time, and with the development of deeper bonds with some members of these households, invitations and visits stopped being triggered only by major social events. Women would call me and tell me to go and visit them "*bash takli shi haja mezyana*" (so you [get to] eat something good), the assumption being that, away from my family, I was eating badly and was lonely at mealtimes. These visits could last three days or two months, depending on the tempo of invitations, my relationship with the family, and whether specific events were taking place in a certain home or village—the return of a migrant husband, the birth of a new child, kin negotiations surrounding the marriage of a daughter, the selling of family land to a migrant neighbor, and so on.

People's offers of hospitality were as complex as they were touching. The fact that I was a young, unmarried foreign woman made this hospitality even more powerful, as some households, and especially some household heads, saw it as their duty to ensure my safety and take care of me in all my movements. *Dyafa* (hospitality), however, could be negotiated and managed, and very rarely did I feel like a "captive guest" (Swancutt 2012, 103) without the possibility of carving out my space in the web of relations that quickly formed around me. With its characterizing "versatile unpredictability" (Herzfeld 2012, 210) that other anthropological writings have ascribed to it (Candea and da Col 2012; Dresch 2000; Herzfeld 1987; Rabinow 1977; see also Elliot 2020), hospitality in many ways defined my field site, as it was through the many offers of "*aji l darna mrehba bik*" (come to our house, you are welcome) that the direction, timing, and rhythm of my movements across the Tadla were defined—and through which my ethnographic material slowly emerged.

Over time, the initial sense of directionless movement between "arbitrary locations" (Candea 2007, 167) that accompanied the first stages of my fieldwork dissipated, and although my work invariably remained multisited, or, rather, multihousehold, my movements took on a certain pattern, with certain families, and in particular certain family members, becoming so-called primary interlocutors—or, more simply, friends, though I am aware of the unresolved complexities of using (as well as avoiding) the concept of friendship in the context of research (Gay Y Blasco and Hernández 2020). These were specific people and households—such as the Ghzaouli family, or the household of Hasna and her daughter Sakina, whom we will meet in chapter 1, or the wives of migrants Salima and Habiba at heart of chapter 3—whom I would visit with more frequency and with whom I would spend more time and share more intimate dimensions of our lives. Rather than providing a holistic perspective on Moroccan migration, I have come to see the different relationships that I formed with these households and people as precious partial openings to the complexity of migration and of social life in the Tadla (Candea 2007).

When I was not moving between households, my fieldwork consisted mainly of trying to engage with and participate in family daily routines. Although I did get better at this over time, the clumsiness and oddness that my hosts spotted in me, even when carrying out the simplest tasks (peeling potatoes, say, or sweeping the floor), never allowed my participation to be completely "ordinary" (cf. Rabinow 1977). I tended to follow the routines of the women of the family, which generally involved getting up very early in the morning to knead the bread dough, preparing breakfast for the rest of the household, washing up, cleaning the house, preparing lunch, and so on until the evening, with a few welcome pauses (depending on the household) to watch an episode of a favorite Turkish/Egyptian/Mexican TV series, or for drinking invigoratingly sweet mint tea and chatting with neighbors and relatives passing by. Along with daily chores, I accompanied women to the weekly souk, to the hammam, to see doctors, to the bank, on visits to neighbors and relatives, and so on. In the evenings we watched TV with the rest of the family, listened to stories told by the older relatives, went for strolls to the medina, and, in the summer, sat outside the house, chatting with neighbors and catching the evening breeze.

The subject of this book, "the outside," permeated my fieldwork. People would invoke *l-brra* during a conversation, tell me a story about their migrant brother, ask me advice about a visa application, or get me to listen to a song about *l-harag* (the burning—i.e., undocumented migration). *L-brra* was *there* all the time—in the Italian cooking pans, in the trips to a Western Union branch to collect a husband's remittances, in the distraught conversations about a neighbor's son's death in his attempt to cross into Europe. It became clear to me quite early on that my methodology could not be limited to, say, formal interviews about *l-hijra* (migration)—*l-brra* was intrinsic to daily life, and my research demanded close listening to such intimate presence. Explicit questions were of course asked, particularly in the earlier stages of my fieldwork, both about the nature of *l-brra* (though see chap. 6 for a discussion of the limits of descriptive questions and answers about "the outside") and about the migratory desires of my hosts, neighbors, friends, and acquaintances. However, my ethnographic understanding slowly emerged mainly through informal conversation, careful listening, and close engagement in daily routines.

My periodic returns, in between family visits, to my rented room in Zafiah became important moments for ethnographic reflection. Here I got to spend some time with the recordings I had managed to take during my trips across the Tadla as well as to discuss with the young women I lived with events that I found unclear, interesting, or troubling. These gripping collective exchanges, which generally also involved other students and acquaintances who were regularly coming by the house, often developed into deep, intense debates about their and my varied understandings of issues ranging from Islamic feminism to peasant versus urban versus migrant existence, and have become key ethnographic and conceptual guides for this book.

People and Voices

Overall, the protagonists of this book are from relatively similar backgrounds: from modest rural households (ʿrubiyin [or ʿrubiya]—peasants, as they are sometimes called disparagingly in Casablanca or Rabat, and as they often describe themselves with a hint of both pride and irony) whose close relatives live abroad. In most cases, the household economy of these families depends mainly on remittances supplemented at times by the employment of other (mainly men) household members—either in the countryside (e.g., fruit picking) or in the Tadla's bigger towns (e.g., construction work). The book is also the result of encounters with people from very different backgrounds and biographies: the *mdiniyen* (city dwellers) like Amal Ghzaouli, my Zafiah "gatekeeper," who live in the big urban centers of Casablanca and Rabat and who return from time to time to the Tadla to visit their relatives, the Zafiah middle- and upper-middle-class families I mention in chapter 5 who have sent their offspring to study *f l-brra* (in the outside), the young teachers we will meet in chapter 2, who have moved from their Amazigh mountain villages to work in state and private schools in the Tadla and beyond. Depending on the topic, these multiple voices are at times evoked together and at times carefully distinguished to trace the distinctive textures *l-brra* takes in different lives in the area.

Although the book draws on a variety of voices, not all the relevant voices are there, nor are all voices given equal weight in my writing. First, this work is mainly the result of my encounters, engagements, and exchanges with Tadla women, and a lot of it, though not all, is written from the perspective of these engagements. During fieldwork, I always interacted, when possible, with all the members of the households I visited and engaged with different generations and differently positioned kin members. Invariably, however, when it came to deeper bonds and greater levels of (mutual) trust, these were generally with women. This was mainly because of the more intimate spaces we shared. I generally shared a room with the women of the family—unmarried women, widowed women, or, as we shall see in chapter 3, women whose husbands were abroad. I accompanied women to the hammam and the gynecologist; I stood around while they cooked dinner and got on with their daily routines. Although I did get close to some men during my stay, particularly older household heads and young boys, this was a very different kind of closeness, based on mutual respect rather than on the sharing of intimate spaces.

Second, this book is mainly focused on nonmigrant women. In other words, this is mainly a study about the relatives of migrant *men*. Although migration of women from the Tadla has always existed (on Moroccan migrant women, see, e.g., Ait Ben Lmadani 2018; Cheikh and Péraldi 2009; El Ghali 2005; Salih 2003), it is mostly men who leave, and it is men who generally leave first, to be joined later (at times) by their wives. As I explain in the chapters to follow, in the Tadla, migration remains, in large part, a male affair.

Third, migrant men are also, in a sense, absent from this book. Indeed, although a great part of this book is about migrant men, very little of it is written from a migrant's perspective. This is not only because of my greater access to and intimacy with women. It is also because migrant men are mostly absent from the daily life of the Tadla: to study migrant men in the Tadla is to study the "presence of an absence" (Agamben 1999, 179). Because of their fleeting presence in the Tadla, I was not able to develop the kinds of relationships I shared with their nonmigrant relatives, making the perspectives of the latter take center stage in this book. This partiality reflects the very nature of an emigrant field site where migrants are, by definition, mostly absent and where their subjectivities are often spoken, shaped, and judged by others—as Sayad (2004, 125) writes in his work on the Algerian migration to France, "the paradox of the science of emigration is that it appears to be a 'science of absence' and of absentees." However, it is true that the absence of migrants' voices can be seen as a shortcoming of the book, and it is a luxury to be able to find some of these voices in other anthropologists' work on Moroccan and North African migration (e.g., Capello 2008; Ilahiane 2003; McMurray 2001; Sayad 1999; Schielke 2020; Silverstein 2004a)—a body of work that should perhaps be seen as this book's unwitting companion.

A final preliminary reflection on field and method relates to my identity as a researcher. It is not always easy to determine how different dimensions of who we are and who we are perceived to be shape our ethnographic work in different ways and at different stages of our research trajectories. There are certain elements that for me have always been obvious determining factors in my work in Morocco—for example, my gender, my nationality, my family status, my *gauriya* (Western, white foreigner) positioning. But there is nothing essentially obvious or given about any of these identity markers—they have always been deeply situational, relational, and unsettled, part and parcel of the situational, relational, unsettled nature of anthropology itself. For example, I have already hinted at some of the ways in which being a woman shaped my doctoral fieldwork. But what probably defined me more obviously as a specific kind of person, at least in certain situations and encounters, was that I was an unmarried and childless woman in a context where, as we will see throughout the book, family status matters a great deal in the definition and recognition of personhood (see also Crawford 2013; Kapchan 2013; Rignall 2013).

Similarly, the fact that I come from a place that many in the Tadla have left for, and many others are waiting and hoping to move to, undoubtedly played a role in my ethnographic work (see also Chu 2010). But it is difficult to assess the extent to which my *brrania* (from "the outside"/foreigner) origins affected and affect the nature of my relationships in and with Morocco. My impression is that the people I know and meet in Morocco mainly see my foreignness as both a vulnerability, and thus tend to put me under their protection, and as a sign of relative ignorance, and thus see it as their duty to explain to me, say, a complex passage in the Quran or what they identify as a specific Moroccan (or, depending on the context, Muslim, Amazigh, Arab, peasant, or simply *dyalna* [ours]) practice or norm. In other words, I have never felt that I generate particular interest by virtue of being from "the outside." I suspect that if my origins were rooted in a different, less familiar "outside," reactions to my presence would perhaps be different. But decades of migration have generated a sense of familiarity with Italy and with Italian words, currencies, customs, and, indeed, researchers—a familiarity that, I think, makes me also more familiar.

As well as this, my *brrania* status does not tend to generate, apart from in a few scattered cases, particular requests for help to reach "the other side." During my fieldwork people would ask me to accompany them to the Italian consulate in Casablanca or to help them with visa applications and other bureaucratic procedures, but rarely did people ask me to involve myself in their quest for *l-brra*. I am unsure whether this was out of respect, pride, or kindness—or because they thought me too young, naïve, and perhaps socially unconnected to be of any real, practical help in their migratory projects. The fact is that my connection with *l-brra* is rarely mentioned in these functional terms, even by people I know are eager to leave, making my personal and research relationships more easily inhabitable on this front. But the glaring disparity, and its deadly consequences, between myself and the protagonists of this book when it comes to access to "the outside," and to travel more generally, remains an unavoidable specter in my work and what ultimately pushes me to write with resolution and care.

Finally, there are many other dimensions of our identity as ethnographers that are less obvious, or that emerge only in specific encounters, or that reveal themselves years after an exchange has been experienced, reflected upon, even written about and published. For example, the first stories I collected as a young student about motherhood and repeated miscarriages in the Tadla (chap. 3) really hit home for me much later, when I myself went through two painful miscarriages. I do not know whether I would have understood these stories more or less had I experienced pregnancy and loss before rather than after my doctoral fieldwork. Just as I do not know whether this experience might have made, as many Moroccan friends suggest, Islamic conceptions of destiny more immediately comprehensible to me, and perhaps even made redundant my whole conceptual detour in chapter 4 on Max Weber and Ash'ari theology in my attempt, as Marisol de la Cadena (2015, 4) frames it, to translate what I was being told "into what I could understand." Either way, the point I am trying to make here is that recognizing our relational positionality and its multiple roles in the production of anthropological knowledge is not always straightforward and settled—and perhaps never should be (see Covington-Ward 2016; Neale Hurston 2009; Strathern 2004)—but rather is a lasting process that informs the very nature of this book.

The Chapters

The book develops around six chapters, each exploring different ways in which migration and life permeate and constitute one another in the Tadla. I begin, in chapter 1, Tempos of Life, by tracing how *l-brra* implicates itself in the pace, rhythm, and tempo of everyday life in the Tadla and the complex ways in which bureaucratic, political, and economic regimes operating in Europe permeate the area. I focus in particular on the ways in which the rhythms of migrants' returns and departures shape the unfolding of both kinship relations and intimate bodily practices, *l-brra* becoming both imaginative frame and inescapable content of family relations and bonds of love and care. In chapter 2, The Outside Inside, I take a closer look at "those who go"—one of the local expressions for migrants, fundamental figures in the Tadla's imaginative and intimate reckoning with migration. I trace how *l-brra* permeates migrants "from within" (*men l-dakhel*) and develop an argument about migration as above all a manner of deep, constitutive transformation—one that, socially speaking, is as potent as it is perilous. In chapter 3, Wives of Elsewhere, I trace the textures life acquires for those married to these intimately transformed men and show how the "wives of the outside," as women married to migrants are sometimes called in the Tadla, grapple with the everyday practicalities of absence and waiting, the decades-long migration of their husbands permeating the understandings of themselves as gendered subjects. Developing further the analysis of migration's constitutive role in the formation of specific forms of subjectivity, in chapter 4, Beautiful Futures, I focus on a younger generation of women, unmarried university students, and trace the ways in which they imagine themselves as specific kinds of modern, gendered, and pious subjects in and through *l-brra*. Tracing the complex intersection between migratory desires, romantic ideals, and Islamic notions of divine destiny, I show how *l-brra* plays a constitutive role in the ways in which young women prepare themselves for a livable future. Bringing the book's argument full circle and returning to the controversial figure of the migrant introduced in chapter 2, in chapter 5, The Gender of the Crossing, I reflect on the complex meaning and practice of manhood when it is intersected with the powerful entity of "the outside." I focus, in particular, on the emotional, structural, and physical work required of Moroccan migrant men in order to remain men despite all odds, and frame masculinity as a particularly precarious achievement. It is through these precarious bodies that migration reveals itself most powerfully as an enthralling and tragic balancing act, where the stakes are as high as can be: differences between life and death, achieved and failed manhood, future and futility. In chapter 6, The Outside, I build on the ethnography of previous chapters to reflect on the beguiling place/concept/power at the heart of the book and on the multiple meanings and textures it acquires in Tadla daily life. I focus in particular on the peculiar ethnographic and conceptual resistance *l-brra* poses to its own theorization and address the possibilities and limits of defining and framing both *l-brra* specifically and the phenomenon of migration more generally. I develop the question of the theorization of migration further in the conclusion, Migration as Life, where I address the problems *l-brra* poses to dominant understandings of migration and outline the possibility of a different kind of ethnographic thinking about contemporary migrations—one that is able to capture the constitutive and contingent relationship between migration and life and thus develop a conceptual and political imagination of migration that is both humble and expansive.

Notes

1. Names of cities, town, and villages, as well as those of admirative areas, are spelled following the Moroccan 2014 census (HCP 2014).

2. For clarity and consistency, throughout the book I use the terms *migration* and *migrants* rather than the more specific *emigration* and *emigrants* (and *immigration* and *immigrants*). This is also because there is a sense of permanency in the formal English definitions of both emigration ("the act of leaving one's own country to settle permanently in another and immigration" [Oxford Dictionaries]) and immigration ("the action of coming to live permanently in a foreign country" [Oxford Dictionaries]) that, as we shall see, does not fit well with the experience and imagination of transnational movement addressed in this book. I do use *emigration* in a few cases where the direction of migration is key for the discussion—e.g., "emigrant neighborhoods" rather than "migrant neighborhoods" to indicate that many people from these areas live abroad, or "emigrant household" rather than "migrant household" to indicate that one or more family members live abroad, a defining attribute for the whole household, as I discuss in chapter 2.

3. The use of the definite article before *brra* varies from speaker to speaker and also depends on sentence construction. The article is present in sentences such as *l-brra hsen men hna* (the outside is better than here) and *'endu l-brra fih* (he has the outside inside [him]) but may be dropped in phrases such as *men brra* (from outside) or *men l-brra* (from the outside). In certain cases (e.g., *dyal [l-]brra*, of [the] outside) it can be difficult to tell whether the article is not there at all (*dyal brra*, of outside) or whether it has been incorporated into the sound of the particle *dyal* (of) but still part of the meaning (*dyal l-brra*, of the outside). In these cases, I have not used the article in the transliteration in order to reflect how the phrase sounds, but I have included the article in brackets in the English translation (of [the] outside) to evoke both meanings.

4. De Haas (2007b) shows that until 1973, the greatest constraint on international movement for Moroccan nationals was posed by the difficulty of obtaining a passport rather than by European migration policies.

5. A parallel if distinct migration movement is that of the Moroccan Jewish population who migrated in large numbers to France, Israel, and Canada after the 1948 creation of the state of Israel and the 1967 Six Day War. Morocco's Jewish population is estimated to have decreased from approximately 250,000 to contemporary figures of about 5,000 (de Haas 2014). For historical and ethnographic accounts, see Aomar Boum (2013), Emily Gottreich (2020), Mohammed Kenbib (1994), and Lawrence Rosen (2016).

6. Up to the 1970s, Moroccan international migration had mostly involved three areas of the country: the northeastern Rif region, the southwestern Sous region, and the internal areas located at the southeast of the High Atlas Mountains (de Haas 2007b).

7. The colonial phosphate extraction activity in the Tadla town of Khouribga from the 1920s onward attracted numerous laborers from the surrounding countryside who subsequently settled in the town with their families (Capello 2008).

8. On the systematic transformation of the Mediterranean Sea into a space of migrant death and its historical and racial logics, see, e.g., Marie Bassi and Farida Souiah (2019), Nicholas De Genova (2018), Gabriele Del Grande (2010), Charles Heller and Lorenzo Pezzani (2014), Khalil Saucier and Tyron P. Woods (2014), and SA Smythe (2018).

9. To protect the anonymity of my interlocutors, I have changed all personal names and have modified or omitted features that may make them identifiable. I have not specified the names of the Tadla towns, neighborhoods, and villages where I conduct research, and I refer to the town where much of my fieldwork is based as Zafiah, which is an invented name. I have also left out

details that could compromise my interlocutors—for example many of the routes that are used for travel without migration documents.

10. Darija is spoken alongside different varieties of Tamazight, or Berber, the indigenous language of the country; *Fusha*, or Modern Standard Arabic, the standardized Arabic understood across the Arab world and the language of news broadcasts and scholarship in Morocco; French, the dominant bureaucratic and schooling language until very recently and the second or third language of many Moroccans; Spanish, in the northern and southern areas of the country that used to be under Spanish rule; and, finally, English and other languages, increasingly spoken by students and Moroccans involved with tourism or international trade (Crawford and Newcomb 2013, 9).

1

TEMPOS OF LIFE

"I was engaged for only five minutes," Hafida always declares bitterly when she tells me the story of her rushed *'ers dyal brra* (marriage of [the] outside). Originally from an Amazigh mountain village of the Middle Atlas, now in her late thirties and living in a small Tadla town with her in-laws, Hafida married a distant migrant relative at eighteen. The whole wedding was a rushed affair: her newlywed (and newly met) husband had only two weeks left in Morocco before his Italian migration documents expired. The unnegotiable temporalities of *le-wraq dyal brra* (the papers of [the] outside) meant that just a couple of days separated Hafida's engagement and the wedding ceremony. This was nothing like what she had expected for this key moment of her life—she had imagined her engagement as a period packed with romantic intimacy and indulgent frills, just like the engagements portrayed in the Turkish and Mexican TV series, dubbed or subtitled in Arabic, she eagerly follows on the small television in her in-laws' living room.[1] "We did everything quickly. . . . 'The outside' doesn't wait . . . one day I was a girl [*bent*], the next I was married [*mzawja*] . . . just like that." Hafida snaps her fingers loudly.

One of the most striking ways in which *l-brra* implicates itself in the life of the Tadla is by directly and indirectly modulating local regimes of time, affecting the pace, rhythm, and tempo of the area. Stories like Hafida's are very common in the Tadla—critical life events are hastily fast-forwarded, artificially prolonged, or suddenly paused to accommodate *l-weqt dyal brra* (the time of [the] outside). *L-brra* implicates itself in the experience of time in the Tadla both by transposing to the area specific "outside" regimes of temporality (European national holidays, factory shifts, bureaucratic rhythms) and by generating specific textures of local temporality through regulating the punctuated arrivals and departures of significant people, things, and information. In other words, *l-brra* becomes both a temporal landscape operating through uncompromising logics and regimes and an imposing temporal agent in its own right, one that needs to be intimately reckoned with on a daily basis.

In this chapter, I begin to trace how *l-brra* operates and is operated upon in the Tadla by tracing the ways in which it affects the pace, rhythm, and tempo of local life. *L-brra* influences a variety of local temporal dimensions, with effects that, as we shall see, go well beyond those of regulating (or *de*regulating) time, as people, life cycles, and intimacies are inevitably swept up in the process. The temporalities of villages, neighborhoods, households, and people in the Tadla work in awkward synchrony with the regimes of temporality of *l-brra*: the dates of Italy's national holidays, a Spanish town's factory shifts, the bureaucratic rhythms of European migration policies, and so on. But it is not only the temporal rhythms of *l-brra* that have derivative effects on the Tadla. Specific actions, events, and decisions that take place in *l-brra* also have deep temporal reverberations in local life in the Tadla. The sudden decision of an Italian employer to sack a Moroccan worker, a vote in the Italian Parliament on a new immigration law, a husband's visit to a Spanish Western Union branch, the signing of a new work contract in France: these are all singular events that, while located abroad, have all kinds of effects on individuals, households, and neighborhoods in the Tadla. One of the most palpable effects, though by no means the only one, is that of temporally structuring, or *de*structuring, the unfolding of life in the Tadla.

The temporality of *l-brra* and of its critical events (Das 2005) contributes to defining not only the tempo and rhythm of the passing of time in the Tadla but also time's specific textures and qualities. For example, there are always long periods in the Tadla when migrant husbands aren't returning, money isn't arriving, and the intermediary between the consulate and the visa applicant isn't calling, during which people will say "*matandirsh walu*" (I don't do anything), "*a tangles u kantsenna*" (I just sit and wait), or "*hadshi l-weqt dyal l-mut*" (this is the time of death/dead time). This "inactive" and "dead" time is regularly interrupted by *l-brra*'s intermittent materializations: the return of a migrant boyfriend, the arrival of remittances, the outcome of a visa application. As we shall see, these human and material arrivals to the area generate qualitatively different regimes of time, unlocking intense economic, bureaucratic, and intimate doings, where inactivity is suddenly unthinkable, and days, hours, and minutes are packed to the brim with action. *L-brra*'s intermittent presence, in this sense, regulates the very succession of different qualities of time in the Tadla.

Perhaps "punctuating," rather than "regulating," is a more effective concept for capturing the local temporal workings of *l-brra*. "Punctuated time" is how Jane Guyer (2007) defines contemporary temporal perspectives on the near future, which, she argues, is "being reinhabited by forms of punctuated time, such as the dated schedules of debt and other specific event-driven temporal frames" (2007, 409). In the Tadla, the concept of "punctuated time" becomes useful not only for designating the specific event-disciplined temporality that characterizes people's reckoning with *l-brra*—waiting for the arrival of money from abroad, for the next phone call from a migrant son, for news from a European consulate. The idea of "punctuated time" is also useful for describing the ways in which *l-brra*'s intrusions abruptly interpose, interrupt, and divert the progression of time in the Tadla, resulting in a punctuated—rather than cyclical, sequential, or cumulative—time. These outside punctuations find themselves enmeshed in a multitude of overlapping local regimes of temporality, dictated by biological cycles and ritual rhythms, tempos of kinship relations and national calendars. *L-brra*'s punctuations also come to be enmeshed in what Dale Eickelman (1977, 50) describes, in his early essay on temporality among transhumant Tadla inhabitants, as the "several alternative temporal concepts" coexisting in the area—from sacred ones regulated by the mosques' daily calls for prayer to colonial ones regulating official timekeeping to agrarian ones determining the rotation of rural markets.

My argument in this chapter is thus not that *l-brra* is unique in its ability to modulate time, nor that it overrides other strands of local temporality existing in the Tadla. Rather, my aim is to show how *l-brra* powerfully materializes itself in and through time—both by inflecting the tempo of daily life and by redefining time's qualities and textures. *L-brra*'s influence over the temporality of the Tadla can be considered at different scales of abstraction, with each scale revealing different forms of complexity (Strathern 2004). In this chapter, I trace this multiscalar and multitemporal work of *l-brra* by first focusing on the tempo of major life events such as marriages and pregnancies, then on the temporality and development of whole kinship structures. I then move to the ways in which *l-brra* permeates the very rhythms of individual bodies. I close by addressing the distinctly unpredictable nature of *l-brra*'s temporal intrusions at all scales and suggest that, by inflecting a key axis of existence such as time, *l-brra* powerfully infuses the most intimate dimensions of social, conjugal, and individual life.

Bureaucratic Blues

"When they come, everything changes—you'll see it with your own eyes!" In the lead-up to my very first Tadla summer, people warned me with increasing frequency that everything was soon going to change. They were making reference to the summer visits of migrants, when the Tadla regularly fills up with returnees visiting their families and hometowns (see chap. 2). The warning was exactly right. Even to an outsider like myself, it is clear that when migrants return to the Tadla, things change. The prices of vegetables and meat in the markets skyrocket, as does the price of the *ness-ness* (half-half—i.e., half coffee, half milk) men order regularly at cafés. New building sites appear everywhere, and construction work on partially built houses resumes. European-plated cars suddenly fill the streets, and people start wearing foreign-looking clothes, shoes, watches, and jewelry on their evening strolls. Something in the rhythm of life of towns and villages changes when migrants return from *l-brra*, and it is a change in both speed and intensity. Suddenly, there is more noise, more parties, more meat in the couscous, more cars on the streets, more weddings, and more men at the all-male cafés and in the mosques.

L-brra affects the temporality of the Tadla in a variety of ways, but its temporal influence is most palpable in its power to regulate, both directly and indirectly, the comings and goings of migrants in the area and the length of their absences. Migrants' absences and temporary visits affect daily rhythms and future projects, wedding dreams and the timing of pregnancies, and the tempo of intimacy and household economies. Through migrants and the rhythm of their transnational movements, *l-brra* becomes an intimate aspect of the ebb and flow of Tadla life. This is especially the case when *l-brra* comes to influence the timing and length of focal events such as engagements and marriages and the tempo of defining moments such as births.

In the stories about her rushed marriage, Hafida describes not only her fast-forwarded engagement for the sake of *le-wraq* (papers/documents) but also how the pre-engagement negotiations were also extremely hurried *pour l-weqt dyal brra* (for [French] the time of [the] outside). Hafida's parents were told that Salah, the prospective groom, was ready to pay any amount for their daughter's bridewealth, as long as everything could be organized quickly (*deghya*), as he had to return to Italy within three weeks for his *permesso* ([Italian] short for *permesso di soggiorno*, Italian residence permit). Hafida's parents agreed to speed up procedures, and within three weeks the engagement and wedding parties were over. Salah left for Italy just a few days after the wedding.

Hafida explains to me that Salah had been unlucky with his *permesso* renewal that year: *huma temma* (those [people] [over] there) had granted him only a six-month renewal to his residence permit instead of the usual twelve months. He had not managed to get his *congé* (holidays [French]) until just a month before *l-weqt* (the time—i.e., the expiry date printed on the residence permit). So, despite his intention to get married during this particular trip home, Salah couldn't stay in Morocco for long, as he had to be back in *l-brra* before the document expired so he could apply for yet another renewal.

With the remarkable precision demonstrated by most people I know in the Tadla when it comes to discussing *l-brra*'s bureaucratic systems, Hafida's narrative about her wedding is structured around the temporality of *l-brra*'s immigration laws, residence permits, and holidays from work. Using Arabic, Italian, and French bureaucratic terminology, Hafida eloquently recounts how certain key moments of her life have proceeded in parallel with *l-weqt dyal brra* (the time of [the] outside), as people in the Tadla sometimes call it.

As mentioned above, wedding stories like Hafida's abound in the Tadla. The general pattern of weddings involving those who go (*huma lli kaimshiw*—see chap. 2) sees migrants returning from *l-brra*, marrying a young woman—often from their extended family (paternal cousins remain the favorite candidates) or someone chosen by the family—and then returning to *l-brra* shortly after the wedding as the bride moves in with her parents-in-law in the migrant's family household (McMurray 2001; Salih 2003). While the intention to get married evolves gradually over time—the whole migratory venture being, in many cases, rooted in the hope of having a decent future marriage—the actual wedding arrangements often need to be rather quick, especially for men who have an uncertain legal status in Europe. For these men in particular, sometimes a snap evaluation of the future needs to be made while visiting home, and decisions on whether and with whom to get married need to be made in a matter of days. This is why things are often set up for migrants in anticipation of their return—enquiries are made about young unmarried women in the area, sometimes a bride is chosen, and the first organizational plans for the wedding proceedings are already beginning to evolve by the time the migrant son or brother visits from Europe. Sometimes engagement parties take place without the groom-to-be. And, although I have never come across it myself, I have heard stories of actual weddings taking place in the absence of migrant grooms unable to leave *l-brra*.

Time is thus compressed and expanded in close parallel with Italian, Spanish, French, and other "outside" working calendars and the unforgiving rhythms and logics of *l-brra*'s governmentalities and bureaucracies of migration. A migrant's engagement with his fiancé may last a decade because he is working without a proper employment contract in Italy, which means he cannot apply for a work visa, which in turn makes him an "undocumented migrant" in the eyes of the Italian state—the final outcome of this causal chain being that the migrant fiancé cannot leave Italy because he risks being unable to return. On the other hand, as in Hafida's story, an engagement may last just a few days because the fiancé-cum-husband needs to return to *l-brra* before a vital document expires.

What this intersection between married life and bureaucratic rhythms reveals is that there is a particular temporal and emotional quality to what other anthropologists have identified as the power of bureaucratic regimes and states of law to shape the everyday (Buch Segal 2016; Kelly 2007; Tuckett 2018; Verdery 1996). Yael Navaro-Yashin's (2007) notion of the affective powers of documents, developed in her work on Turkish-Cypriots' reckoning with identity verification and travel papers, can in a sense be taken a step further with reference to the Tadla. Here, not only do documents have emotional power over people but they also regulate the economy of emotions between people, dictating wedding plans and romantic imaginaries.

L-brra's influence on the timing of focal events such as engagements and marriages has effects that extend beyond the realm of conjugal emotion, however. The temporality of *l-brra*, which migrants make operative in the Tadla through their arrivals and departures, also structures the speed and rhythm of people's movement through different fundamental life stages. By structuring the temporality of people's movements within a web of consanguine (related through blood) and affine (related through marriage) relationships, *l-brra* ends up affecting the very tempo of kinship.

The Tempo of Kinship

In his critique of structuralism, Pierre Bourdieu (1977, 1990) puts particular emphasis on what he calls the "detemporalizing effect" of structuralist analyses of practice, including practices pertaining to the realm of kinship. This critique was developed most famously in his discussion of Claude Lévi-Strauss's (1987) analysis of Marcel Mauss's theory of the gift, where Bourdieu sought to show that the detemporalizing effect of structuralism was "never more pernicious than when exerted on practices defined by the fact that their temporal structure, direction, and rhythm are *constitutive* of their meaning" (Bourdieu 1977, 9).

In the Tadla, the "temporal structure, direction, and rhythm" of kinship practices are definitely constitutive of their meaning in Bourdieu's sense, and But when kinship is intersected by *l-brra* this deep temporal character is exceptionally clear. It is particularly when *l-brra* disrupts ideal and idealized temporalities of kinship that the crucial role of time reveals itself most strongly—and, in turn, when *l-brra*'s constitutive role in local life by virtue of its hold on certain strands of temporality emerges most starkly.

Khadija's life trajectory provides a powerful example of this. In her forties and from a rural village a few kilometers outside Zafiah, Khadija married her paternal cousin Aziz when she was sixteen. Khadija did not get pregnant on the night of her wedding as everyone hoped, nor in the days preceding her newlywed husband's departure for *l-brra*. This meant that for the first few years of her married life, she was in the precarious position of being a childless daughter-in-law in her husband's household (more on this in chap. 3). Khadija says that she held her breath for three years, which is the time it took her husband to obtain the legal status he had temporarily lost in Italy, without which he couldn't return to Morocco. As Tadla women often explain to me, the birth of a child, particularly a first child, is a fundamental step in carving out one's place in the in-laws' household. Confirming a popular argument in the kinship scholarship regarding the defining role, particularly in patrilocal/virilocal settings,[2] of motherhood for daughters-in-law (Donner 2003; Empson 2011; Inhorn 1996; Vlahoutsikou 1997), Khadija echoes many women I know when she tells me that "before, you are nothing [*walu*] . . . but when you give birth you become family."

It is in this sense that I see *l-brra* inflecting the tempo of the development of kin relations in the Tadla—by regulating the coming and going of migrants, *l-brra* is also regulating the position of nonmigrant women like Khadija within their own local web of relations. Women like Khadija can find themselves "stuck" for years in the position of childless daughter-in-law in their in-laws' household; on the other hand, a woman's position in a family household can change abruptly with the unexpected return of a husband and the birth of a child nine months later. When it comes to migrants' kinship relations, one's position as girl (*bent*) rather than woman (*mra*), as married woman (*mzawja*) rather than mother (*'umm*), as father (*abb* [or *bu*, or *bba*]) rather than grandfather (*jedd*), is directly inflected by *l-brra*, which can either freeze or rapidly advance a whole set of relationships. When a migrant does return and marry a fiancé or conceive a child with his wife, it is as if a whole set of relationships and the people within them are jolted forward. *L-brra* generates a peculiar sort of "intervallic leaping" (Pedersen 2007, 317) between different stages in a life cycle and between different positionings within a web of kin relations.

Indeed, one could go as far as arguing that through its abiding influence on the temporal development of kin relations, *l-brra* plays a key constitutive role in defining the people who form and are formed by those relationships. Having or not having a child, being engaged or formally married, being a father or a grandfather, generate not only different positionings within a kinship network but also a different positioning of the (gendered) self— indeed, a different actualization of the self (cf. Barlow 1994; Fortes 1978; Joseph 1999; vom Bruck 1997a). Perhaps the clearest illustration of this existential significance of kinship positioning can be found in the case of brides' reproductive trajectories and in a mantra women always repeat to me in the Tadla: "*ila matwledish, matkunish*" (if you don't give birth, you are not [there]/you don't exist), a poignant observation about the precarious social/individual existence of migrants' wives in particular, which I develop further in chapter 3.

So, migrants' returns from *l-brra* are not only emotionally important but also key in the emergence and validation of specific (familial) people. Returns are, in this sense, subject-forming events in Caroline Humphrey's (2008) sense of the term, events that "bring about the sudden focusing or crystallization of certain of the multiplicities inherent to human life and thus create subjects, if only for a time" (2008, 359). But while Humphrey speaks of events as moments when "singular personalities burst into the field of vision" (357), and thus as moments creating singular subjects, here I see returns (and departures) as also creating fundamentally relational subjects, key in the development of major social projects, such as the constitution and reproduction of lineages and of the people formed within and through them.

L-brra is clearly not acting in a vacuum with regard to other forces, from the biological to the divine, that impose specific temporalities on the rhythm of lineage, conjugal, and intimate ties. Infertility, divorces, and marital arguments, to name but a few examples, are all equally capable of bringing the temporal progression of my interlocutors' familial and personal life to a halt, and, more generally, infusing the whole process with unpredictable and indeterminate rhythms and tempos. Indeed, my proviso on this point can be expressed in relation to Jennifer Johnson-Hanks's (2002, 2005) broader critique of the use of the life stages model in anthropology. Mounting a critique against the idea that life events such as adulthood and parenthood can be treated analytically as inherently coherent, clear in direction and fixed in outcome, Johnson-Hanks has suggested that a life course is better framed as something "founded in indeterminacy and innovation," as most life events are "negotiable and contested, fraught with uncertainty, innovation, and ambivalence" (2002, 865). This is certainly an important reminder of how generative leaps and halts are constitutive elements in people's life courses quite independent from the influence of an entity-cum-force like *l-brra*. However, my sense is that *l-brra* produces these temporal rhythms and tempos in a specific way and with specific kinds of effects, interrupting, with a distinctive kind and quality of force, processes that are conceptualized (and certainly idealized) as being relatively fluid and *'adi* (normal)—*in primis*, the movement of kinship status from fiancée to wife or, even more crucially, from wife to mother. It is precisely because of the importance my interlocutors give to these processes that *l-brra*'s temporal intrusions assume such imposing significance, as they affect those very "vital conjunctures" (866) that shape their personal and relational identity.

In fact, although Johnson-Hanks's critique of the idea, dominant in the social and demographic sciences, of clear, distinct, and predetermined life stages is useful at an analytical level, it does not necessarily reflect the preoccupations of my Tadla interlocutors. As I understand it, my interlocutors expect and desire life stages, particularly those of marriage and reproduction, to be fixed in direction and clear in outcome. The idealized movement from one life stage to another is part of those "essentializing practices" discussed by Michael Herzfeld (1997, 144) in reference to Greek masculinity, practices that both give form to and make apparent the presence of a (gendered) self. By interfering with the temporality of these essentializing practices, *l-brra* unavoidably becomes a crucial player in people's lives.

The significance and scale of such interference are not the same for everyone in the Tadla. *L-brra* certainly inflects in more powerful ways in the temporality of the life course of those young women who, for a combination of reasons, are engaged but not yet married or married but childless. Similarly, the return of a migrant husband affects a woman who already has two or three children (and, importantly, a son) to a different extent than it does an engaged or childless young woman. In other words, the scale of *l-brra*'s impact is very much determined by one's specific life circumstances. But as any one person's life trajectory affects, both relationally and pragmatically, the rest of her family members, it is also true that the temporal influence in an individual's life has repercussions on a much wider network of related people. So, while *l-brra* intrudes in people's lives with different degrees of intensity, it is also invariably influencing the rhythm and tempo of entire segments of kinship relations.

It is important to mention here that people generally identify *l-brra* as the temporal agent causing the peculiar rhythm of the transnational movement of migrant relatives even in cases where other elements are also at play. Some women know, for example, that it is not always just *le-wraq* (the documents) that prevent their husbands from returning home. Although it is rarely stated explicitly, it is often implicitly acknowledged that the rhythm of husbands' returns, for example, is also determined by factors that go beyond bureaucracy: lack of money, shame, involvement with an Italian woman. These different elements that directly or indirectly determine the temporality of visits all fall under the inclusive concept-cum-place of *l-brra*, which is invariably identified as the entity that orders (or *dis*orders) the timing and duration of migrants' visits—and thus what is inflecting *l-weqt dyalna* (our time, also used to refer to present times—see Eickelman 1977).

Whether determined by bureaucratic regimes, migrants' own choices, or an assortment of different causes lumped together under the term *l-brra* by my interlocutors, the effects of migrants' arrivals to and departure from the Tadla are not limited to the temporality of major life events alone. As I now go on to explore, these movements also inflect the tempo, speed, and quality of more routine and ordinary actions in the daily life of migrant households—and, in doing so, come to accelerate and decelerate regimes of actions of individual bodies.

Moving Money, Moving Bodies

Migrants' arrivals in the Tadla are generally accompanied by an intense escalation of doings. This escalation often also characterizes the days and weeks preceding the returns, when emigrant households become the setting for a flurry of activities, centered especially around the body. When the return of a migrant husband is imminent, for example, most women I know pay a special visit to the local hammam, the public steam bath. Although visits to the hammam are regular, particularly in the more rural areas of the Tadla, the trip to the hammam preceding a migrant's arrival is characterized by a particular degree of meticulousness and care. Migrants' sons and daughters are scrubbed by their mothers or aunties more vigorously than usual, using *sabun dyal brra* (soap of outside), saved specially for the occasion. Wives of migrants carefully cover their skin with henna *mezyana* (good/good quality) and then with even more care rinse it away, because, as they explain to me, men *lli kaimshiw* (who go) have somehow come to dislike the smell of henna on their wives. Hair is brushed energetically, hands and feet meticulously soaped and rubbed, and skin scrubbed vigorously with a hard sponge. The actions carried out at any regular visit to the hammam are on these occasions both amplified and intensified and are performed with a particular kind of care and precision.

A number of other body-related actions are performed or intensified by migrants' close relatives in preparation for the arrival. Toenails are cut, and hair is trimmed and at times treated with products *dyal brra* (of [the] outside). Hafida, whose *brra*-inflected marriage we encountered earlier, once told me she was saving money to "*ndir snani*" (do my teeth—i.e., go to the dentist) for her husband's next visit. Hafida, generally an abundant eater, also always goes on a diet (*régime* [French]) in preparation for her husband's returns, and bread becomes scarce at mealtimes a few weeks before the expected arrival (only to become plentiful again when her husband is home).

Actions performed on the body itself are accompanied by actions for adorning it. Makeup and perfume are exhumed from drawers, and "good underwear" from *l-brra*—generally a gift from migrant husbands that is left religiously untouched while they are away—is prepared for the husband's return.[3] Clean jellabas are taken out of wardrobes for all members of the family, and clothes without holes or stitches are retrieved from top shelves. As far as wives of migrants are concerned, the timing and extent of this beautification and adornment are crucial. Making oneself beautiful too early—that is to say, too far ahead of a husband's arrival— will raise questions about who the beauty is intended for. Making oneself beautiful too late will simply leave a woman *mawajdash* (unready/scruffy) for her husband's return. Actions are thus carefully synchronized with the tempo of migrants' arrivals and departures, particularly those of migrant husbands.

Indeed, the change in bodily rhythms produced by migrants' arrivals to and departures from the Tadla is deeply intimate for their wives. Friends and acquaintances regularly refer to the peculiar pattern their sexual lives take by virtue of "the outside." As we shall see in the following two chapters, migrants' wives are deeply and explicitly aware of *l-brra*'s direct and indirect interference in the intimacy of conjugal couples. These concerns are also of a temporal nature, as sexual intimacy in particular is often unambiguously related to the temporal patterns of *l-brra*. The long periods of time (months, years, and sometimes even decades) when migrants are away and relations between husband and wife are on pause are punctuated by the intense intimacy of migrants' periodic presences, when sexual expectations, obligations, and desires often have to be compressed into only a few weeks.

The fluctuations of intimate and sexual rhythms, based on the tempo of migrants' arrivals and departures, are not in any way a private affair between husband and wife. Indeed, the rhythm of a whole household often adjusts to the rhythm of the temporarily reunited couple. This is the case particularly in extended households, where limited space is shared by a varying number of people—usually the migrant's parents, children, and unmarried siblings, but at times also cousins and grandparents. The distribution of bodies in these houses alters with the arrival of a migrant man. Migrants will reappropriate for themselves the *bit n-n'as* (the room of/for sleep; the bedroom), which, in rural households, is often the only room with a door and a bed instead of the traditional Moroccan long divans. This is a room that migrants will have often furnished in Italian or Spanish style, or, more generally, in a *style dyal brra* (style [French] of [the] outside) when they first got married. When the migrant is away, the room is generally used by a variety of different people and for a variety of different activities—from drying hard wheat (*gmeh*) to storing anything from clothes to scooter parts. When migrant men come home, they settle in the room with their wife, and the rest of the household members readjust, reorganizing their daily activities in the remaining spaces. Indeed, parents-in-law, children, and whoever else lives in the house tend to spend much more time outdoors during the first days of the migrant's return. Children are sent on endless errands or told "*sir tl'ab*" (go play!), and adults find things to do outside the house in order to leave intimate time and space to the couple, *bash ikunu mejmu'in* (so they [can be] together).

Activities and movements in a household are thus reorganized around migrants' arrivals and departures in order to carve out a physical and temporal space for the married and long-separated couple. This space is by all means artificial, not only because of its temporal juxtaposition to the general daily routine, but also because, rather than being an integral part of the ordinary life of a household, this intimate space has to be actively and explicitly created in order to exist.

There is generally no particular sense of embarrassment or erotic innuendo accompanying the intimate adjustments to a household's organization when a migrant returns home. These adjustments are part and parcel of a somewhat pragmatic attitude that combines discourses on conjugal sexual duty and need with comments of a temporal nature about there being no time (*makaynsh l-weqt*). However, when talking with migrants' wives or with other members of emigrant households such as sisters or mothers, it is clear that these intimate rhythms are not always conceived of and experienced as '*adi* (normal). For example, as I discuss in the following chapter, women refer to the temporary burst of sexual activity generated by their husbands' return not only with longing (at times) and irony (always) but also with hints of shame and unease. Sexual intimacy between husband and wife, considered a mutual duty (including a religious one—see Roded 2006; Smid 2010, 44), seems at times to lose its naturalness because of the awkward and erratic temporal rhythm it acquires through *l-brra*. Long periods of sexual inactivity, which at times undermine women's very conceptualization of themselves as wives and women (chap. 3), are dotted with sporadic periods of intense intimacy—an intensity that is seen as having the power to transform and even distort an otherwise integral aspect of married life, changing its very nature.

It is not solely through the movement of migrants that *l-brra* comes to inflect regimes and rhythms of bodily actions in the Tadla. The periodic appearance/arrival of information, gifts, documents, and money from *l-brra* also contributes in fundamental ways to the structuring and nature of activities in households and neighborhoods. The arrival of remittances in particular has a special kind of influence on the rhythm and quality of life in emigrant households. To illustrate this, let me briefly focus on a household in the Tadla I know well and trace how intimate bodily practices, and their specific rhythms and intensities, are periodically triggered by the arrival of *l-flus dyal brra* (the money of [the] outside).

L-code

"*Ja l-code! Alice, ja l-code!*" (the code has come [or arrived]! Alice, the code has come!). Sakina, the eight-year-old daughter of a longtime friend in the Tadla, is jumping around me excitedly with her mother's mobile phone in her hand. I have been staying with Sakina and her mother for about two weeks and have been told repeatedly about the imminent arrival of a text from *l-brra* with *l-code* (the [Arabic] code [French]), the numerical code that allows people to collect money sent from abroad at a local Western Union branch. I have even been involved, unwillingly, in delicate telephone negotiations over this *code* between Hasna, Sakina's mother, and her husband, a migrant in Italy. Hasna's husband has been calling her nearly every day, and after a few minutes of heated discussion, he will tell his wife, "*Duwwezlia l-gauriya*" (put me on with the *gauriya*, the Western foreigner). In his impeccable Italian, learned in his ten years in Italy, Hasna's husband will tell me how his wife "*non capisce niente*" (doesn't understand anything) and "*pensa che i soldi, qui, sono gratis*" (thinks that money, here, is for free). Once the telephone call is over, Hasna will tell me how her husband "*mafhemsh walu, ga'!*" (doesn't understand anything)—"he thinks that life, here, is [for] free [*fabour*]."

L-code has the power to trigger endless transnational arguments in many of the emigrant families I know in the Tadla. As revealed by the exchange between Hasna and her husband, these transnational negotiations often precipitate a clash of contrasting economic analyses of "the outside" and "the inside," rooted in the interlocutors' different spatial and imaginative stances. *L-code* triggers not only transnational but also localized tensions. In nonnuclear family arrangements, just one member of the household (generally a brother or a father) receives either the remittances or the code that gives access to them. As is often stressed in the migration literature (Akesson 2009; de Haas and van Rooij 2010; King, Dalipaj and Mai 2006; Pedersen 2013), the hierarchical and gendered access to the incoming foreign money can generate tensions, spoken and unspoken accusations, and complex conflicts in emigrant households.

Along with tensions and conflicts, the arrival of remittances also produces a shift in both the rhythm and quality of a family's regimes of action. In Hasna's household, for example, made up of herself, her daughter, and her mother-in-law, Sakina's excitement over the arrival of *l-code* becomes the prelude to about two weeks of intense, accelerated activity for everybody in this small, all-female household. This intense, accelerated activity begins the moment *l-code* is received: following is a description of what happens in the immediate hours following the code's arrival.

Upon receiving the text message with *l-code*, Hasna, her mother-in-law, and her daughter rush to their respective compartments in the shared wardrobe to extract *lebsa dyal brra* (clothes of/for [the] outside)—clothes that, as I mention in the introduction, are not worn for the usual, familiar outdoors of the neighborhood or local *hanut* (shop/corner shop), where people often wear their indoor pajamas, or even the weekly market, where an old jellaba worn over pajamas will suffice. Once the clothes of the outside are chosen, the women start getting ready to leave the house. In a way that recalls the preparation for the arrival of a migrant son, husband, or father, Hasna encircles her eyes with kohl, Sakina's hair is brushed and plaited, and the mother-in-law secures her headscarf with precious-looking pins. Once this careful preparation is complete, the women head in the direction of the main road to town, taking care not to dirty their clothes as they cross the muddy fields surrounding their house. On the road, they hail a horse and cart and negotiate the price for a lift into town. On reaching the town, they quickly walk to the *grand taxi* rank,[4] rush to the next taxi leaving for the neighboring town, and cram themselves in with the other passengers. After a thirty-minute drive, they leave the taxi and walk to the town's Western Union branch, where Hasna reads out *l-code* to the man behind the counter. The women wait in tense silence for the clerk to find *l-code* in the system and then watch his hands vigilantly while he counts the money out. The money is then carefully folded and tucked away in the pocket of the mother-in-law's apron, ever present underneath her jellaba. Once the money is secured, the three women slowly start heading back to the *grand taxi* rank, and the reverse journey home begins.

I briefly describe here the multiple practices triggered in Hasna's household by the arrival of *l-code* to give a sense of the instant effects of *l-brra*'s intrusions on domestic rhythms and movements within and beyond the home. These effects do not end with the collection of the money, however. The geographical, physical, and technological process required for transforming *l-code* into money described above is generally followed by the process of transforming this money into other local things. The days following the trio's visit to the neighboring town's Western Union branch are characterized by a flurry of economic activities. These include paying off the household's debt with the local corner shop; buying cream, honey, and other expensive foods; paying overdue bills; buying new school clothes for Sakina; purchasing a new cooking pot at the market; and so on. The Western Union visit also generates other kinds of activities that are only indirectly economic and more in the realm of morality and kinship (cf. Parry and Bloch 1989). For example, *l-code* allows Hasna to pay for a coach trip for herself and her daughter to the neighboring village to visit her mother and siblings. Thanks to *l-code*, and without informing her husband and mother-in-law, Hasna is also able to pay for her mother's visit to a *kuwway*, a traditional healer practicing cauterization (see Kapchan 1996, 30). While Hasna is spending the money her husband has sent following their lengthy negotiations, she is also nurturing and fortifying fundamental relationships with her own kin—a crucial practice in virilocal emigrant settings like the Tadla, as we shall see in chapter 3.

Within a fortnight, all the money *l-code* has generated is gone. Once these two weeks of intense expenditure are over, activities in Hasna's household significantly slow down, visits to relatives become less frequent, and the presence of special foods at mealtimes visibly diminishes. Hasna starts hinting to her husband over the phone that money is needed and that a new *code* from *l-brra* must be sent soon. Arguments once again begin to punctuate the transnational phone calls between husband and wife, increasing exponentially in heatedness and intensity as the economic and familial activities decrease in pace and vigor with the dwindling money supply. "Here we go again," Hasna whispers to me, covering the phone with her hand as she inaugurates a new cycle of conjugal negotiations.

Money Time

The effects of remittances on so-called sending areas such as the Tadla have received close attention from migration scholars, governments, and aid agencies alike. Moving beyond the "development versus dependency" paradigm that dominated the discussion on remittances until the late 1980s—what de Haas (2007a) describes as the either/or models of "migration optimists" (for whom remittances, and migration more generally, meant economic, political, and even cultural development of poorer countries) and "migration pessimists" (for whom remittances meant South-North dependency, inequality, and brain drain)—anthropologists in particular have paid increasing attention to the subtle and varied impact of remittances on emigrant households and communities (see, e.g., Akesson 2009; Atekmangoh 2017; de Haas and Rooij 2010; Lopez 2015; McMurray 2001; Pedersen 2013). Despite this diversification and nuancing of focus, rarely is attention given to the temporal effects of these transnational monetary movements, and, more specifically, to the ways in which they influence the tempo and intensity of daily, ordinary activities. An exception to this can be found in studies like Julie Chu's (2010) ethnography of Chinese migration, where she traces how overseas remittances increase and intensify local ritual life (Chu 2010, 171–216; see also Dusenbery and Tatla 2010; Gardner 1993b; Gardner and Grillo 2002). However, what emerges from tracing the arrival, transformation, spending, and eventual extinguishing of *l-code* in households like Hasna's is that the temporal effects of remittances in the Tadla are not limited to major religious and ritual moments. Here, the movement of remittances, just as that of migrants, seems to play a key role in the very rhythm of the everyday, transforming temporarily the tempo, intensity, and quality of more ordinary, everyday activities—from the frequency of family visits to the rhythm of bodily adornment. We have seen with Hasna how the arrival of remittances can trigger an abrupt, multidirectional acceleration of activities, temporarily interrupting daily rhythms and affecting the orientation, tempo, and speed of practices that go well beyond the strictly economic realm.

Hasna's adventures with *l-code* show that remittances coming in from *l-brra* require local work in order to become operative in emigrant areas. Indeed, the reason why I describe in such detail the women's movements from the moment *l-code* appears on Hasna's phone is because I wish to show the web of practices required by *l-code* in order for it to become *flus* (money) and then the kinds of work (economic, emotional, relational) this *flus* in turn produces. The process required for the transformation of *l-code* into money in particular shows how *l-brra*'s intrusions need work—and work of all kinds—in order to be made locally operative. Arrivals from *l-brra* need to be actualized, translated, managed, distributed, and contained, and this mediatory work in itself affects the timing, rhythm, and orientation of actions and doings in the Tadla. Indeed, *l-code* is already inflecting the temporality of Hasna's everyday life even before it becomes operative through the derivative effects of its expendability. I would argue that what happens explicitly with *l-code* takes place, at times less palpably, with all kinds of *brra* intrusions in the Tadla, including those of returning migrants themselves. When a migrant returns home, his relatives and family members need to readjust swiftly, rearranging their positioning (both physical and hierarchical) within the household and the orientation of their actions and doings. This readjustment of roles, priorities, and orientations can be considered the necessary work required to actualize what the returning migrants are meant to be: fathers, husbands, sexual partners, heads of households. Just as with *l-code*, these returning mobile bodies need to be carefully mediated. The economy of respect, duty, dependency, intimacy, and power requires work in order to make these returns operative (in emotional, economic, and relational terms) and not just alien and problematic events.

The work required to actualize *l-brra*'s temporal intrusions, be they migrants or remittances, brings to mind the practices of Moroccan religious mediums or even learned Islamic scholars (*fuqaha*)—figures who, in a variety of ways, translate, mediate, distribute, and manage the intrusion or presence of the (transcendental) outside for the human world and its requirements (see Spadola 2014, 2015). Indeed, from this standpoint, *l-brra* directly evokes religious cosmologies where, as J. Lorand Matory (2009) writes with regard to the Other Place of the Yoruba Atlantic religion, "health and ritual order . . . depend not simply on the existence of the faraway Other Place, but on the management of the arrival, presence, and departure of its personnel and powers" (239; see also Holbraad 2012). Part of *l-brra*'s power lies precisely in the fact that it enters, on various levels and in different ways, the here and now of the Tadla, making the mediation and management of its presence a key factor for personal well-being and the smooth flow of social life.

This mediation and management are far from straightforward. This is not only because *l-brra*'s intrusions are characterized by a peculiar kind of power and force that are by definition complex to handle. It is also because *l-brra*'s materializations are, fundamentally, unpredictable. There is no predictable rhythm to the ways in which *l-brra* appears in the Tadla, nor to the way it accelerates and decelerates local life. Readjustments made for the return of a migrant husband, as well as those made for the arrival of remittances, do follow a recognizable pattern. However, the how and when of these adjustments varies significantly, as does their impact in daily life each time they are performed. This is why *l-brra* is in many ways perceived as *dis*ordering, rather than ordering, time.

Disordered Time

Women often smile and respond "*llahu a'lem*" (only God knows, also *ya'lem llah*) when I ask about their husbands' next visit. This is generally the answer I receive also with regard to other outside appearances, such as the arrival of the next *code* or the outcome of a visa application. There is a tangible unpredictability surrounding the course of family relations, the household economy, and, indeed, one's personal life trajectory when these are intersected by *l-brra*. There is always the possibility that a husband will visit, a text-cum-money will arrive, or news will break in the neighborhood of new visa application rules in Europe. This constant potentiality makes it impossible to frame *l-brra*'s punctuations in the Tadla in terms of the production of an ordered, cyclical temporal pattern.

This unpredictable temporality is particularly striking when it comes to the timing of migrants' visits. Migrants are often unable to say for sure when they will return home and how long their visits will last. For those with unstable employment and/or legal status in particular, it is extremely difficult to predict the pattern of visits and departures. Everyone knows when it is most likely for men living "outside" to return. Everyone knows, for example, that if a migrant relative has a stable job in Italy or Spain, he will probably have some free time to visit home over the summer months.

However, summers are gray areas of possibility rather than times of certainty, not least because only a small proportion of Tadla men have stable jobs and regular holidays in *l-brra*. Some summers, migrant relatives will not come back at all, other summers they will stay for four months instead of the expected three weeks, and sometimes they will simply show up in the middle of December. Husbands, boyfriends, and brothers may show up without warning and then sometimes also disappear without warning. *L-brra* behaves at times like an unpredictable organism, spitting out and then reabsorbing relatives, friends, and neighbors without warning. Many people I know in the Tadla speak of their relatives' visits from abroad in terms of a highly unpredictable sequence of appearing and disappearing acts from the fog of *l-brra*: for many, the sudden accelerations and decelerations *l-brra* instantiates in their lives are erratic and unpredictable, based on an erratic and unpredictable time—*l-weqt dyal brra* (the time of [the] outside).

Not everything is ungraspable and unpredictable, of course. There are some migrants, for example, who plan their visits well in advance, and their kin always know when they will arrive and leave. The mother of Meriem, my roommate when I lived in Zafiah, even receives in advance a copy of her migrant son's plane tickets. On one of my visits to Meriem's village in the Atlas Mountains, her mother showed me a worn photocopy of a ticket reservation with the date and time of her son's arrival in six months' time. Meriem's mother kept this piece of paper in the inside pocket of her apron, which she never parted company with. From time to time, she would pause in her household chores, sit down on a chair in the kitchen, and take the piece of paper from her apron pocket, carefully stroking it open on her lap. I once saw her silently cry while folding and unfolding the photocopy of her son's plane ticket. She couldn't read what the paper said—like many women of her generation in the area, Meriem's mother couldn't read and write—but she knew what it meant. At times, she would simply put her hand on her stomach over the pocket where the ticket was, as if to absorb the tangible proof that her son was coming home soon, the piece of paper becoming a concretization of both a unique type of relationship between mother and son and a key temporal landmark for the organization of the family.

However, most people in the Tadla speak with uncertainty about the timing of their relatives' returns from abroad, making Meriem's mother's temporal knowledge an exception rather than the rule. At times, there is a real sense of weariness surrounding the ticking of this outside clock that influences and (dis)orders daily life and routines. It is also an exceptionally special ticking, one that reminds people that their lives are compelled to follow not only the time regimes of the neighborhood, of ritual ceremonies, of children's schools, and of the calls of the muezzin from the nearby mosque. The ticking of the outside clock reminds emigrant households of the special possibility they have, along with a heavy obligation, of following the progression of other time(s), too. But the nonnegotiability of *l-weqt dyal brra* (the time of [the] outside) is also seen as something that can sever as well as produce possibilities. The time of *l-brra*, after all, determines when one will next see a migrant husband, son, or brother, and for how long his absence will have to be endured, when the outcome of a life-changing visa application will arrive, and when intimate and economic practices related to remittances need to be activated. Indeed, the fact that the timing of these punctuations often feels uncontrollable and unpredictable further heightens *l-brra*'s hold on people's experience of time.

Times of the Outside

In her work with Palestinian families of political detainees, Lotte Buch Segal (2013, 2016) argues that Israeli bureaucratic procedures take on a specifically temporal dimension in the everyday lives of Palestinian households. She traces how the lives of detainees' wives in particular are tied to "enduring presents" (2013, 122) where they find themselves endlessly repeating the same bureaucratic procedures with uncertain outcomes, such as applying for permissions to visit their husbands in jail, which generates a sense of existing in a permanent present where time does not progress and, instead, cyclically repeats itself. Analyses of the intimate interlocking of bureaucracy and local experiences of time resonate strongly with emigrant Morocco. Here too, bureaucracy, alongside other direct and indirect manifestations and reverberations of *l-brra*, acquires a specifically temporal dimension, affecting the local experience, reckoning, and understanding of time. But rather than tying the Tadla to an "enduring present," as Buch Segal argues for Palestine, *l-brra* and its bureaucratic rhythms and regimes here become key agents in the temporal progression of the present. *L-brra*'s punctuations—be it migrants, the money they send, rumors of a new migration law, or the outcome of a visa application—push or shove different strands of the "now" in the Tadla. Time is pushed forward, backward, or sideways in relation to more or less normative, more or less expected, and more or less desired temporal and intimate trajectories. This *brra*-infused temporal progression is neither linear and "standardized" (Barak 2013, 5) nor consistent and predictable. Time, or at least those strands of time enmeshed within *l-brra*, moves through what could be termed a series of hiccups, jumping from one migrant visit to another, from one remittance to another, and from one visa rejection to another. These hiccups, or punctuations, are experienced as erratic rather than cyclical, uncertain rather than repetitive or predictable. As I have said, they recall, in this sense, Guyer's definition of "punctuated time," made of events that are "qualitatively different rather than quantitatively cumulative" (2007, 416), although these particular punctuations, rather than being mere perceptions of the near future, intrude in the very progression of the now in its multiple forms, transforming both the nature and tempo of daily activities.

By inflecting the timing, rhythm, and tempo of practices, events, and relationships, *l-brra* powerfully modulates the way people reckon and experience time in the Tadla. In doing this, *l-brra* joins more established time regimes already operating in the Tadla, from the Muslim lunar calendar regulating religious ceremonies, to the Gregorian calendar popularized under French and Spanish colonization, to the Agrarian calendar (also referred to as the Julian or Berber calendar in the literature) regulating rural cycles and solar feasts. As Eickelman (1977) argues in his article on conceptions of time in the Tadla of the 1970s, and as the anthropological work on temporality in Morocco continues to testify (e.g., Abu-Shams and Gonzalez-Vazquez 2014; Amahan 1988; Crawford 2008; Ilahiane 2005), multiple temporalities have always coexisted in the country. *L-brra,* I argue, contributes to this multilayered local timescape with a specific kind of intimate force, becoming both a key temporal coordinate and a powerful temporal agent in the ticking of local life.

To give a sense of this local ticking, in this chapter I have focused on the qualities and effects of *l-brra*'s punctuations. In chapter 3, I focus on those long periods between these punctuations, when migrant husbands are not returning, remittances are not arriving, and visa applications are being endlessly processed, and focus on women married to migrants and the kinds of gendered selves that emerge while waiting for *l-brra* to actualize itself. Before I do this, however, I must introduce the primary agents, or conduits, of these economic, emotional, and structural punctuations: migrant men. The next chapter introduces the complex figures of *huma lli kaimshiw* (those who go) and begins to trace the ways in which they bring *l-brra* into the most intimate spheres of everyday existence in the Tadla.

Notes

1. The romantic and prolonged engagement that Hafida desired for herself does not necessarily reflect "traditional" conceptualizations of marriage in Morocco, where the *khotba* (engagement) often plays a minor role and is principally a time of negotiation between kin groups rather than a period of romance between fiancés. See Edward Westermarck (1914) for an early engagement with marital and premarital rituals in Morocco.

2. Patrilocal (marriage in the father's place of residence) and virilocal (the form of postmarital residence in which a couple move to the home of the husband) are sometimes used interchangeably in the anthropological literature. In the stricter sense, "patrilocal" is often taken to imply residence in a patrilineal group generated by virilocality repeated through the generations (Barnard and Spencer 2010).

3. "What am I meant to do with these in the fields?" Hafida once said, laughing while showing me a set of undersize "made in Italy" underwear her husband had brought her from *l-brra*.

4. *Grand taxi* are cars that carry up to six passengers and make trips between towns.

2

THE OUTSIDE INSIDE

It is a warm summer evening in a small village of the Tadla, and we are sitting with a few women from the neighborhood outside Saida's house. The women are discussing the recent circumcision celebration of a villager's son when an ear-splitting blast of music from a nearby alleyway abruptly interrupts the conversation. Everyone pauses to listen until Saida murmurs bitterly, "So the animals have arrived!" (*iwa jaw l-hayawanat*). A couple of women smile and nod at Saida's comment; one of the younger girls hints at a dance move with her hips in response to the music. Another woman, after reproaching the girl with a half-hearted "*hshuma!*" (shame [on you]), replies to Saida, or maybe to the music, with a long sigh and the versatile expression, "*ya rebbi*" (oh my Lord).

"The animals" Saida is referring to are the returning migrants who at the beginning of every summer start to trickle back into the Tadla. The loud music comes from the sound system of the wedding between, Saida explains to me, "*shi bent dyal l-huma*" (some girl from the neighborhood) and "*Mohammed lli kaimshi brra*" (Mohammed who goes [to the] outside). These weddings are a leitmotif of Tadla summers, when the soundscape of villages and towns is permeated by loud *she'bi* (popular) music from wedding celebrations, and roads become unruly motorways teeming with foreign-plated cars carrying white-clad brides and newlywed migrants. At the center of this yearly nuptial commotion are migrants: *huma lli kaimshiw brra* (those who go [to the] outside), or, as Saida harshly calls them, "*l-hayawanat*" (the animals). Saida is not the first person I have heard referring to returnee migrants and their behaviors as animallike (*bhal hayawanat*). Many people in the Tadla, directly or indirectly, talk about returning migrants as odd, strange, simultaneously attractive and troubling beings who are somehow distinct from the rest of nonmigrant *bnadem* (human beings/people).

These complex characters are fundamental figures in the area's imaginative and pragmatic reckoning with *l-brra*. It is often by engaging with returning migrants that people in the Tadla assess *l-brra* and its powers: the power to transform humble into arrogant; to enrich, uplift, or madden. This practical imagination moves in both directions, however, and while returning migrants are important mediums for understanding *l-brra*'s multiple properties and oddities, *l-brra*, on the other hand, plays a central part in determining the ways migrants are both conceptualized and reckoned with at home. This is not only because people's longing for *l-brra* makes those who move toward it valuable, albeit complex kinds of people and nourishes the expectations others have of them. It is also because contact with *l-brra* is seen as fundamentally transforming migrants into specific kinds of beings who come to possess some of the intangible qualities of *l-brra* itself. *L-brra* is said to affect migrants' appearance and speech, behavior and mood, and seductive powers and intuition, somehow permeating their very constitution. In short, migrants have *l-brra f dakhel* (the outside inside). Through them *l-brra* becomes, rather than a simple destination, an invaluable personal quality.

Having the outside inside is unavoidably a mixed blessing. In this chapter I trace how *l-brra* is what makes migrants special kinds of people—unrivalled marriage prospects and powerful seducers who are allowed to bend or circumnavigate norms of propriety and behavior. But migrants' specialness also manifests itself in other more sinister ways. Migrants' behavior is described as arrogant, strange, uncanny (*ghrib*), and their temporary visits home are often awkward, sometimes even unwelcome. By having *l-brra f dakhel* (the outside inside), migrants are conceived as being fundamentally different from anyone else in the Tadla, and this otherness is both admired and despised, desired and envied, making the figure of the migrant liminal and even controversial (cf. Nyamnjoh 2011; Sayad 1999).

Developing my analysis of the intimate temporal work of *l-brra* from chapter 1, in this chapter I discuss the complex characters who travel to and from this powerful space-cum-entity. I begin with the multivocal narratives that circulate in the Tadla about "those who go" and proceed to consider how migrants are seen as special kinds of people in the area and the implications this has for social life, starting with marriage arrangements with local women. Unpacking the different dimensions of this specialness reveals that not only wealth and status but also *l-brra* itself distinguishes and qualifies migrants in the area; the constitutive changes instantiated by *l-brra* invariably evoke classic anthropological themes of transformational rituals, where the very core of those involved is permanently affected.

Wondrous Stories

Stories and storytelling are powerful mediums through which knowledge about migrants is produced, circulated, and stored in the Tadla. Captivating, wondrous, and at times bizarre stories about "those who go" circulate regularly in the area, intersecting and feeding into stories about *l-brra* itself and its multiple properties. Stories span many different genres, ranging from narratives about migrants' crippling homesickness to tales about the riches and possibilities migrants encounter the moment they set foot on *l-brra*'s shores. Moroccan, Tunisian, and Algerian *she'bi* (popular) and Raï music, where themes of migration and exile play a dominant role, contribute substantially to this migratory narrative landscape (see Moktary 2008; McMurray 2001, 98–109; Souiah et al. 2018). *She'bi* songs about migration, the ceaseless background accompaniment to evening marketplaces and youths' everyday activities, crisscross with stories told by returning migrants, discussions about migration on national TV and in the local press, and stories about *l-brra* circulating within and beyond emigrant households. These multiple narrative strands come together to form a specific kind of knowledge about *l-brra* that is fundamentally mediated by those who are able to move between *hna* (here, also *hnaya*) and *temma* (there): migrants.

Stories about migrants in the Tadla range from the wondrously miraculous to the depressingly bleak. I have consistently heard both of great men who made it in *l-brra* and became rich, powerful, and morally strengthened and of men who were met with nothing but ruin, desolation, and alcohol after their departure. These stories are skillfully evoked, told, and retold in the Tadla when discussions about *l-brra* emerge. Mohammed, a man in his late fifties from a small village in the Tadla countryside who is always willing to hold forth on *l-brra* in a colorful way, regularly draws on a rich plethora of stories to substantiate his view that migration "is for bad people" (*nas l-khayebin*). He also draws on a variety of these stories to prove to his listeners that *l-brra* has the power to turn even the best Moroccans into bad/ugly (*khayeb*) individuals—the story about his friend the gardener is the one he uses most to illustrate this point.

Mohammed's friend left for Italy in the late 1990s. He didn't need to go—Mohammed always points out when he tells this story—he had a job tending his town's public gardens and could have built a life in Morocco. He had, however, *l-brra f rasu* (the outside in his head), Mohammed says: he was one of those people who find *l-brra* irresistible and simply had to leave. Mohammed's story about his migrant friend consists of a long list of terrible things that happened to him *f l-brra* (in the outside). This list is tweaked each time the story is told and very much depends on Mohammed's mood when telling it, as well as the point he wants to make with it. However, the story always includes three fundamental elements: (1) an Italian woman the gardener married so he could apply for Italian citizenship and who methodically ruined his life; (2) the gardener's involvement in drug dealing in Italy that somehow resulted in him losing a leg (either because of drug abuse or because of an accident—this part of the story has always been unclear); (3) the gardener's current situation: in a wheelchair and living with his new wife, a young Moroccan woman from his hometown who married him in order to get a spousal visa for Italy and subsequently found herself living in a depopulated, isolated village in the Italian countryside. Mohammed always ends this grim migration story by punching the ground with both fists and stating, "*Wellah* [I swear by God] . . . your own country [*bladek*] . . . that's the only place where you can be happy."

But Mohammed's personal stash of migration stories is not all bleak events and unlucky, injured protagonists. Like everyone else in the Tadla, Mohammed also has very positive stories to tell about *l-brra* and migrants, stories with happy endings and admirable people. His favorite one, perhaps, is about another friend of his, from the nearby phosphate town of Khouribga, who sent his two young sons to Europe in the early 2000s on one of the boats regularly crossing into Spain from Tangier. The story goes that when they made it to Spain, the boys (aged twelve and ten at the time) were fed, schooled, and looked after—"*kollshi fabour, khti!*" (all for free, sister!) Mohammed often repeats with a broad smile—and are now living a successful life in Spain.

The different registers Mohammed uses to speak about these two migrant trajectories—the tragic trajectory of the town gardener, the thriving trajectory of the two Khouribga boys—shows how different forms of knowledge are stored side by side in people's narrative repository about both *l-brra* and those who travel to it. Mohammed's stories also reveal the complex ways in which knowledge about migration and its protagonists is produced and reproduced through different kinds of narratives and storytelling. Stories about drugs, deceit, and physical decay alternate with stories of success, hope, and matchless possibilities. The story about the two migrant boys in particular provides a precious window into the kinds of imageries that surround migrants in the Tadla. First, the story shows how travelling to *l-brra* can be associated with a specific kind of cleverness (*'qel*). Mohammed is full of admiration for his friend's and his sons' ability to fool *l-brra*'s generally incomprehensible system. The relationship existing in "the outside" between parental authority and state jurisdiction is often discussed in the Tadla as being both weird and unpredictable. Astonished accounts of Moroccan nationals being sent to jail in Europe simply for slapping their misbehaving children are frequent in the Tadla. Migrant men sometimes tell me they are reluctant to take their families to "the outside" because they are concerned that their children will become rebellious and disrespectful. They tell me that there, if a son goes to the police and reports his father, the police will invariably take the son's side. A migrant in his early forties once said to me, "How am I going to raise my children in such madness? If a father's word is nothing, and some policeman who is still a child himself [*shi bulisi baqi weld*] can tell me how to be the head of my own house. . . ."

In Mohammed's story, however, his friend's family somewhat heroically manages to turn this odd, "mad" system against itself. In the story, the arrival of two young boys on *l-brra*'s shores produces, almost magically, accommodation, food, healthcare, and a future. Here, the whole Spanish system, from its idea of moral parental behavior and its interference with fatherly duties to its migration laws, is outsmarted. Both the migrant boys themselves and their parents are praised in the narration for being able to play norms of hospitality and childcare, outlandish as they may seem, to their advantage. But along with the admiration for migrants' *'qel* (cleverness/mind/intelligence) and the forms of knowledge produced about *l-brra*'s systems through it, Mohammed's story also taps into the specific kind of suspension of disbelief that is activated when stories about migrants are told in the Tadla. The first time Mohammed told me about his friend's sons, I was surprised by the uncritical way he recounted such a happy ending story. I had become accustomed to the energetic way my acquaintances critically analyzed and carefully dissected any story, gossip, or account that came their way. However, different scales of evaluation, and indeed different styles of telling, listening, and recounting, are applied to stories about migrants and *l-brra*. In his seminal analysis of Algerian migration to France, Abdelmalek Sayad makes a rather bleak analysis of this type of storytelling of/about places like *l-brra*: "The collective misrecognition of the objective truth of emigration . . . is maintained by the whole group, the migrants who select the information they bring back when they visit their home village, the former emigrant who 'enchants' the memories that they have kept of France, and the candidates for emigration who project onto 'France' their most unrealistic expectations" (Sayad 2000, 167). Sayad places what he terms the "collective lie" (147) of migration—of which both migrants and nonmigrants are guilty—at the very heart of the production and reproduction of the Algerian emigration to France of the mid-1970s. I am unsure as to whether the language of "objective truth" and "collective lie" is analytically effective in a context like the Tadla, where *l-brra* constitutes a complex place of and for the imagination, situated in radically diverse expectations and desires, and signifying multiple hopes and trajectories. As we have already seen, I find the language and analytics of hope, imagination, and possibility more revealing when reckoning with the complexity of *l-brra* and its irresistible traction (see also Elliot 2020). Nevertheless, in his attempt to unpack the role of storytelling in the reproduction of migration, Sayad is tackling head-on a kind of disjuncture between migrant experience and migrant narration, and between migrant narration and local forms of critique, tangibly present also in the Tadla. What is particularly telling in the case of Mohammed's story is that the suspension of ordinary judgment regarding the truthfulness of a successful migratory plot is extended to a suspension of ordinary judgment on the behavior and moral conduct of the migrants themselves.

Indeed, Mohammed's story about the ingenious young migrants addresses another key fact about migrants in the Tadla—namely, the moral exceptionalism that surrounds them. In Mohammed's story, a father is described as sending his two sons on a potentially fatal trip to Spain. Everyone in the Tadla knows about the deadly dangers of *l-harag*, literally "the burning" (Pandolfo 2007), the concept used to refer to the clandestine crossing of the Mediterranean. Everyone also knows that *l-brra mashi bhal hna* (the outside is not like here) and that the journey's destination, as well as being desirable and exceptional, is unfamiliar and dangerous. The practice of sending sons or daughters to another household to improve their life chances or to work as domestic laborers is not uncommon in the Tadla—see, for example, Vanessa Maher's (1974) classic study of fostering in the Middle Atlas, David Crawford's (2010) more recent work on young Amazigh villagers employed in urban labor, and Mary Montgomery's (2019) ethnography of women domestic workers in Rabat. In the Tadla, at least, children are generally sent to familiar settings—to a member of the extended family or to wealthier acquaintances. Mohammed's friend, however, had sent his sons to "the outside," conceptualized in many senses as *ghrib* (strange/

unknown/uncanny) par excellence, and the exact opposite of family and familiar (cf. Pandolfo 2018). The fact that he had sent his children to *l-brra* rather than to any other nonfamiliar place/space somehow transforms what would otherwise be classified, in the Tadla and definitely by people like Mohammed, as careless abandonment into dutiful and clever care. Because *l-brra* is involved, an exceptional mode of conceptualizing a father's duties and responsibilities is activated in the narration. Ordinary moralities of kinship are partially suspended in the story, and the emigrant family's breach of hegemonic norms of parental responsibility are accepted, understood, and even set, at least in some sense, as an example.

I return to this peculiar suspension of ordinary judgment below, where I address the question of how and why migrant men are considered optimal marriage partners in the Tadla despite their often low-status origins and perceived smug behavior. Before this, another key aspect about migrants needs to be introduced—namely, the distinctively ambiguous way that migrants' doings in *l-brra* are discussed and assessed back home.

Hazy Doings, Vengeful Knowledge

The circulation in the Tadla of exceptionally detailed stories about migrants is coupled with a contrasting sense of vagueness and ambiguity about migrants' daily doings in "the outside." At the beginning of my first stay in the Tadla, I regularly asked the people I met what their relatives, friends, and neighbors did in Europe. The reply would often be a shrug and a dismissive "*kheddam* [or *kaikhdem*]" (working, employed) or "*gales*" (sitting—i.e., out of work). When I tried to press my interlocutors to elaborate on their answers—where does he work, what job does he do, is it tiring, is it safe, has he changed jobs over the years?—I would often get "*ma'arftsh khti*" (I don't know, sister) as an answer, and the conversation would then move to another topic. In some cases, people simply did not want to tell me. In many cases, however, I feel my interlocutors genuinely did not know—and, more importantly perhaps, did not necessarily want to know—what their husbands, sons, cousins or neighbors did in *l-brra*. While knowledge about *l-brra* and its workings (from bureaucratic, chap. 1, to cosmological, chap. 6) is often strikingly precise in the area, a complex kind of hazy knowledge surrounds migrants' activities on the other side of the sea.

Everyone in the Tadla has, of course, a rough idea of what "those who go" do abroad. Everyone knows, for example, that migrants in Spain and Italy usually work in the construction industry, in factories, in agriculture, or as vendors in markets and on beaches. However, people do not necessarily know what exact jobs their husbands or sons do at any specific moment. This kind of not knowing does not generally stem from an impossibility to find out what relatives do on the other side—if anything, in many cases it feels purposeful and cultivated rather than an inability to know. Nor is this hazy knowledge always linked to a reluctance on the part of migrants themselves or their families to disclose the activities that allow them to survive in *l-brra* and send back remittances. My sense is that an important dimension of this specific kind of haziness is linked to the fact that knowing exactly what migrants do in *l-brra* is often considered inconsequential, even unimportant in the Tadla. What counts is a relative's status as a migrant and whether he works or "sits"—though even the latter counts to a lesser degree, as what really matters and qualifies is that someone has reached the other side successfully (see chap. 5). The rest— how a migrant makes money, how many hours he works in a day, exactly where and how he lives—is of secondary importance. Whereas in the Tadla it makes a considerable difference whether a husband is a seasonal worker on the land or, say, an electrician, or whether a father decides to marry his daughter to a cobbler or a teacher, for men who are in *l-brra*, these differences are of relatively limited importance, and it is acceptable to possess just hazy knowledge of their doings *temma* (there). Their qualifying characteristic is, as I explore below, "the outside" itself rather than their specific activities there.

Different reasons may be given for the hazy knowledge surrounding migrants' doings in *l-brra*. Not knowing is partly linked to a rather stoic acknowledgment that *temma mashi bhal hnaya* ([over] there it's not like here). People see little point in classifying and differentiating individuals and their jobs on the basis of the same classificatory regimes that work in Morocco. Khadija, the wife of a migrant living in Spain, made this clear once when I asked her about her husband: "I think he works in construction [*le-bni*]. I think he said that once. But construction isn't like what you see here, so I'm not sure. Even if he did say construction, I wouldn't know what it means out there. I've heard that there, builders have clean clothes [*hwayejhom nqiyin*]. So I don't know. . . ."

The haziness I refer to is of course also linked to a desire to gloss over the fact that migrant relatives may be employed in low-status jobs (if at all) and involved in underground commercial (and other) activities. Given the negative stories circulating about migrants' activities abroad and the knowledge about the kinds of jobs available for *nas dyalna* (our people—i.e.,

Moroccans and more generally North African/Muslim migrants) in Europe, it is not entirely surprising that people, particularly when first meeting me, tend to gloss over their relatives' activities in *l-brra* and participate in the production of a specific kind of hazy knowledge about "those who go." With so many negative images circulating locally about young Moroccans selling drugs in Europe, for example, the mothers and sisters of young migrants in particular generally take great pains to stress that their sons and brothers are not involved in dealing drugs, saying "*huwa mashi weld l-ghobra*" (literally, "he isn't the powder's child"—i.e., someone who makes money selling drugs in *l-brra*). However, while relatives in the Tadla tend to be clear about what their sons or brothers are not doing in *l-brra*, what these young men are involved in on the other side of the Mediterranean Sea is often difficult to ascertain. This haziness applies to migrant relatives more generally, and specific questions on the nature of the jobs of close relatives are often answered, if at all, with a vague "*ybi' u yshri*" (he buys and he sells), meaning that the man in question is involved in some kind of commerce. What exactly he "buys and sells," and from and to whom, is seen as an odd question that is often met with a shrug—an observation Katy Gardner (2008) also makes in her work on Bangladeshi migration to Britain, where she argues that it is the actual connection with *bidesh* (foreign countries), rather than one's specific commercial (or other) activities in Britain, that matters and qualifies migrants. I stopped asking specific questions about employment in *l-brra* a few months into my first stay in the area, particularly when I realized that in the Tadla, saying that one's migrant son or husband "*ybi' u yshri*" is met with an understanding nod of approval by the listener, and no further questions are asked.

Importantly, not everyone is so vague when discussing migrants' doings in *l-brra*. Some people happily volunteer damaging information about migrants' activities abroad. As I have mentioned, stories circulate continually in the Tadla about Moroccans in *l-brra* doing degrading jobs, living in degrading conditions, and eating degrading foods. This negative discourse often arises on specific occasions—for example, when nonmigrants comment on migrants' arrogance during their return visits to Morocco, where they are accused of showing off their flashy cars, expensive clothes, and extremely high offers of *sdaq* (bridewealth). "They live like animals in Europe and then come here and prance around like princes," I often hear people say. These unforgiving comments draw eclectically on information originating from migrants themselves, newspaper and TV programs about Moroccan migrants' lives abroad, and stories recounted in the souk or *qehwa* (coffeehouse), all combined with a sort of vengeful imagination of the nonmigrant population. When commenting on migrants' matchless offers of bridewealth, their loud, excessive wedding parties, and their gestures indicative of careless wealth—leaving excessively generous tips for waiters, buying excessive quantities of meat at the butcher's, and so on—some people invoke the discourse of animallike lifestyle of migrants abroad and use this narrative to attempt to undermine migrants' appeal in terms of wealth and status.[1]

It is often unmarried, educated men who invoke these vengeful narratives about migrants' unworthy doings in *l-brra*. These are either men from the same rural areas of the migrants in question who have made their way through the Moroccan education system and become state-school teachers or men from a slightly higher position in the social hierarchy of a given village or neighborhood, whose families own a small business in town or larger plots of land in its surrounding countryside. These men consider themselves inherently superior to peasant migrants, either because of their intellectual work, something highly valued in the Tadla, or because of their inherited higher social status. The fact that their migrant neighbors—and, indeed, their migrant relatives—are surpassing them in wealth, prestige, and ultimately even rank makes this class of nonmigrants particularly prone to using the discourse of migrants' inhuman status abroad as a way of reminding themselves and others of their own superior humanity.

However, with a few important, vengeful exceptions, such as those above, generally speaking it is haziness that characterizes discussions of migrants' doings abroad. Considering the low-status jobs that many Moroccans have in Italy (see Capello 2008; Dal Lago 1999) and indeed the dehumanizing effect their stay in *l-brra* is sometimes described as having on them (I will return below to this specific language of nonhumanity reserved for migrants), it comes as no surprise that my acquaintances and interlocutors often choose to change the topic of conversation. I would argue, however, that there is more to this than simple discomfort or silent omission. What men are doing abroad simply is not, in many cases, the point.[2] In conversations between family members and neighbors, I have very rarely heard someone ask what a son, brother or husband does in *l-brra*. At times, people may ask, "*Wash kheddam?*" (is he employed or does he have work?), and, after receiving a yes or a no, the conversation will move on to other topics. *Kayn f l-brra* or *huwa 'la brra* (he is in "the outside") is what matters, what people are interested in, and what ultimately qualifies the person in question. In this sense *l-brra* takes the semblances of a "qualisign"—a quality that is, as in Charles S. Peirce's (1998) classic definition, both an embodied sign and a value signifier (cf. Chu 2010). I explore this in more detail below through the classic example of migrant marriage arrangements, where the one trait that seems to ultimately count is the groom's connection with *l-brra*.

Extraordinary Spouses

L-brra's power to qualify people in specific, special ways emerges most strikingly in marriage arrangements. When a prospective groom *lli kaimshi brra* (who goes [to the] outside) approaches a household asking for a daughter's hand, the complex procedures I have witnessed in marriage arrangements between nonmigrants—the intense questioning, the long periods of negotiations between the families of future groom and bride, the careful evaluation of the man's background and lineage—often seem to disappear. Though of course exceptions and variations exist, a man's relationship with *l-brra* often seems to override other characteristics of his personhood. In other words, being, say, a *'rubi* (peasant, but also, disparagingly, a country bumpkin, unsophisticated) or illiterate, or of uncertain employment status, or even of unclear family background, is not a determining factor when a household is evaluating a marriage offer from a migrant man.

My friend Jihane's nuptial story is a good example of the above. Jihane has a secondary school diploma and is the daughter of the manager of a local business. At eighteen, she married Salah, a *'rubi men le-'rubiya* (a peasant from the countryside—an ironic repetition Jihane uses to stress the peasant origins and essence of her husband) who had crossed into Italy as a teenager. A friend from the neighborhood had told her that her brother Salah was back in town for a while and was looking for a bride. Jihane agreed to think about it, and two days later her friend, accompanied by her brother and mother, showed up at Jihane's home to discuss the marriage with her father. Jihane's father had initially resisted the offer—the future he had in mind for his daughter was not marriage with a *'rubi* from Fqih Ben Salah, an agricultural town in the Tadla that, for people like Jihane's father, is synonymous with peasantry, illiteracy, and mass emigration. Despite his initial reluctance, however, Jihane's father eventually accepted the migrant's offer. A week later the agreement was sealed between the two families, and Jihane was getting married: Salah had to rush back to Italy before his Italian *wraq* (papers/documents) expired.

When Jihane first told me the story of her marriage, I was struck by the class and, more generally, social differences between the bride and groom. In a context where formal education, far from universal in Morocco (see chap. 4), is an invaluable attribute, and where state or privately employed educated people take great pains to distinguish themselves from the 'rubiya (peasants) around them, often starting with their own kin, Jihane's marriage arrangement seemed quite striking. An exceptional evaluation had been made of the groom by virtue of his connection to l-brra, making the other characterizing features of his personhood virtually irrelevant, or at least likely to be ignored.

I have come across many cases like Jihane's in the Tadla, where migrants with unclear family lineages at home and even less clear jobs in l-brra are granted the hands of educated, more urban daughters. It is, of course, difficult to generalize, as each marriage arrangement has its own peculiar biography, but it is fair to say that a migrant prospective husband is rarely turned down by a family in the Tadla. During conversations with me, criticism is often vented against parents who "give their daughters away" to migrants. These parents are often portrayed by onlookers as either naïve or selfish (or both) and as putting their own interests before those of their daughters. I am sometimes taken aback by these spiteful comments, not least because they are often voiced by acquaintances who themselves have at least one daughter married to a migrant. People often portray their own family stories of migrant weddings as being different, exceptional, or, in any event, unrelated to the judgment expressed regarding other households. Perhaps this is another manifestation of the constant moral oscillation—constitutive, as I discuss also in chapter 6, of the ways people speak about l-brra more generally—between damning and admiring conceptualizations of migrants. Either way, the fact remains that a neighbor or relative may be harshly criticized for granting his daughter's hand to a "peasant migrant" by someone who's daughters are all married to migrant men. And while the migrant marriages of others are critiqued, migrants seem to be desirable grooms for one's own family.

The fact that migrants are seen, ultimately, as desirable sons-in-law is linked to a variety of factors. Migrants' access to wealth through their employment in l-brra plays an important role in these marriage arrangements, where not too many questions are asked, and where migrants get away with marrying women of sometimes quite different social statuses. The bridewealth that migrants are able to offer is often on an entirely different scale compared to what nonmigrant men in the area are able to put together. This creates a paradoxical social scenario, classic in many emigration settings (Chu 2010; McMurray 2001; Sayad 1999), where educated and respectably employed men are unable to generate the kind of bridewealth afforded by migrant men with little or no education and employed in low-status jobs. As Hamza, a young teacher I know in Casablanca, often tells me, only half-jokingly I suspect, "Those who go, Alice, they are our real ruin [*ruwina*] . . . not corruption, not unemployment. . . . Those who go are Morocco's real problem!"

On paper, Hamza has all the requisites for being a desirable husband. He is well educated and has a stable job in a private secondary school in Casablanca, meaning he can guarantee a decent standard of living and dignified social status to his future wife. However, this ideal nuptial setup is ruined by, as he puts it, "*l-hayawanat dyal brra*" (the animals of [the] outside). In his native village in the Tadla, where he is hoping to find a wife, the bridewealth "rate" has risen dizzily over the last ten years, making it hard for a man who has not left Morocco to be able to compete financially with migrants.[3] "They come back with very little time and lots of money," Hamza said once, summarizing the situation for me. "They knock on the door of the first pretty girl they spot and offer such a high bridewealth that the parents would be fools to refuse. They have no time to discuss and negotiate with the parents of the girl; if the parents ask for more money they agree straightaway, because they want to have the wedding party before they set off again for 'the outside,' you understand? They make normal people who negotiate bridewealth because we have to, and because it's tradition, Alice, look mean [*sqram*]." Hamza's words echo what many authors writing on migration have argued—namely that migrants are able, by means of foreign-accumulated economic, social, and cultural capital, to buy into and displace more longstanding forms of status and hierarchy (see Gardner 1995; Ghannam 1998; Gilsenan 1996, 265 -97; McMurray 2001; Persichetti 2003; Salih 2003, 53 -80; Sayad 1999). My sense, however, is that the different forms of capital that migrants offer, displace, and symbolize only partially explain their desirability as marriage partners and, more generally, their distinctive "specialness" in the Tadla. At the risk of contradicting my nonmigrant acquaintances like Hamza, who put the difference between themselves and migrants down to a question of wealth, I would argue that what a migrant is offering his future wife and her family is not just more money or any other kind of more conventional capital but something of *l-brra* itself.

With this I am referring not just to the concrete, legal possibilities to reach *l-brra* that a migrant husband can potentially offer his wife and her family. The legal regime in Europe is such that marriage to a legally resident migrant is one of the very few ways available to people in the Tadla to reach *l-brra mashi b l-flouka* (not by boat—i.e., legally, with documents), making migrant spouses valuable intermediaries for *l-brra*. However, it is not solely the pragmatic possibility of moving to *l-brra* that "those who go" embody. Indeed, particularly in the more rural areas of the Tadla, wives of migrants rarely end up joining their husbands in *l-brra*. This is because their husbands often remain undocumented migrants throughout the marriage and thus are not able to *dir le-wraq* (do the documents—i.e., submit a family reunification application to the local migration authorities). It is also because some men feel ambivalent about their wives joining them in *l-brra*, and may postpone the decision over the years. Either way, as we will see in the following chapter, premarital promises of migration to *l-brra* often do not deliver in the time and way expected. The parents and the young prospective spouses are aware of this—they have seen it happen time and again in their neighbors' and relatives' households, and they have heard countless stories about the hardships endured by migrants' wives.

Despite this common, shared knowledge, "those who go" continue to embody something that nonmigrants simply cannot, and this inevitably places them in a qualitatively different category—or league—from any other man. My sense is that what distinguishes them is no less than *l-brra* itself. Once a man leaves for *l-brra*, *l-brra* becomes an inextricable part of who he is in relation to others. This makes the conceptualization of *l-brra* as a place of difference, betterness, and possibility spill over on and in the people who have managed to reach it. *L-brra* becomes an intangible quality of those who leave for it, affecting in fundamental ways the kinds of evaluations (both positive and negative) reserved for them in the Tadla. Indeed, my sense is that the extraordinary attitudes encountered in Mohammed's stories about migrants above, the hazy knowledge that is attached to migrants' doings in *l-brra*, and the passionate, contrasting views surrounding "those who go" in the Tadla all emerge from the complex pragmatic and imaginative conceptualizations of *l-brra*. These include the common understanding that *l-brra* has the power to fundamentally transform migrants from the inside out or, perhaps more accurately, from the outside in—a transformation to which I now turn.

Intimate Transformation

A classic comparison is made in the migration literature between the transformational powers of migration and those of traditional initiation rites (e.g., Ali 2007; de Haas and van Rooij 2010, 45; Jónsson 2008; Kandel and Massey 2002). In particular, parallels have been drawn between the changes migration brings to a migrant's social standing (gender and social maturity, for example) and those neophytes undergo through initiation. The changes people in the Tadla identify in migrants could be also compared, in a sense, to those produced by initiation rites—which, as in Victor Turner's (1967) classic analysis, affect the very core of those involved. In his work on Ndembu male circumcision ceremonies in northwestern Zambia, Turner famously critiqued the common definition of initiation rites as processes that involve merely conveying "an unchanging substance from one position to another by a quasi-mechanical force (as sociologists we would be inclined to see)" (Turner 1967, 102). In contrast to this mechanistic view, Turner boldly defined initiation rites as "ontological transformations" (102). He wrote that in the liminal period of male rituals, when young Ndembu boys leave for the bush and are secluded from the rest of the community, as well as during the *mukanda* (the boy's circumcision ceremony), initiates are "believed to change their nature" (102). Turner argues that the arcane knowledge boys receive from the elders during these initiation rituals "is not a mere acquisition of knowledge, but a change in being" (102), as it "transforms them from one kind of human being into another" (108).

While devoid of any specific kind of ceremonial or sacred language (see chap. 6), the kinds of transformations people in the Tadla identify in returning migrants recall in important ways Turner's definition of ritual. Tadla residents identify in migrants not only a change in wealth and status but also core transformations concerning the very features that define migrants' personhood. As in Turner's definition of ritual, there is something ontological in the way the migratory process, and more specifically *l-brra*, operates—affecting, for good or worse, the very being of those involved.

One obvious indication that *l-brra* comes to affect and qualify migrants is that it features in the very ways they are designated as people. Migrants are rarely referred to in the Tadla without *l-brra* being mentioned. Indeed, the term for migrant—*muhajir* in Modern Standard Arabic, also *zmagri* in Darija/Moroccan Arabic—is rarely used in local parlance. People who have migrated are referred to as *nas lli kaimshiw brra* (people who go [to the] outside), shortened, as we have seen, to *huma lli kaimshiw* (those who go) and other interchangeable permutations: *huma lli kaynin temma* (those who are "there"), *huma temma* (those "there"), and so on. So, for example, Said, my neighbor when I lived in Zafiah, is never referred to simply as Said but always as *Said lli kaimshi brra* (Said who goes [to the] outside), abbreviated sometimes to *Said lli kaimshi* (Said who goes). The house where his family lives, built gradually over the years during Said's summer visits, is a *dar dyal brra* (house of [the] outside), and the neighbors refer to the whole family as *nas lli kaimshiw brra* (people who go [to the] outside).

Migrants themselves tend to incorporate *l-brra* into their social personhood. A returnee migrant visiting the Tadla will often introduce himself by saying "*ana kayn f l-brra*" or "*ana f l-brra*" (I am in the outside). A declaration of absence, of not being just in Morocco where one has temporarily appeared, *ana f l-brra* is as much a description of who one is as of where one lives. *Ana f l-brra* leaves ambiguously open whether the person in question has only partially returned home and whether his "being" can be in any way separated from the place-cum-entity of *l-brra*. Indeed, *l-brra*'s ability to capture and retain parts of those who leave for it is made explicit at times. Some people in the Tadla liken, for example, *l-brra* to a powerful woman with whom migrants enter intimate relationships that change them to the very core. This image of "the outside" as a feminized and powerful entity is not uncommon in North African (see Ben Jelloun 2009; Sayad 1991). Sayad reports a retired Algerian laborer living in a Parisian banlieue phrasing this imaging with bleak clarity: "France, I'm gonna tell you, is a low-life woman, like a whore. Without you know it, she encircles you, she takes to seducing you until you've fallen for her and then she sucks your blood, she makes you wait on her hand and foot. . . . She is a sorceress. She has taken so many men with her. . . . She has a way of keeping you a prisoner" (cited in Bourdieu and Wacquant 2000, 176). In the Tadla, *l-brra* is also at times identified as a feminized and lustfully attractive entity. Women married to migrants ironically point out to me that their husbands are married to *l-brra* rather than to them: "*huwa mzawj bih, mashi biya ana*" (he is married to "it," not to me). With this, they allude not only to the possibility of their long-absent husbands having sexual encounters (if not full romances or even parallel married lives) while away but also, possibly more radically, to the feeling that their husbands' relationship with *l-brra* itself is of a much more intimate and determining nature than the one with their own wives.

People detect the transformative effects of this intimate relationship between migrants and *l-brra* when men come back to visit their hometowns and villages. First and foremost, signs of *l-brra* are identified on migrants' physical bodies. Skin color and texture are monitored closely—"*jeldu mashi bhal jeld dyalna*" (his skin is not like our skin), a friend once told me, nodding toward a man walking past us. "*Huwa f l-brra*" (he's in "the outside"). Migrants' skin is at times described as becoming fairer and softer, *bhal l-brra* (like the outside). This physical change is attributed to a variety of factors, from *l-brra*'s different sunrays to the different kinds of food migrants eat *temma* (there). However detailed the explanation for such striking transformation, it is always accompanied by the idea that it is "the outside" per se that is manifesting itself on migrants' skin. A migrant is thus clearly identifiable to my acquaintances simply, as they put it, *men l-brra f jeldu* (from the outside on/in his skin).

L-brra's interference with migrants' bodies doesn't seem to stop at the surface of the skin. Women married to migrants often mention to me how their husbands, when they return home, behave in strange ways, speak strange words in their sleep, and demand strange ingredients in their meals. The strangeness women detect in their husbands is seen only in part as the result of learning new behaviors *temma* (there). Strangeness is also traced back to the ability of *l-brra* itself to permeate migrants' bodies and minds and make them act in peculiar ways. After all, it is common knowledge in the Tadla that *l-brra* can *dkhel f bnadem* (enter into people/humans).

L-brra's ability to affect people *f l-dakhel* (within/inside) was first brought to my attention by Samira, a young woman married to a migrant man. I happened to be staying at her house in the outskirts of Zafiah during one of her husband's yearly visits home. One day during my stay, an argument broke out between the couple while we were having lunch. After a few minutes of heated discussion, Samira's husband lost his patience and banged his open hand on the table, making his elderly mother, who also lived in the house, shriek with fear. The angry gesture put an end to the conjugal discussion, and Samira started clearing the table with a tray and moved to the kitchen. I quickly followed her, mainly out of embarrassment for having witnessed something I knew I wasn't supposed to see as a nonkin guest. "*Sheftih?*" (did you see him?), Samira whispered to me when I entered the kitchen. She was making reference to her husband's angry outburst, which had surprised us all. "'*Endu l-brra fih*" (he has the outside inside him), she told me, and then continued, "*Men nhar li msha, huwa mashi 'adi*" (since the day he left, he has not been normal/himself).

Using the traditional idiom of spirit possession, Samira told me that her husband was "*mqiws*" (touched). Being touched, in Moroccan Darija, means being struck or possessed by a *jenn* (spirit).[4] A person can be stricken by a *jenn* for a variety of reasons—for having angered it, for being in a place known to be inhabited by *jnun* (spirits, sing. *jenn*)—for example, near a source of water—or for being in a particularly vulnerable emotional state (Pandolfo 2007, 352). The effects of being stricken or seized by a *jenn* are considered varied in the Tadla and depend not only on the kind of *jenn* in question but also on its specific desires and moods. A *jenn* can make humans fall ill, seduce them, make them feel pain in certain parts of the body or even paralyze them, affect their emotional state, control their love life, and, more generally, make them behave in peculiar ways. By transposing this language of spirit possession to her husband's behavior, Samira was qualifying the relationship between her migrant husband and *l-brra* in a specific way: she was identifying *l-brra* as the kind of thing that can take over one's being, just like a *jenn*. Samira pointed out to me that since he had been touched by *l-brra*, her husband walked differently and spoke differently; his skin was becoming fairer and his eyes a little darker. Samira told me that her husband's mood had changed radically, and he would sometimes have strange outbursts of rage like the one I had witnessed over lunch. "*Safi, l-brra dkhel fih*" (that's it, the outside has got inside him), Samira would say throughout her husband's stay every time he raised his voice or became excessively angry.

By identifying *l-brra* in her husband's mood and being, Samira, together with recognizing *l-brra*'s peculiar transformational powers, was of course also making a powerful although indirect criticism of her spouse. *L-brra* often emerges as an idiom—even a discursive genre (cf. Kapchan 1996)—through which people in the Tadla express their discontent, be it economic-cum-existential, as we will see in chapter 6, or interpersonal, as will emerge, for example, in women's discussions of marriage and family in chapter 3. However, it would be a mistake to write off too swiftly women's discourses about *l-brra fih* (the outside inside him) as merely functional tools employed by frustrated wives to complain about their irritable husbands. The problem with such an analysis—which recalls, incidentally, the classic anthropological analysis of spirit possession as a structural functional "societal valve," sensu I. M. Lewis (1971)—is that it would grossly overlook these women's very explicit concerns (and wonderment) about the palpable effects of *l-brra* on those returning from it, starting from their own husbands. There is no question for the women I know in the Tadla that *l-brra*'s effects on their migrant husbands are very real indeed.

Possibly because of the intimate nature of *l-brra*'s effects, it is often in intimate encounters with returning husbands that women experience these very real effects most directly. "*Sheft l-brra fih f l-byt*" (I saw the outside in him in the room—i.e., the bedroom), women say when I ask them about their husbands' returns. Some will describe how they can sometimes spot *l-brra f 'eynih* (in his eyes) or how *l-brra* makes their husbands act in strange, unexpected ways "*mlli buhadna*" (when we're alone). "*Bayna blli l-brra dar lih shi haja*" (it's clear/obvious that the outside has done something to him).

Different Animals

The figure of the *hayawanat* (animals) that opens this chapter reappears at times in these intimate discussions about migrant husbands. Either in reference to the unnatural bursts of conjugal intimacy dictated by *l-brra*'s erratic temporality we encountered in chapter 1 or to describe the peculiar, unnerving behavior of a returning migrant husband, women sometimes conjure up the figure of the *hayawanat* just as Saida did to describe her migrant neighbors and Hamza does to debase his migrant marriage rivals. While it is always difficult to untangle metaphors from actual ontological statements—the two are permanently and mischievously tangled when it comes to *l-brra*—the different ways and contexts in which migrants are spoken of as animals in the Tadla does point to a specific kind of difference nonmigrants identify in them. As we saw in the opening scene of this chapter, the term *hayawanat* is not limited solely to vengeful descriptions of migrants' lives abroad. In certain narrative contexts or in specific situations migrants are said to have become different kinds of beings while away.

In the summer of 2009, I visited the relatives of a Moroccan family friend living in Italy in his hometown, close to Zafiah. I still have vivid memories of the visit because while I was there, I found it impossible to sleep at night. For nearly three weeks, I spent the nights listening, with the rest of the family, to the noise of engines, the screeching of tires, and the loud *she'bi* (popular) music coming from cars roaring up and down the narrow dirt alleys of the neighborhood. The cars that kept my hosts and myself awake were of a special kind, with Italian and Spanish number plates. As my hosts explained to me, they were driven by "those who go to the outside," who had returned for the summer and spent their time cruising around their hometown in their four-wheeled symbols of success. One night, two or three days into our sleeplessness, the household's great-grandmother, generally too weak to speak, spurted out in a feeble voice that emerged from the side of the room where she lay day and night, "*Wullau hayawanat*" (they've become animals).

Something in the elderly woman's tone surprised me. There was something in the way she used the word *hayawanat* that drew my attention to the fact that "animals" is not only about a moral condemnation but also about something deeper and more intangible, something about the kind of beings migrants may become. As perhaps already clear from its scattered appearances in this chapter, the term *hayawanat* is used in a variety of different contexts in the Tadla and to refer to a variety of different characteristics identified in migrants and their behaviors—either witnessed directly when they are home or imagined while they are abroad. In all cases, however, *hayawanat* is used to differentiate the speaker from migrants.

It is this act of differentiation that I think is important, as it reiterates a key quality of migrants in the Tadla: their constitutive difference by virtue of their contact with *l-brra*. My interlocutors' use of the term *hayawanat* allows me to draw on another African context of migration where the parallel between migrants and animals is made explicit and where the risk of migrants becoming animals is voiced directly. I am referring to West African bushfalling, the term originally used for hunting in the forest and today the local word for migration in a number of West African settings (Alpes 2012; Gaibazzi 2015; Nyamnjoh 2011; Ngwa and Ngwa 2006). As Maybritt Jill Alpes (2012, 91) writes with regard to Anglophone Cameroon, bushfalling is "the act of going out to the 'wilderness' (bush) to hunt down meat (money) and bring back home the trophies." Francis Nyamnjoh speaks of cases where the hunter/migrant himself can become game by virtue of his contact with the bush/*whiteman kontry*: "The hunt and distance farming make sense only to the extent that the hunter or farmer is able to return home at the end of the day. Those who transform the hunting ground . . . into a permanent home run the risk of being accused of having sacrificed kin or having themselves been converted into game by the intended quarry" (Nyamnjoh 2011, 708). Nyamnjoh's observation about the risks of bushfalling in Cameroon recall in interesting ways the transformational risks and possibilities associated with travel to *l-brra* in the Tadla. Whether leaving for "the bush" or "the outside," migrants in both ethnographic cases risk becoming permanently affected by their powerful destination. Indeed, the parallel to be drawn here regards not only the animal trope present in both settings—though clearly with different implications and perhaps degrees of literality in a hunting context like that discussed by Nyamnjoh—but also the fact that migrants are conceptualized, both in Cameroon and in Morocco, as becoming the elsewhere they have left for. In both cases, migrants can become "the other side."

The fact that so-called sending communities perceive migrants as fundamentally different and changed is a recurrent theme in much of the migration literature. Sayad's pioneering exploration of the colonial, cultural, and existential dimensions of twentieth century Algerian migration to France, for example, provides a disturbing insight into the effects of this exodus on migrants themselves, whom he describes, without mincing his words, as a "double absence" that does not exist either at home or abroad (Sayad 1999; see also Sayad 1988). Other authors have traced the reintegration difficulties migrants encounter when they return home—the mixture of positive and negative feelings migrants are greeted with (Osella and Osella 2000), migrants' disappointment in realizing their exclusion from "home" (Mandel 1990), and the inevitable, often painful difference that emerges between those who have stayed and those who have left (Miller 2008).

What is striking about people's interaction with migrants in the Tadla is that the difference identified in returning neighbors, friends, even husbands is associated, in part at least, with the complex powers of *l-brra* itself. Migrants are not considered different solely because they have learned new kinds of behavior abroad or have stayed away too long and forgotten local ways of being. As we have seen, together with these estranging elements, migrants are perceived as being affected by *l-brra* itself, as being permeated by some of *l-brra*'s impalpable qualities and thus as being different—strange, incomprehensible, changed, as well as inescapably special—because *l-brra* is effectively penetrating and transforming them. They have, in short, *l-brra f dakhel* (the outside inside). This is what makes Turner's intuition about the "change in being" of initiation rituals so valuable for thinking about migration in the Tadla. People's interaction with migrants reveals how migration here cannot be framed, to paraphrase Turner, merely as a mechanical force that transfers an unchanged person from one position (e.g., nonmigrant, boy, poor) to another (e.g., migrant, man, rich). Rather, migration reveals itself here as a transformational force in precisely the deep, ontological sense Turner theorized for Ndembu rituals. I return to the gendered implications and complications of such a transformation toward the end of the book, where I trace how *l-brra* becomes part and parcel of migrants' very masculinity. To conclude the present discussion, let me consider a key implication of migrants' transformative contact with *l-brra*—namely, the role it plays in people's imagination and conceptualization of *l-brra* itself.

Imaginative Bodies

I have used this chapter to introduce *huma lli kaimshiw* (those who go), fundamental figures in the Tadla's imaginative and pragmatic reckoning with *l-brra*. My focus has been primarily on the different kinds of palpable and impalpable effects that *l-brra* is observed and imagined to have on migrants. Observation and imagination, however, are bidirectional: the imagination of *l-brra* informs the conceptualization of migrants, but, equally, intimate interaction with, observation of, and stories about migrants directly feed into the imagination of *l-brra*. Migrants are in this sense key "technologies of the imagination" in the Tadla, defined by David Sneath et al. (2009, 19) as "social and material means by which particular imaginings are generated" and thus integral protagonists of the "heterogeneous processes by which imaginative effects come about in social life" (19).

Anthropological work on the imagination (e.g., Bryant and Knight 2019; D'Onofrio 2017; Mittermaier 2011) increasingly argues for closer ethnographic attention to the social and intimate workings of the imagination—the "pragmatics of imagination," as Diana Allan (2014, 140) calls it in her work on Palestinian "dream talk" in Shatila. My sense is that the interaction between migrants and nonmigrants in the Tadla constitutes an important "live" example of the practical and pragmatic workings of the imagination. Through migrants and their "cyborg bodies"—part Moroccan, part *brra*; part familiar, part strange—people in the Tadla come to imagine, and indeed experience, *l-brra*, its properties, and its effects. Donna Haraway's (1991) classic use of "cyborg" as metaphor for hybrid of machine and organism, creature of both fiction and lived social reality, powerfully captures migrants' hybrid qualities—part familiar (husband, son, neighbor) and part "outside" beings who behave, look, and speak in unexpected, wondrous, even unsettling ways. It is through the interaction with these complex migrant bodies, their stories and myths, their gifts and cars, their styles and speech, that people in the Tadla form a specific kind of knowledge about "the outside," a specific kind of understating of what *l-brra* is and what it is able to do: financially, physically, emotionally.

While migration studies have long pointed out migrants' contribution to the formation of people's imagination of the elsewhere, the literature generally focuses on the narrative and material culture of migrants' returns—stories, reports, and memories of "the other side," gifts, clothes, and conspicuous consumption back home. Here, however, it is not only the material signs of wealth and success migrants (sometimes) bring home, nor is it only the wonderous and bleak stories migrants recount or that are recounted through them about *tmma* (there), that provide people in Tadla with imaginative material about *l-brra*. One of the fundamental ways in which migrants produce imaginations of and knowledge about *l-brra*—one of the key ways in which they are, indeed, "technologies of the imagination"—is also through their own unavoidable transformation. By engaging with migrants who have *l-brra f dakhel* (the outside inside), people in the Tadla are in a sense engaging firsthand with *l-brra* itself.

Migrants are not the only technology of the imagination of *l-brra* available to people in the Tadla. Kuwaiti satellite channels broadcasting US TV series (Ossman 1994), tourists going off the beaten track to explore Atlas Mountains villages (Bennani-Chraïbi 1994), and palpable or elusive remnants of the French Protectorate—from French-speaking Moroccan elites to French-sponsored development projects (Crawford 2008)—are just some examples of the many imaginative technologies linking the Tadla to *l-brra*. Migrants, however, are different kinds of conduits from satellite TV channels, tourists, and even traces of French colonialism. As we started to see in the previous chapter and will see throughout the rest of the book, migrants bring *l-brra* into the most intimate spheres of people's lives, from kinship structures all the way to the intimacy of conjugal bonds. This intimate power is perhaps most palpable in the lives of those who are married to migrants—so much so that, as we shall see in the next chapter, they sometimes speak of themselves as "married to the outside."

Notes

1. See David McMurray's (2001, 65) discussion of a parallel "status competition between those who leave and those who stay behind" in the Moroccan frontier town of Nador in the 1980s. McMurray focuses on the ways in which the traditional Nadori elite, having to reckon with the threat to their social status posed by a new troubling class of rural, illiterate, but rich migrants, tried to undermine migrants by reinforcing their cultural and symbolic superiority (literacy, contacts with high officials, age-old social prestige, taste, and so on). McMurray also shows, however, that toward the end of the 1980s, traditional elites and petit bourgeois were slowly losing the exclusivity to determine and control what signified "higher social status" to the new moneyed emigrant families.

2. What migrant women do is also, in some cases, not the point. It does, however, depend, as with men, on the specific situation. A woman leaving Morocco on her own is subject to both implicit and explicit questioning about her intentions while a woman joining her husband is generally subject to less moral scrutiny.

3. As is the case for many of my young interlocutors, Henrik Vigh (2009) argues that one of the main reasons for migration in his Guinea-Bissau field-site is the possibility it offers to overcome the "schism between the culturally expected and the socially possible" (95) by allowing men to accumulate enough resources to marry and start a family. The relationship between migration and marriage here acquires an additional dimension: by becoming, through migration, socially possible for migrants, marriage becomes, in parallel, *un*achievable for nonmigrants.

4. *Jnun* (in Moroccan Arabic: *jenn* [singular]; *jnun* [plural]) are supernatural beings mentioned in the Quran that live in a world parallel to humankind. They can be neutral, good, or evil and have the power, among other things, to make humans fall ill and to possess them and seduce them. See Vincent Crapanzano's (1980) classic ethnographic account of the popular *jenn* in Morocco Aisha Qandisha, and, for contemporary engagements with *jnun* in Morocco, Lawrence Rosen's (2016, 93–166) gentle account of *jnun* and other spiritual entities through the words of a longtime interlocutor and friend in Sefrou; Emilio Spadola's (2014) *The Calls of Islam* on spirit trance, exorcism, and mass mediation in Fez; and Stefania Pandolfo's (2018) *Knot of the Soul* on Islamic theological and medical reasoning on the soul and its afflictions.

3

WIVES OF ELSEWHERE

"Ana, Alice, ana mzawja b l-brra" (I, Alice, I'm married to *l-brra*), Salima declares with a sad smile. Salima, a Zafiah woman in her thirties, married Karim at sixteen. Three weeks after the wedding, Karim left for Italy and has never been back since. Salima tells me that something went wrong with his papers when he returned to Italy after the wedding and that since then, he has been living as a *clandestino* (undocumented migrant [Italian]) in Italy, making it impossible for him to leave the country. When I first met Salima, Karim had been away nearly twenty years—"I'm not married to my husband; I'm married to the outside," Salima always says. By marrying Karim, Salima also entered into an inescapable relationship with *l-brra*, the entity that encompasses her husband and anchors him away from her. Karim's protracted absence testifies to his valuable link with *l-brra* and is also the manifestation of the painful flip side of this special link: a presence in *l-brra* necessarily entails physical absence *hna* (here). The encompassing link between Karim and *l-brra* means that interactions between Salima and her husband are mediated by *l-brra*, a mediation so powerful that at times it takes center stage, strongly conveying the sense that *l-brra* may be the real object of Salima's relationship and her husband simply its conduit.

This chapter is about the intimate connections women like Salima come to form with *l-brra* through their migrant husbands. Continuing my exploration of *l-brra*'s operative force in the practical and imaginative unfolding of life in the Tadla, I trace how *l-brra* engenders specific subjectivities and relations not only for those who leave but also for those who stay, willingly or unwillingly. Taking Salima's melancholic remark on her marriage as a starting point—"I'm married to the outside"—I trace how a conjugal link with a migrant instantiates a sustained and complex relationship with *l-brra* itself, a relationship that I term of *intimate distance*.

In particular, I trace how such intimate distance with *l-brra* can call into question, expand, or alter a woman's very personhood in the Tadla, revealing how migration, as well as modifying gender relations as the literature on the "left behind" argues, may also be producing specific and precarious gendered subjects.

Ambiguous Absence

"This isn't a normal life, Alice. A wife is meant to be close to her husband, not alone like me. There is always an empty space inside me, and I can't fill it up." Salima tucks herself deeper under the blankets, and after whispering "*buonanotte khti*" (good night [Italian] sister [Arabic]) in my direction, she goes silent. I can't see her in the pitch darkness of the room, but I know her eyes are still wide open. For the past two hours we have been talking in the dark about her faraway husband, while the rest of the house is asleep. Lying next to us on the blankets spread out on the floor for the night is Salima's nine-year-old niece, who dozed off at some point during the conversation. In the room next door, Salima's mother-in-law and her three sisters-in-law are also sleeping. The gentle snoring of Salima's brother-in-law reaches us from another room he is sharing with his paternal uncle and his nephews. As often happens in these virilocal family settings where women are surrounded by their husbands' relatives, Salima tells me the story of her married life in stolen pockets of time and space: late in the night or early in the morning when everyone is asleep, on the flat roof or terrace while hanging clothes, on the way to the corner shop to buy milk or bread. Stories are often abruptly interrupted by the arrival of an unwanted or potentially problematic listener. Many of the migrants' wives' narratives I have collected in the Tadla are of a distinctly intermittent, patchy nature, often consisting of allusions and brief comments that are then developed and clarified, at times even weeks later, when another opportunity arises for talking without being seen or heard by the woman's relatives. In these many intermittent stories, absence—the materialization in the Tadla of a husband's presence in *l-brra*—is a constant, imposing theme.

To marry a migrant in the Tadla is, in many ways, to marry an absence. Between the irregular visits of migrant men I described in chapter 1, there are long periods, sometimes even decades, when husbands are not physically present and their wives *kaimshiw buhadhom* (go/walk alone). As I mentioned in the introduction, migration in the Tadla is mainly a male affair, and although women's migration from Morocco is significant (see, e.g., Ruba Salih's [2003] study of Moroccan migrant women in Italy), in the Tadla it is predominantly men who leave—or leave first, anyway. As we saw in the previous chapters, men in the Tadla generally emigrate as young unmarried *drari* (boys) and often marry young women of their local or neighboring area during one of their return visits when they have accumulated enough money and resources in *l-brra* to pay for the ceremony and the bridewealth and meet the rest of the bride's family's requirements.

In most cases I know, a fundamental underlying aspect of the marriage negotiations between the families of the future bride and groom is the understanding that the migrant man will *iddiha* (take her) as soon as possible, meaning that she will move to *l-brra* to live with her husband. The degree to which families insist on this aspect of premarital negotiations varies significantly, as does the degree to which families have the knowledge, status, and connections to make these requirements specific and effective. While in some households, a vague promise of "*gha nddiha*" (I'm going to take her) has been enough to marry a daughter to a *rajel lli kaimshi* (man who goes), other households may well ask to see a copy of the aspirant husband's work contract in Italy before even considering the union. Either way, explicitly or implicitly, *l-brra* is a fundamental component of the bridewealth offered by a migrant. But while other parts of the bridewealth are either for immediate use and consumption (money, jellabas, blankets, jewelry) or to be kept safe in case of a divorce, *l-brra* is a more ephemeral component and rarely actualizes itself in the way and time expected of it. For various reasons, marrying a migrant man necessarily involves a certain amount of waiting for the promised "outside" to materialize, which in turn involves a certain amount of waiting for one's conjugal life to become (or begin to become) *'adi* (normal)—the term women use to describe a life where husband and wife live in the same household and country and where a married woman is not *dima buhadha* (always alone).

While waiting for *l-brra* to materialize—mainly in the form of a *ricongiungimento* (family reunification document [Italian])—women married to migrants live a peculiar kind of conjugal life in the Tadla, where husbands, most of the time, are physically absent. This absence—punctuated, as we have seen, by sporadic presences—translates as a whole series of existential concerns, practical adjustments, and refined strategies on the part of women. The absence is productive in many ways, although what it actually produces is viewed with a great deal of ambivalence.

Present Absence

Absence is in many ways an achievement in emigrant settings. In her study of Chinese migration, Julie Chu (2010) describes how the striking emptiness of villas built by migrants on the rural outskirts of Fuzhou palpably contrasts with the overcrowded houses around them—a daily reminder for those who are not yet migrants of the luxuriousness of absence. In the Tadla, absence is something to aspire to. And just as with the imposing empty villas in emigrant Fuzhou, absence is constitutive of presence in a variety of other realms. First and foremost, absence in the Tadla testifies to one's presence in *l-brra*. It testifies to one's ability to leave, to one's courage to cross the sea, and to one's success in developing a sustained relationship with *temma* (there). Secondly, and linked to this, while physically absent migrants leave an indelible mark—or "trace," as Jacques Derrida (1976) calls the "mark of the absence of a presence" (Spivak 1976, xvii)—in intimate, social, and architectural landscapes back home.[1] By migrating, men distance themselves from what they conceive as an insignificant (and economically poor) presence and become a powerful "present absence" through building a family house, developing an independent household, sending over European money and gifts, and so on. The more time men spend in *l-brra*, the more they become present in their household and neighborhood.

Absence in this sense is valuable not only to the migrant persons but also to those connected with them by blood or marriage. The absence of a son, brother, husband, or father bears witness to the fact that a whole household—even a whole kinship group—has a tangible link, a relationship, with *l-brra*. In this sense, then, a migrant's relationship with *l-brra* is partible, or at least shareable, with others, particularly with related others. As I discussed in the previous chapter, a household with its breadwinner abroad is often termed a *dar dyal brra* (house of [the] outside) in the Tadla. Equally, a family that includes one or more migrant members is referred to as a family that "goes to the outside"; the migrant status of one member (especially if the family head) becomes the defining characteristic of the whole household. The migrant's absence from a household or kin network brings the household's connection with *l-brra* to the fore and crystallizes it.

The fact that the absence of the household head (*mul d-dar*) qualifies and defines a whole household is, of course, the reflection of a more general understanding by which the social, religious, and political standing and lineage of the head is made the defining characteristic of the whole household and its members—something Suad Joseph (1993, 467) frames as "patriarchal connectivity" (see also Buch Segal 2016; Crawford 2008; Davis 1983). Migration smoothly inserts itself in this type of kinship reckoning, and the migrant qualities of a close relative or spouse trickle down (or across) to others in the Tadla, making the movement of one family member the significant and qualifying characteristic also for those related to them. As well as being a defining characteristic, a migrant's absence also constitutes an indisputable possibility for those related to them, as it invariably implies one's own possible future presence in *l-brra*. People know that kinship and spousal links with a migrant are crucial for a "paper route" (Chu 2010, 110) into *l-brra*.

A relative's absence from the Tadla and presence in *l-brra* is considered a possibility also because it means that there will always be somebody *men l-'a'ila* (from/of the family) to provide a certain bridge, legal or otherwise, with and within *l-brra*—the quality and certainty of this bridge depending greatly on one's kind of kinship tie, as Alessandra Persichetti's (2003) study of the reproduction of agnatic/patrilineal solidarity in the emigration patterns of a Tadla town shows so well. Last but not least, absence in the Tadla means a possible future presence in *l-brra* simply because, as people repeatedly tell me, "*hadshi mntaqi*" (this is logical). As my Zafiah neighbor Hassan explained to me once, "A woman has to be with her husband, a son with his old parents, a child with his father. So, everyone will go, one day. *Hadshi li kayn u safi!* [This is how it is and that's it!]" Echoing Hassan's words, people often tell me that it is simple logic (*mntaq*) that if the man is not coming back—and few are—then, some day in the not so distant future his closest family will be in *l-brra*. (An important reminder that familial logic is considered to be ultimately more powerful even than the logic[s] of "the outside," despite the latter's deadly frontiers and brutal bureaucratic hurdles.)

Absence is thus a powerful connection and connector to *l-brra*. Wives of migrants know this, as does everyone else in the Tadla, and their discussions of absence are highly contextual, often carefully attuned to the audience they are addressing. In many cases, having a husband in *l-brra* makes all the difference, and lamenting an absence also means reiterating one's privileged positioning, each utterance containing multiple layers and addressing multiple interlocutors. However, despite the intrinsic worth of being married to an absent migrant husband, a link with *l-brra* also has negative reverberations on life in the Tadla, and migrants' wives are often awkwardly positioned in the social life of the area. This means that for as much as absence is valued, it is also in many ways despised by those women who interact with it directly and on a daily basis.

Lacking Life

Women's attitudes toward their husbands' absence are complex and irreducible to a single stance, and they develop, change, and fluctuate in tandem with other elements and dimensions of their lives. Women who lament their husbands' absence will also complain quietly when their husbands return for their brief visits, as temporary presence can also be problematic (see chap. 2 and chap. 5). For instance, Nejma, a woman in her fifties whose husband has been coming and going from Italy throughout their married life, always makes a point of telling me how her spouse is not necessarily a welcome presence: *"ngullik saraha, ybarzatni"* (I'll tell you the truth, he annoys me), she says to me, adding that she prefers it when he is not around: *"nemshi buhdi hsen"* (I go/I walk alone; it's better). Other women I know rejoice ironically about their husbands' absence, particularly when the husband in question is described as especially irascible—*"rjal huma ghir mashakil benti"* ([listen] my daughter/child, men are just problems), they will tell me. However, there is always also a sense of loss and danger accompanying women's interaction with and discourses about absence—something that transcends how much a woman enjoys being alone and makes reference to the deeper consequences and implications of absence.

A husband's absence is seen as having the power to taint other elements and relationships and somehow comes to encompass life as a whole. A husband's physical absence seems to produce the absence of many other elements, both tangible (money, physical contact, protection) and more ephemeral (happiness, health, normalcy). It generates absence in a more general sense, both less precise and more encompassing, and women speak of their lives as lacking (*naqs*) something both specific (the physical presence of a husband) and general (the sense of not living life how it should be lived: *hayati naqsa* [my life is lacking]).

In Arabic, the verb *naqis* means to diminish, to lower, to be defective (in something), and the noun *naqs*, which stems from it, means lack, defect. *Naqis* conveys the sense of something missing, a lack of something, and can refer to "being lowered," "imperfect," "short of supplies" (Juntunen 2002, 128). *Naqs* is often used in a Tadla household as a criticism of the taste of tea or food: *atay naqs* (tea is lacking—i.e., it does not have enough sugar);

naqs melha ([food is] missing/lacking salt). It is to this sense of lack, of there being something missing, that women refer to when discussing their migrant husbands. Connoting a "qualic" parallel (Munn 1987) between their life and insipid meat or bitter tea, they are openly expressing how the absence of one single ingredient can affect the quality of life as a whole.

The theme of *hayat naqsa* (lacking life/life lacking something) is always present when my interlocutors discuss their husbands' absence—and this applies also to those who ironically state that they are happier when their husbands are not around. The theme of *hayat naqsa* goes beyond a wife's socially expected expression of sorrow for a faraway husband and signals something deeper about the way a woman's relationship with *l-brra* inflects her life in the Tadla. Indeed, the idea of *hayat naqsa* goes well beyond the feelings of unhappiness for the absence of an individual husband.

Women do speak of missing their husbands as individuals and recall with fondness and often sadness the brief moments they have spent together. They will tell me stories of their husbands' romantic gestures, proudly show me the presents they have received *men brra* (from outside), and talk about their husbands' beautiful eyes or distinctive voice. Together with a sense of melancholia and longing for their own husbands, however, women repeatedly refer to the problematic physical absence of the structural figure of a *rajel* (husband/man) in their lives. This absence is problematic not necessarily because women need or want a *rajel* next to them (though many do) but because of the specific situation and positioning the absence of a *rajel* generates in their daily life. As sad and *khayeb* (ugly) as the absence of one's individual husband may be, it is the absence of *a* husband that, in certain situations at least, matters most. In other words, it is their positioning as *mra bla rajel* (woman without man) that women most lament. This in many ways underscores their claims about having a hard (*s'iba*) life, as their grievances refer directly to the normative religious and social discourse on the family, in which a man's rightful position—*blastu* (his place)—is seen as being next to his wife and kin.

However, it is not just to validate their claims (including, importantly, those of departure) that women speak in terms of a structural rather than individual absence. There is serious concern about the sustained absence of a husband—and about the expected and unexpected, immediate and long-term consequences of this absence—that goes beyond the absence of a specific individual and makes reference to the precarious position of a *mra bla rajelha* (woman without her husband). These concerns are largely oriented toward women's familial relations and the delicate balancing act between different attachments they must perform and embody by virtue of their intimate distance with *l-brra*.

Scattered Kinship

Cohabitation with affines requires a careful and complex balancing act on the part of a migrant's wife. In the Tadla, a woman entering a new household must quickly learn to respect and be respected, establishing a fragile compromise between deference and defenselessness (cf. Sa'ar 2001). The absence of a husband makes this balancing act particularly demanding. Not only is a daughter-in-law's traditional positioning as an outsider unmediated by her husband's presence—"*ana buhdi deddhom*" (I'm alone against them), women will say when discussing their in-laws. A woman's link with *l-brra*, objectified in her husband's absence, also makes her a somewhat temporary household member, and the lingering possibility of her departure exacerbates her precarious position. The delicate process of integrating a daughter-in-law into a new household is thus rendered more complex by the fact that a woman married to a migrant is inextricably linked to *l-brra*, together with being linked to her original household, from which, as we shall see, she never completely parts.

The precarious positioning of a migrant's wife emerges most explicitly in her relationship with her mother-in-law. The dangers associated with mothers-in-law, widely acknowledged throughout Morocco, take a troublesome turn in stories about migrant families. In the Tadla, it is an obvious fact of life that the relationship between mother and daughter-in-law is, at the very least, a fiery one. Songs, films, jokes, and nursery rhymes all refer to the mother of the husband/husband-to-be as a hard, demanding, and cunning troublemaker (see Guessous 2007, 91–94; Mernissi 1988; Rassam 1980). Stories about mothers of migrant men, however, often have a darker twist to them and reach greater extremes, as if the migrant's absence allows the darkest of schemes to be played out and makes precarious relationships run wild.

Stories of mean, controlling mothers-in-law—women who monitor their daughters-in-law's every movement or who carefully ration their daily food and water, for example—are popular in the Tadla. Migrants' wives have told me of mothers-in-law who don't give them enough to eat, force them to carry out exhausting cleaning duties when they are heavily pregnant, steal their money, refuse them medicine or forbid them from going to the doctor, visit a *shuwwaf* (person adept at magic) to make them fall ill, and so on. But a mothers-in-law's most dangerous power is generally linked to her ability to *'emmru rasu* (fill his head)—the expression used to refer to a mother-in-law's (and other relatives') ability to fill a migrant's head with gossip and manipulated information about his wife. This skill is seen as particularly dangerous because it has the power to convince a son, for example, to divorce his wife, cut her remittances, or take a second wife.

So, a migrant's wife's precious relationship with *l-brra*, crystallized in her husband's absence, also makes her position in her in-laws' household precarious and peripheral and exposed to tangible and intangible threats. Consanguine kin play a fundamental role in counterbalancing this positioning. Women married to migrants rely heavily on their blood relatives for assistance with child-rearing and household chores, for support and protection in the case of arguments with their in-laws, for financial help (albeit rarely), and for simple company ("*bash mankunsh dima buhdi*" [so I'm not always alone]). The fundamental role of matrilineal/maternal kin ties in determining a married woman's life chances, vividly described in Vanessa Maher's (1974) early ethnography of the Moroccan Middle Atlas, takes on particular significance in the life of a migrant's wife. In the early 1970s, Maher wrote that women in the Middle Atlas, "having no economic prospects within the market economy and no security through their conjugal relations to men, for marriage is very unstable . . . come to depend on their female associates" both through "uterine kinship ties and patron-client relations" (1974, 222). These female networks of support and exchange are also acknowledged in later ethnographies of Morocco (e.g., Capello 2008, 47–94; Kapchan 1996; Newcomb 2009). These studies, however, also highlight important social and historical departures from Maher's early work, starting from women's increased access to the formal and informal market economy (Kapchan 1996) and the nuclearization of Moroccan families (Newcomb 2017). Both processes significantly rescale women's reliance on transversal female ties.

However, for many migrants' wives in the Tadla, participation in the market economy and processes of family nuclearization are often not an option,[2] making their situation strikingly close to Maher's description of Middle Atlas married life in the 1960s. A husband's absence in many ways seems to hinder these national gendered trends, which are often described in the Moroccan and Middle Eastern literature as bringing about key changes in women's positioning in the family and society. On the one hand, as a friend explained to me once, there is very little point in nuclearizing (*tskun buhdek* [(you) live alone]) with a husband who is never home. Even in those cases where women have their own conjugal house to live in—a request appearing increasingly in marriage negotiations, particularly in the Tadla's more urban centers—migrants' wives often opt (or are made to opt) to live with the husband's family or, rarely, with their own. On the other hand, the absence of the husband's watchful eye, even when delegated efficiently to others, makes migrants' wives' chances for employment outside the home slim, as men—and, more importantly, their families in the Tadla—often disapprove of their wives' participation in the market economy during their absence. Some women do engage in small-scale informal trade—for example, by doing sewing and embroidery jobs from home or selling to neighbors items of clothing or jewelry bought in small batches with part of their remittances. But wives of migrants are not generally employed outside the home, nor do they tend to participate in the informal economy of the marketplace, as do the pioneering women vendors, herbalists, and magic experts of Deborah Kapchan's (1996) classic ethnography of the souk of Béni Mellal, one of the Tadla's main urban centers.

The impracticality of nuclear arrangements—often the first step toward major independence from both birth family and in-laws—and their complex implications when they do occur (women living on their own with young children, for example), coupled with the complexities of seeking employment as a *mra dyal brra* (woman of [the] outside—i.e., married to a migrant), significantly intensify these women's reliance on family networks. Indeed, the relation/reliance on consanguine kin discussed in the anthropological literature on Morocco is here intensified to such an extent that migrants' wives at times even move back to their fathers' households during their husbands' prolonged absences, defying both the virilocal norm of the area and the expectation that women become, through marriage, their in-laws' responsibility.

The strong reliance on consanguine kin generated by a husband's absence is not without risks. Salima's story provides a telling example of the dangers involved. Salima has not been on speaking terms with her father for a very long time because of a longstanding dispute with her father's second wife. From the moment her father married a second wife, Salima says, there have been "*ghir mashakil*" (only problems/trouble) in her childhood home. These problems escalated dramatically when, during an argument, her father's second wife hit Salima's mother, who ended up in a hospital, and Salima reported the event to the police. Although the police report came to nothing, Salima's father swore he would never speak to his daughter again, outraged by the way in which she had exposed his marital and household affairs to the local authorities.

On one of my visits to Salima in 2011, she was desperately trying to gather *le-wraq* (the papers) for an Italian tourist visa application so she could join her undocumented husband abroad. No one in her husband's household was prepared to help her, neither with the cost of her numerous journeys to the Italian consulate in Casablanca nor with the financial statements required for the application. To apply for a tourist visa, Salima needed to provide proof of a financially stable situation in Morocco—thus, from the Italian immigration authorities' perspective, providing sufficient assurance that she was not intending to overstay her visa. Lacking financial resources of her own, and with no bank account and thus bank statements that could prove she was economically independent (which, indeed, she was not), Salima had turned to *darna* (our home—i.e., the consanguine home) for help. Through the mediation of his two wives, she had repeatedly asked her father for a declaration that he would officially take on the responsibility of her travels and her economic status.[3] Her father, unrelenting, repeatedly refused. Salima's mother, probably worried for her own positioning in her husband's household, had very early on withdrawn from the mediation between Salima and her father, claiming that she could do nothing to help and reminding Salima that "*endek 'a'iltek daba*" (you have your family now—i.e., Salima's in-laws).

In her critical essay on consanguine relations in the Middle East, Amalia Sa'ar (2001) makes an important observation on the ways in which anthropological scholarship on gender and kinship has left largely untouched the assumption that the consanguine family represents a locus of empowerment and protection for married women. She points to the tendency, particularly in the early feminist literature on the Arab world, to highlight women's "skilled utilization of their blood rights for . . . lifelong support within the patriarchal group" (723). In her ethnography of Palestinian families in Israel, Sa'ar shows how women's entitlement to protection from their consanguine kin is more limited than what might be assumed (see also Stafford 2000). Focusing on cases of "failed familial fidelity" (724), she shows how married women are often unable to obtain support and protection from their blood relatives, particularly at times of conjugal crisis or financial difficulties.

As Sa'ar argues for women in Palestinian households in Israel, Salima's story shows that support from kin is not something migrants' wives can take for granted in the Tadla. As with all kinship relations, consanguine relations are complex and need constant work and attention in order to be effective (Carsten 2000)—these are not networks automatically providing solidarity and protection simply by virtue of shared blood. Wives of migrants are hit particularly strongly by the complexity of consanguine relations, as these wives often depend more than other women on these particular ties. In this sense, then, women's relationship with *l-brra* positions them in situations of potential isolation and loneliness in the Tadla with regard to both their affines (with whom they occupy a particularly peripheral position) and their blood kin (on whom they depend excessively).

So, being "married to *l-brra*" inflects family relationships in particular ways and places specific strains upon them. When a young wife enters a new household, she has to learn how to balance a fundamental attachment to her own family with her incorporation into a new one, taking care never to be either too close or too distant from either. This balancing act between different claims and attachments is complicated by the fact that by marrying a migrant, a woman also enters into a constitutive relationship with *l-brra* itself. Thus, rather than being pulled in two directions (childhood home on the one hand, in-laws on the other), migrants' wives could be seen as being pulled in three: their own blood kin, their husbands' kin, and, abidingly, *l-brra*. Within this triangle of forces, women often find themselves in precarious situations. Though all three are important—indeed, life-determining—attachments, it is not always possible for women to calibrate or "proportion" (Corsín Jiménez 2008) them effectively, and at times they describe how, as a result of these multiple connections, they feel attached to nothing at all.[4]

It is telling that for women caught in this position, actualizing their link with *l-brra* is conceived as the only effective solution. Once "in the outside," women assure me, "everything is going to be normal/ok [*'adi*]." There is a strong sense that by actualizing one's latent relationship with *l-brra* and thus with one's husband, other relationships—first and foremost with birth family and affines—will in turn be ordered and fall once again within the much-desired realm of normalcy.[5] Until this happens, and while women are still in the Tadla, their position is in a profound sense a precarious one. This precarity, however, is not just because of the web of family relationships that typically encircles migrants' wives. An unactualized link with *l-brra* is seen as affecting women also in a deeply intimate way, generating not only precarious relationships but also precarious beings—and, more specifically, precariously gendered beings.

Gender on Pause

Migrants' wives are popular figures in migration and development scholarship. Classified as "women left behind," a telling example of the kind of patriarchal thinking at the heart of much migration work, women married to migrants are often considered powerful exemplars of migration's impact on gender relations and even "social progress" in emigrant countries. A general hypothesis is often made that the absence of migrant men both requires and allows their "left behind" wives to take on new roles and responsibilities in the household and sending community—a process that, in turn, has the potential to positively affect women's positioning in patriarchal settings and, in the long run, local and even national gender power relations (Brettell 2003; Brink 1991; David 1995; Matz and Mbaye 2017; Taylor et al. 2006). Some studies of migrants' wives have complicated the relationship between men's migration and women's improved social standing by placing it within a specific sociohistorical context, or by considering the longevity, and hence the social permanence, of these processes (e.g., Brettell 1986; de Haas and van Rooij 2010; Lenoël 2017; Mondain et al. 2012); still other work has questioned the existence of such a causal relationship altogether (e.g., Day and İçduygu 1997; Hampshire 2006; Myntti 1984). However, the general hypothesis remains that men's migration can be an important pathway to what the literature refers to as "female empowerment" in emigrant settings. This is the argument found in many studies of Moroccan migration specifically (e.g., Aït Hamza 1995; Ennaji and Sadiqi 2008; Fadloullah et al. 2000; Khachani 2004), which highlight how men's migration ultimately increases the power, autonomy, and responsibilities of "left behind" wives.

In the Tadla, men's migration undoubtedly increases some of the responsibilities and duties put on their wives. This is mainly the case for those women who live separately from their in-laws and family in de facto women-headed households—a very small proportion of my interlocutors. But even for women like Salima who live in extended households, a husband's migration does at times generate specific kinds of responsibilities, increasing, for example, women's interaction with traditionally male arenas such as the local units of the *makhzen*—the Moroccan government apparatus. In the absence of their husbands, women in certain family arrangements, particularly those living with very elderly or very young male in-laws who are unable to take on household responsibilities, deal with state taxes and bank loans, rents, debts, school bureaucracies, relocation policies, and local state officials, acquiring in the process a specific kind of proficiency in administrative and bureaucratic language, style, and movement. When I'm in the area, I often accompany women on their tours of administrative offices—a visit to the Caid (local representative of the central government) to plea for an exemption for an unruly brother-in-law; a quick, deferentially pitched conversation with the city administration neighborhood representative, the *muqaddem*, about problems with an official form; a meeting with the school head about an undisciplined daughter; a trip to the bank to ask for leniency over a delayed mortgage payment. These responsibilities are a direct product of women's relation with *l-brra*, as typically—or at least ideally—relations with the *makhzen* and its emissaries, and with financial, legal, and administrative institutions, are handled mainly, if not wholly, by men.[6]

Significantly, however, women do not speak of these heightened interactions with *hwayej dyal rjal* (men's things) in the enthusiastic terms found in some of the migration and development scholarship. Absence, as the literature points out, does open up specific spaces for women who have migrant husbands living abroad. However, I think the important question lies in whether these spaces are in any way desirable to the women themselves (cf. Mumtaz and Salway 2005). The responsibilities and duties generated by women's particular connection with *l-brra* are framed more often than not as an undesirable additional burden to their already *mashi 'adia* (not normal) life. Indeed, these responsibilities and "new functions" (Ennaji and Sadiqi 2008, 182) are often portrayed as being yet another sign of women's (undesired) departure from normalcy and from a normal life (*hayat 'adia*). Importantly, it is mostly widows and divorcees who deal, on their own, with state offices or banks in the Tadla, indirectly confirming the precarious closeness between migrants' wives and other structurally marginal/liminal women in the area.[7]

Rarely do migrants' wives express a sense of freedom or relief about this marginal or liminal position. Indeed, the question dominating the migration and development scholarship of whether women are empowered by their migrant husbands' absence feels somewhat out of place in the Tadla. "Female emancipation," understood in the secular-liberal tradition as an enactment of women's agency in the face of male hierarchical power, is not the most urgent concern for the women I know (cf. Mahmood 2005). In the Tadla at least, migrants' wives' most urgent concerns are not oriented toward freedom from relations of gendered subordination but rather toward remaining a gendered person against all the odds—despite the distance from one's husband, the dependency on one's father, the sexual inactivity, the pauses in reproductive life, and the risk of repudiation or divorce. If one is to follow my interlocutors' concerns, theoretical reflections on gender in the Tadla should focus not only on how and if gender power relations are shifted by the migration of men but also on how gender itself is formed (or *un*formed) by it and through it. In other words, while the migration scholarship tends to consider migrants and nonmigrants as stably gendered and their relations (generally of power) as potentially shifting through migration, my sense is that migration in the Tadla affects not only the relations between genders but also the genders being related (cf. Strathern 1988)—and it is the latter, rather than the former, that most concerns my interlocutors.

"I have a husband and I don't. I have a house and I don't. I'm a wife and I'm not. I'm a woman and I'm not." This is Fatima speaking, Salima's younger sister who lives in a small Tadla village with her husband's family; her husband, just like Salima's, has been a migrant in Italy throughout her marriage. "My life isn't *'adia* [simple/normal] like the life of other women," she often tells me. Many women I know in the Tadla express this complex sense of simultaneously being and not being. *Being* is a deeply gendered notion here, and in a way one becomes a worthy person—a person worthy of being a person—through enacting, voicing, clinging, and aspiring to certain gender-appropriate modes of being. These modes of being, although definitely not static and monolithic, as portrayed in some of the early anthropological work on the Middle East, are nevertheless grounded in specific, meaningful actions (Peteet 1994), moments (Smid 2010), and relationships (Joseph 1999) that qualify women as gendered subjects— and, in turn, as subject tout court. As I mentioned in chapter 1, for some women, their peculiar relationship with *l-brra* influences precisely those "essentializing practices" (Herzfeld 1997) that makes them recognizable (to themselves and others) as appropriately and properly gendered persons.

Fatima often explicitly voices this relationship between her unactualized connection with *l-brra* and her sense of (not) being a *mra dyal bessah* (real woman), and she has developed a poignant analysis of the effects of her husband's absence on her gendered self. First and foremost, Fatima connects her four consecutive miscarriages to her husband's absence. Fatima regularly refers to her miscarriages in our conversations, and she speaks of them with a mixture of anguish and resentment. She often says that her unborn children knew the father would be far away: "they were right not to come out," she once told me. "They knew they would grow up without a father, like Ahmed [her only child]." Fatima explains, pointing to her womb, that something is wrong inside her: "*kollshi mkhallat fiya*" (everything is mixed/tangled inside me). She explains that this is because "*kollshi maqlub f hayati*" (everything is confused/topsy-turvy in my life) and repeats what I have quoted above: "I have a husband and I don't. I have a house and I don't. I'm a wife and I'm not. I'm a woman and I'm not." For Fatima, the causal link between her *maqlub* (confused/upside-down) life and her *mkhallat* (mixed/tangled) insides is crystal clear. The causal link works the other way as well—her tangled insides, unable to give birth, make her life even more upside down: her inability to have other children is the most distressing, and in many ways socially and existentially threatening, element of her *mashi 'adia* (not normal) life.

Absence does not affect solely Fatima's womb. Her body is periodically overcome by different kinds of pains and illnesses, and often simply everything hurts (*kollshi darni*) because, as she explains to me, "*hayati mashi 'adia*" (my life is not normal). She sees her husband's absence from her life and her own absence from *l-brra* as the main cause of her ill health: "[it's] because I'm not there with him!" Tiredness, stress, overwork, stairs, germs, heat, humidity, her mother-in-law, the sun. . . . These elements are always invoked as being involved in making her unwell. But it is her husband's absence, and the more general absence of *l-brra* from her life, that she identifies as the overriding cause of her illnesses. By some ironic coincidence, I am often under the weather myself when I visit Fatima, and our friendship has developed over the years by exchanging complaints about our poor state of health while tucked under three or four blankets, watching Arabic-subtitled Turkish and Mexican soaps. Fatima will always say that I fall ill in Morocco because I miss my mother and my country. And when Fatima's neighbors come round for tea, they all agree with her that I am ill because of *l-ghorba*, the state a migrant is known to suffer when away from home. Abdelmalek Sayad provides an evocative description of the concept of *l-ghorba* in the Maghreb: "In the traditional logic, *el ghorba* is associated with 'sunset', darkness', distance and isolation (among strangers, and thus with their hostility or contempt), with exile, fright (that caused by the night and by the fact of getting lost in a forest or in a hostile natural environment), with confusion (due to losing one's orientation), with misfortune etc." (Sayad 2000, 167). In the Tadla, the term *l-ghorba* is often used as a synonym of migration, as becomes clear from listening to popular musicians singing about *wlad l-ghorba* (boys/youths of *l-ghorba*—i.e., migrants) (Moktary 2008). Though not a migrant, Fatima tells me how she, just like me, suffers from *l-ghorba*. The absence of her husband, her miscarriages, her everyday life in her in-laws' household "*buhdi*" (on my own), sleeping alone every night "*bhal mra bla rajel*" (like a woman without a man/an unmarried woman), all make her suffer from *l-ghorba*, from a sense of isolation, exile, distance, and loss of orientation. "I don't know what I'm doing here," Fatima sometimes tells me.

"Here" (*hna/hnaya*) does not refer solely to the Tadla or to her husband's household but more generally to her place *f l-ʿalam* (in the world), to the precarious situation of being and simultaneously not being a wife and a mother—elements necessary for existing, in her eyes, as a purposeful person. "The truth is, Alice, I'm not a woman (*ana mashi mra*)." Although Fatima says this with irony, I have always felt that she means it, at least in part. Many women point out to me that their lives as migrants' wives fall short of what a woman is supposed to do and be. By making impossible certain crucial essentializing practices—from intimacy to reproduction to sharing life with one's husband—their peculiar conjugal relationships can call into question their position as grown women (*mra*) altogether. "*Tannʿas buhdi*" (I sleep alone) is one of the most effective ways women use to convey—to myself and to other women—their sense of peculiar misplacement in their lives. While sometimes celebrated with big fits of laughter, the long periods of sexual abstinence that I discuss in the previous chapters are also invoked as a very tangible reminder of the awkward misplacement of one's gendered body, a misplacement directly produced by one's unactualized connection with *l-brra*.

Given this, it is perhaps unsurprising that there is a sense of urgency characterizing women's waiting for *l-brra* to actualize itself in their life. Women consider their precarious familial and gendered positionality in the Tadla a temporary state of affairs, one that is expected to change in the very near future. Migrants' wives' lives are characterized by a pervasive expectation of imminent change: one's marriage to "the outside" is meant to become, very soon, a *zwaj ʿadi* (normal marriage) where spouses will live together, where empty spaces will be filled by physical presence, and where one's intimate distance with *l-brra* will finally become simple closeness.

Waiting for the Outside

Migrants' wives' peculiar conjugal relationships, stretched between the Tadla and "the outside," make *l-brra* a constant possibility, and waiting for this possibility to actualize itself is a constitutive element of daily life. Life is permeated by a sense of intense waiting not only for the next outside appearance, as we saw in chapter 1, but also for a stabilizing, definite, and definitive event to take place: a movement to "the outside" or a husband's permanent return to the Tadla. Although there are cases in the area of successful migrants who have returned to the Tadla to live with their wives and kin (though these permanent returns are not common and are never uncomplicated—see chap. 5), most women I know considered this a very improbable and not particularly desirable scenario in their own case and see their own movement to *l-brra*, often the original conjugal agreement, as the event that will restore normalcy to their lives and personhood. "When I'll be there with him, everything's going to be *mezyan* [ok/fine/good]," my friend Habiba, who has been planning her departure to *l-brra* throughout her marriage, tells me every time we meet. For Habiba, as for other women I know, there is a sense of urgency to her waiting: she feels her husband's absence and her anomalous life are slowly eating away at her. Habiba is constantly waiting for something to change, to happen, to evolve. She sees her own waiting as qualitatively different from the waiting of other people who surround her, as she knows that her conjugal link to a migrant makes the possibility of "the outside" imminent and *mntaqi* (logical). She once explained this to me through a striking *Animal Farm*-like phrase: "everyone here is waiting for 'the outside,' but I am waiting more than anyone."

Waiting is not necessarily the shameful activity Xiang Biao (2014) describes in Northwest China, where it is increasingly evaluated in moral terms. In his study of an emigrant community, Xiang highlights how waiting generates deep temporal anxieties and goes against an embodied time-as-money ideology where rushing becomes a necessary essence of being (see also Crawford 2008; Hage 2009, 3; Pardy 2009). This, Xiang shows, implies that a kind of secrecy and embarrassment are interwoven in people's endless waiting to migrate from their villages. In the Tadla, on the contrary, waiting is an integral and very explicit component of women's lives. Unmarried women, whether employed or unemployed, university educated or with no school education at all, are often described as "waiting beings" (*kaitsennaw* [they wait]): waiting for marriage and adult life to begin. At times, this trope is used in demeaning ways—for example, by educated young women when commenting on other women in their family who have left school and are now at home "just waiting for a husband." However, *galsa* (sitting—i.e., not working/staying at home) is often used to describe a state of affairs—indeed, for many, an appropriately gendered one (see chap. 5)—rather than being a negative observation.

So, Habiba's waiting isn't necessarily a strange state to be in, nor is it unusual (see also Rignall 2013). However, as she herself points out, there is a specific quality to her waiting that distinguishes it from, on the one hand, the kind of waiting in which unmarried women engage and, on the other, that of other aspiring migrants populating the Tadla. Her conjugal link makes her waiting special and her "prospective orientation" (Reed 2011, 528) especially concrete. Habiba distances herself, for example, from young men sitting at cafés and waiting, as she sees it, for *l-brra* to come their way. Alone or in groups, sitting at outdoor tables drinking coffee, smoking cigarettes, and watching people walk by, these men "*kaitsennaw l-brra*" (wait for *l-brra*), Habiba whispers to me, keeping her eyes to the ground and walking quickly past the male-populated cafés. She says the same of young Sub-Saharan African migrants waiting for an opportunity to travel to Europe whom she encounters in the Tadla's bigger towns and sees on national TV in Rabat and Casablanca. "*Ana mashi bhalhom, ana ghadya!*" (I'm not like them, I'm going!) Habiba tells me. *L-brra* has already come her way through her marriage, and all she needs to do now is wait for that connection to actualize itself. In this sense, then, women married to migrants like Habiba are not *waiting for* migration as they see others doing, but simply *waiting out* their time in Morocco for *l-brra* to finally actualize itself in their lives (cf. Hage 2009; Reed 2011).

However, because the timing and route of this actualization are indeterminate—women can indeed wait decades for it—*waiting for* is never completely eradicated from the women's orientation. Thus, for women in the Tadla, the certainty of future mobility is made up of indeterminate routes and passages—women know they are going (and thus are waiting out their time in the Tadla), but they don't know when and how (and thus are also waiting for those decisive events to take place).

Life is thus permeated by a specific mode of certain but indeterminate anticipation of *l-brra*. This specific kind of anticipation "continually redirects attention towards the fact that something has to still happen and become" (Reed 2011, 528; see also Miyazaki 2004; Robbins 2004), and perhaps because of the distinctive juxtaposition of certainty and indeterminacy that characterizes it, this anticipation often nurtures rather than hinders *brra*-oriented action in migrants' wives' everyday lives. Indeed, although Habiba and other women married to migrants, particularly those who do not work, describe themselves and are described by others as "sitting and waiting," both "sitting" and "waiting" are ripe with doings, purpose, and activity (cf. Liebow 2003). These are not only the everyday activities of baking bread, cooking, cleaning, milking cows and harvesting, going to the market, and so on— activities somehow eclipsed by the notion of *galsa* (sitting). Migrants' wives' "sitting and waiting" also involve doings oriented toward migration and the actualization of the possibility incorporated in their conjugal link with *l-brra*. As I now go on to show with the story of Habiba, however, sometimes these doings, rather than translating into trans-Mediterranean movement, produce more expectant waiting—transforming waiting into a lasting texture of life in the Tadla.

Migratory Restlessness

Throughout the years I have known her, Habiba's life has been characterized by periodical migratory activity—moments when her activities, imagination, and actions are purposely oriented toward actualizing her connection with *l-brra*. Though always latent, from time to time the possibility of her departure erupts on the surface, making her movement to Europe feel imminent. This sudden heightened possibility can be generated by a variety of factors—a change in the tone of her husband's voice on the phone, news that a new migration law is being discussed in the Italian parliament, a dream where her son is speaking Italian. These events activate a period of intense migratory activities in Habiba's life—she will collect application documents, save money to visit Casablanca migration offices, visit relatives to gather support and information, ceaselessly call her husband in Italy asking him to sign and send over a variety of documents and statements, set up meetings with migration brokers, and spend sleepless nights disentangling the cryptic maze of visa applications. This sense of imminent departure regularly withers away after a few weeks, and the activities accompanying the brief intensification of migratory possibility are always followed by a slow return to the routine activities of low-intensity waiting.

The first time I found myself involved in one of these flurries of migratory activity, I was confused by the dormant reactions of Habiba's close relatives, who live in both Italy and Morocco. There we were, travelling on long bus journeys to the Italian consulate in Casablanca, talking till late at night about Habiba's new life abroad, going into town to get passport photos taken, photocopying papers and statements, slipping *shi haja* (something— i.e., money) into the hands of visa brokers, and so on. Throughout all this migratory activity, Habiba's relatives stood back and watched. Even Habiba's husband was not as involved as I expected he might be.

At a certain stage, the intense activity of preparing and precipitating an imminent departure slowed down, until it came to a complete halt. Nothing specific happened as far as I could tell. It was more a combination of small events: an unexpected hurdle appeared in the bureaucratic process Habiba had initiated at the Italian consulate, her husband's signed statements kept being delayed, an appointment with a migration broker was missed when Habiba's son fell ill, some key papers went missing. For a variety of different reasons, the imminence of Habiba's departure slowly paled before my eyes, and soon she was back to saying—with the characteristic certain but indeterminate tone of migrants' wives in the Tadla—"someday, I'm going." A telephone conversation with Habiba's cousin, who lives in Italy, made me realize that the family was dormant because they predicted the outcome of Habiba's prospective actions toward *l-brra*. Habiba's cousin told me that periods of heightened migratory possibility were dotted throughout Habiba's marriage and that none had resulted in *l-brra* yet: "something always goes wrong, some deadline is always missed, her husband always gets anxious [*gli sale l'ansia* (Italian)] and pulls back. . . . After a bit it all goes back to normal, and Habiba goes back to normal waiting."

For Habiba's relatives, her cyclical efforts to leave seem to be predestined to fail—indeed, it is when Habiba is orienting all of her energies toward leaving that her status as a "stayer" emerges in all its clarity. When Habiba is making no explicit effort to actualize her migratory connection with *l-brra*, when she isn't gathering documents, statements, and passport photos, both she and her family conceptualize her as "waiting to leave." Both her own family and her husband's family speak of Habiba as a future migrant, a future leaver—"she'll be in 'the outside' one day," they assure me—and her husband's absence is the most tangible proof that this is going to happen. However, when this distant future appears closer, when the possibility becomes more tangible, this narrative suddenly switches. It is as if, while Habiba periodically sees glimpses of her waiting for *l-brra* coming definitively to an end, those around her maintain their conceptualization of her as a migrant-to-be and, thus, as someone who waits.

Waiting Personhood

Migratory activity seems to reiterate Habiba's existential quality of "someone who waits." This waiting, however, does not leave Habiba and the other women I know unaffected. In the process of waiting, and in all those movements, activities, thoughts, dreams, plans, expectations, and relationships that make up this waiting, migrants' wives become specific kinds of persons in the Tadla, with a specific kind of relationship with *l-brra*.

While their geographical distance from *l-brra* often remains the same over the years, migrants' wives move closer to "the outside" in many other ways as time goes by. They regularly gather detailed information about *l-brra*, their knowledge of *l-brra*'s bureaucratic systems becomes increasingly accurate as years goes by, and throughout their protracted conjugal relationship with *l-brra* they accumulate an increasing number of outside things, both tangible and intangible—perfumes, pans, words, clothes, magazines, mobile phones, contraceptive ideas, recipes, and bureaucratic loopholes. Most importantly, in their telephone conversations with their husbands, the women speak with *l-brra* every single day. In their active waiting for migration, migrants' wives are dealing directly with *l-brra* and creating a specific type of relationship with it—they are getting to know its rhythms and its flaws, its dangers and its special properties, its currencies and its laws.

People around migrants' wives recognize and validate this precious relationship. Neighbors and kin often come to Habiba's house to ask her advice about documents or the *dwa men temma* (medicine from "there") that their sons have sent them from Italy or Spain. Neighbors and kin also come over to listen to Habiba's stories about Europe, which she has heard from her husband, in the marketplace or in the hammam, or that she just knows ("*a kana'ref!*" [I just know!]). Although she has never been there, Habiba's special connection with *l-brra* and the expectant waiting and specific orientation of her life and thoughts it has produced make her closer than others to *l-brra* itself. Both the relationship with *l-brra*, crystallized in their conjugal link with a migrant man, and the expectant orientation toward it make women like Habiba key connections with, and even extension of, *l-brra* at home.

Intimate Distance

The Tadla's women of [the] outside (*le-'yalat dyal brra*) powerfully testify to the ways in which *l-brra* contributes to the emergence of specific kinds of persons even in the absence of actual migratory movement. The intimate, conjugal connection with *l-brra* permeates women's experience and understanding of themselves as gendered persons in multiple ways: it generates specific kinds of familial and emotional bonds, affecting women's ties with both blood and acquired kin; it shapes the ways in which they imagine themselves as (not yet) women; and it instils their everyday lives with a sense of expectant waiting for "the outside" to actualize itself. Taken together, these elements contribute to making women married to migrants specific kinds of gendered and relational subjects in the Tadla, subjects who are the direct result of their liminal positioning between *hna* (here) and *temma* (there). The liminal position that women like Habiba acquire over their married life, the result of a complex mixture of knowledge and expertise about, expectant orientation toward, and conjugal relations with *l-brra*, is in many ways the manifestation of their intimate distance both to the Tadla and *l-brra*.

Indeed, a peculiar intimate distance ties but also separates women like Habiba, Salima, and Fatima to both home and abroad. Migrants' wives are close to *l-brra* in ways that others in the Tadla simply are not—everyone has the possibility to move, but these possibilities are not all of the same quality, and wedlock is invariably considered a closer type of relationship than, say, mere desire or hope for *l-brra*. At the same time, women married to migrants are not yet close enough to "the outside" to become *huma lli kaimshiw* (those who go). A similar intimate distance ties and separates migrants' wives to the Tadla. Women married to migrants are more distant from the Tadla than others, oriented as they are toward another time and place and linked to *l-brra* through the intimacy of marriage. However, they are not distant enough to be unbound from the everyday of kin and neighborhood relationality.

The women's husbands, on the other hand, are in many ways too close to *l-brra*, a closeness that affects them deeply, as we saw in chapter 2, to the point of making them fundamentally different from the Tadla, their neighborhoods, and even their own families. Migrants' wives are not close enough to *l-brra* to be entirely transformed by it, and this is perhaps the reason why they become accessible and effective mediators between here and there for those around them. Indeed, observed from this perspective, it may even be argued that women's intimate distance from *l-brra*, albeit disquieting, may be a more habitable position than the one occupied by their migrant husbands who, by being too close to *l-brra*, have also become too distant from *d-dar* (home)—though of course such a favorable comparison with the conditions of their migrant husbands hardly reflects the ways in which the women themselves generally see their own positions, as we have seen throughout this chapter.

I return in chapter 5 to migrant men's problematic closeness to *l-brra* and ensuing problematic distance from the Tadla. Before doing this, I wish to address the place *l-brra* occupies in the lives of another group of women in the Tadla: younger women who are yet to enter married lives and for whom *l-brra* plays a key constitutive role in the imagination and precipitation of the future.

Notes

1. In the translator's preface of *Of Grammatology*, Gayatri Chakravorty Spivak (1976, xvii) writes, "Trace can be seen as an always contingent term for a mark of the absence of a presence, an always-already absent present of the 'originary lack' that seems to be the condition of thought and experience."

2. Though see Hein de Haas and Aleida van Rooij (2010) and Moha Ennaji and Fatima Sadiqi (2008) for other Moroccan emigrant contexts where family nuclearization is indeed an option.

3. Both academic literature and legal advocacy highlight how migration rules, laws, and infrastructures systematically position women in a situation of dependence on men; see Janet Calvo (2000) for an early influential analysis.

4. In his critique of anthropology's focus on social relations, Alberto Corsín Jiménez (2008, 194) proposes a model of "proportional sociality" that "takes into account the different ways in which people inflect and qualify their relationships. Proportional sociality tells us the factors by which the stretching out of the social takes place. It talks about how people re-scale their biographical projects." My interlocutors in this chapter could be seen as engaging in the "proportional sociality" Corsín Jiménez calls for—a sociality where "biographical projects" are "re-scaled" by balancing differently scaled relationships. However, the result of these "proportional" efforts is not necessarily rewarding. Indeed, my point is precisely that a "proportioning" of one's connections with affines, blood relatives, and *l-brra* is basically impossible to achieve—an impossibility that bears difficult consequences for the women themselves.

5. See Rebecca Empson's (2011) discussion of the fundamental role in northeast Mongolia of both connections and discontinuities between persons and from kin groups "in order to establish a more singular mode of subjectivity" (147). I would argue that in the Tadla, in order to establish a "more singular mode of subjectivity" one has, first and foremost, to actualize one's relationship with *l-brra* in order to free oneself from the *mashi 'adi* (not normal) connections with consanguines, affines, and husband and establish new and appropriate connections with them. This actualization is in many ways also an envisioned future moment of "subjectification" for the women themselves, in the sense that women see their departure for *l-brra* also as a moment when "*gha nkun ana*" (I am going to become/be me/myself).

6. See David Crawford's (2008, 112–44) compelling ethnography of the relation between Amazigh villagers in the Moroccan High Atlas and state authorities, where he shows how differently positioned people within village and lineage hierarchies interacted in different ways, and with different results, with the state and its local representatives.

7. Caroline Brettell (1986, 95) highlights how, in early twentieth-century Portugal, the "left behind" wives of men who migrated to Brazil were called "widows of the living," while Donna Gabaccia (2006, 190) has shown how the Italian wives of American émigrés of the late 1800s were termed—both by their contemporaries and, later, by historians—"white widows."

4

BEAUTIFUL FUTURES

"You always have to be ready for God." In the cramped rented room she shares with three other students, Zineb is getting ready for an evening stroll in town. Balancing a small plastic mirror on the thin internal windowsill and bending down to catch her reflection, she meticulously rubs white foundation cream on her face. Once a uniform layer of makeup covers her skin, she reaches for lipstick, then mascara, then black kohl for her eyes. She then reaches for a colorful scarf, which she fastens around her head with some of the many pins scattered around the room. She takes a few steps back from the mirror, observes her reflection, and, to the sound of her roommates' exasperated groans, rubs the lipstick away with a tissue and starts applying a different, paler one to her lips. "This is better," Zineb murmurs to herself, satisfied. "Always be ready for God!" she repeats, giving a wide smile to her roommates, who are waiting impatiently for their turns at the mirror. "My husband may be out there today, walking around the medina," she says, now looking in my direction. "If you want to find him (*huwa*), you have to be prepared. Nothing happens if you're lazy." "And nothing happens if you're ugly, either!" Zineb's roommate adds with a smirk. "Or ugly, yes." Zineb nods seriously while checking her lips in the mirror one last time.

By "him" (*huwa*), Zineb means her destined husband. A university student in her early twenties from a village of the Middle Atlas Mountains, Zineb, like her roommates, is apprehensively waiting for her married life to begin. She repeats to me regularly that everything in her life has already been written and that God has already determined who her husband will be. "*Kollshi b l-mektab*" (everything is written), Zineb and other young women tell me when referring to the person they will end up marrying. The predetermined quality of the futures they expect for themselves, however, is not conceived as granting them idleness. The meticulous preparation of the self that Zineb and her friends undertake before leaving their student rooms and walking to the town's old medina—populated, as we shall see, by a wealth of potential migrant husbands—is one of the many actions they perform in view of their predestined futures. Far from an immobilizing "theological fatalism" (Elder 1966, 229), the young women's conceptualization of destiny seems to require, rather than impede, action. Crucially, these actions include being ready for the gaze of a hoped-for migrant husband, which in turn means being ready for a *musteqbal dyal brra* (future of [the] outside) to begin.

This chapter is about young women's desire for a future of the outside and the multilayered work they orient toward this future. This work starts, first and foremost, with and on the self. By combining pioneering academic trajectories, tentative abidance to divinely determined conjugality, and careful beautifying techniques, young women cultivate a specific kind of predisposition, or openness, toward *l-brra* through particular actions, thoughts, and routines. Young women in the Tadla recognize that the future is characterized by inscrutable and nonnegotiable divine plans, *l-brra*'s bizarre and brutal bureaucratic systems, and the unpredictability of love itself. In other words, they recognize that the future is a complex and slippery entity, never entirely controllable or completely predictable. However, in a certain sense precisely because of this unpredictability, they invest a considerable amount of work, time, and thought into fostering specific kinds of *brra*-infused futures.

Prospective work toward an outside future is mainly oriented toward actualizing specific kinds of conjugal lives, as it is mainly through marriage that *l-brra* is imagined as a possibility. In this chapter, then, I explore how *l-brra* emerges both as an idiom through which young women voice specific kinds of relational desires and as an entity that influences the very manner in which they shape their orientation toward the actualization of these desires. In doing so, I trace how *l-brra* emerges here as an active ingredient in the very crafting of gendered, pious, and modern selves rather than simply as an imaginative trope.

Educating the Future

As the summer holidays draw to a close and the cars with Italian and Spanish number plates start streaming out of Zafiah packed to the brim with clothes, almond sweets, and mint rolled up in newspaper, young people from

Zafiah's surrounding countryside and nearby mountains start streaming into the city for the new academic year with their own appliances: gas cylinders and stoves, notebooks and papers, tagine pots and couscousieres, spices, flour and vegetables, and abundant blankets. Young people in the Tadla area wanting to continue their education after high school need to move to university towns like Zafiah for the academic term, as their homes, tucked away in the Middle Atlas Mountains or in the central Moroccan countryside, can be as far as an eight-hour bus ride away from campus. This influx of students transforms the neighborhoods surrounding the university buildings during the months of the academic year.[1] Many families living in the university area rent out a room, a story, a level, or even an entire section of their home to students, who often stay in university dorms (when space is available) for the first year or two and then move to rented rooms for the remainder of their degree courses. Toward the end of a term and just before the beginning of a new one, small groups of students can be seen everywhere in the network of narrow paved and unpaved streets surrounding the university buildings, knocking on doors, enquiring about rooms to rent. Student housing is generally all-male or all-female, and some streets become predominantly populated either by young men or young women on a seasonal basis. The area around the university is, however, quite circumscribed, and so interaction between young men and women is constant either by young men or young women—at the corner shop when buying snacks, in the narrow streets connecting the houses to the main road and the university, and, importantly, through windows and open doors that allow the circulation of voices, music, and the smell of cooking.

What is striking about this seasonal influx of students from the Tadla's rural areas is its high percentage of young women. The recent dramatic change in Moroccan women's involvement in education is clear in national literacy statistics: in 1960, female illiteracy was at 96 percent (78 percent for men) (Elliott 2015, 168); the latest census sees female illiteracy drop to 42.1 percent (22.1 percent for men) (HCP 2014). The generational change in women's education is definitely palpable in the Tadla. My student acquaintances in Zafiah, who mostly come from very modest-income households in either the nearby Middle Atlas or the vast countryside areas surrounding the town, are often not only the first ones in their households to attend university but also in many cases the only women in the family who are literate. Many come from Amazigh mountain villages and towns where women traditionally married very young and were sent to school for a very short time, if at all (Elliott 2015; Hoffman 2006; Maher 1974). Women like my interlocutors are thus, in a sense, the pioneering product of a complex mixture of changing ideas about schooling in Morocco (Boutieri 2016), state-funded schemes aimed to combat illiteracy in more rural areas of the country (Agnaou 2012), and an uneven, hotly debated shift in the conceptualization of women's role in society (Newcomb 2009, 2017). This specific social context and, in more immediate ways, my interlocutors' unique positioning within their own family histories generate complex possibilities and risks for their personal and particularly their conjugal futures—possibilities that give rise to specific ways of imagining and reckoning with *l-brra* itself.

The young women I know in Zafiah have what could be termed a noninstrumental attitude toward education—or, perhaps more accurately, their attitude toward education is not instrumental in the ways that may be expected (cf. Adely 2012). Education (*l-qraya* or *te'lim*) is considered good, important, and interesting, but this does not necessarily mean that women expect they are going to use it—for example, to get a better job or even a better life. [2] This take on intellectual life is in stark contrast to the highly instrumental discourses young men in the Tadla develop on education, where the explicit reason given for proceeding with their studies is earning more money and achieving, as they put it, "a better life like in the outside." Women I know discuss studying in terms of getting a better understanding of things, being modern, and gaining respectability. The quality of their future, however, is seen as depending mainly on sharing their lives with a good husband (*rajel mezyan*) and on God's willingness to provide them with one.

Although young women know that studying will potentially allow them to get a good job, they often tell me that whether they are actually going to work or not ultimately depends on whom and when they are going to marry. Their future working life depends on their husbands' wealth and on their marital living arrangements, including whether the newlyweds will be living with their in-laws. Either way, many young women see employment as a temporary activity that will last either until they get married or until they give birth to their first child. The prospect of having to work after becoming a mother is often seen quite negatively and as a kind of fallback solution if problems materialize along the way. For many, employment is definitely not a life goal. This negative attitude toward having to work is often mixed with a kind of detached admiration for wealthy (or wealthier) Moroccan and European working couples. The idea of a wealthy workingwoman and mother is *chic et modern*. On the contrary, a woman who is not wealthy and who works is conceptualized as simply being unlucky and having married a man who cannot or will not support her or as eschewing her household duties as wife and mother. There are, of course, exceptions to this view—for example, becoming a schoolteacher, as a number of students plan to do, tends to be exempt from this mode of thinking and generally accepted as a respectable occupation postmarriage, though not necessarily postchildren. In general terms, however, women's employment after marriage is seen positively only when it is not a necessity, and thus when it is not seen as compensating for a husband's lack of resources or care.[3]

So, while education is seen as an important step toward a specific kind of modern, educated, and indeed European future, what is conceived as ultimately determining the future's shape and content is the kind of marriage and the kind of man a woman will end up with. Nearing their midtwenties and inexorably moving away from marriageable age, young women are both excited about the prospects that the university has opened for them and anxious about the delay it has caused to the beginning of a married life. But while marriage remains the normative horizon for their lives to come, notwithstanding their pioneering educational trajectories, women also expect their conjugal futures to be qualitatively distinct from those of their mothers and grandmothers—as well as from those of their unschooled peers back home. Overly educated compared to most family acquaintances who would normally be seen as obvious marriage matches, women are both eager to acquiesce to parental authority in matters of marriage arrangements and deeply aware that they must somehow work behind the scenes if they desire something more than marriage with a 'rubi (village peasant). With their characteristic ironic solemnity, students often tell me that studying to get a degree is the easy part of their lives; commencing a married life, and a suitable one, is really the arduous task.

This task is made particularly demanding by the fact that young women consider only certain kinds of married lives suitable and livable. If on the one hand they regularly repeat that their conjugal futures are divinely determined and unknown, they are also very clear on the kinds of married lives they imagine and hopefully expect for themselves. These are, invariably, married lives that are constituted in and through migration.

Outside Romance

Young women share the powerful longing for a migratory elsewhere that imbues the Tadla area and position *l-brra* at the heart of their imagined conjugal futures. They are very clear that only a migrant husband, a *rajel lli kaimshi*, can offer the kind of married life they expect for themselves.

This is not only because marrying a migrant man is what generally makes women's migratory movements both bureaucratically possible and socially legitimate. It is also because students hold complex migratory-cum-conjugal expectations wherein the possibility of reaching *l-brra* is intertwined with the imagination of a specific kind of conjugal bond that migration has come to signify in the area.

The young women often use the expression *'alaqa dyal brra* (relationship/bond of [the] outside) to refer to their desired married future. In doing so they describe their ideal form of conjugality as based on, among other elements, mutual understanding and support, some form of romantic love, and a small nuclear family with relative independence from in-laws. Importantly, when Zineb, whom we met earlier at the mirror, tells me what she expects from an *'alaqa dyal brra*, she roots her description in her analysis of what surrounds her in the here and now of the Tadla and, in particular, in the life of her own mother, who married, at thirteen, an older widower from the neighborhood, as arranged by her parents. The striking difference between her mother's marriage and what Zineb imagines for herself should not be read as a simplistic reversal/refusal of the older generations' way of life, however. Zineb never speaks of her parents' marriage with contempt, and never once has she discussed her conjugal future as a rejection of her mother's marital life. She takes a more evolutionary approach to the matter— her mother married in her time (*weqt dyalha*), and Zineb wants to marry in her own time, which is deeply permeated by *l-brra*. Zineb says she and her six siblings all had a happy childhood, and her mother had a hard but blessed life, as her father was a good man who looked after her till the day he died. He never hit his wife or his children, he never got drunk, and he never went broke. Her mother, Zineb often says, had a good married life. What Zineb wants for herself is a man like her father, with the fundamental supplement of an *'alaqa dyal brra* to unite them, and a man "who goes" to be her partner in such a union.

A defining characteristic of this *'alaqa dyal brra* as imagined by my young Tadla interlocutors is the quality of the communication between husband and wife. Zineb tells me, "I want my husband to speak to me, to tell me if something is wrong at work or with the family, so I can be close to him. . . . You, Alice, you always go to the countryside to do your things [she is referring to my research here]. You've seen how we are down there. . . . Husband and wife don't talk. . . . They live together, but they don't talk."

My experience of the Tadla countryside isn't exactly this. In the families I know, communication between husband and wife takes place constantly through one-to-one conversations, indirect jokes, mocking, arguments, and sharing of food and space. Indeed, I find that in the more rural and poorer households there is generally a more relaxed gendered division of space compared to some of the more urban, slightly richer households in provincial towns like Zafiah (see Kapchan 1996; Mernissi 1994; vom Bruck 1997b).[4] The availability of more rooms in the latter households and the different organization of daily routines within them means that often less space and time—particularly informal time—are shared by women and men compared to more rural households.[5] However, I do agree with Zineb that isolated interactions between husband and wife are more limited in rural settings. In extended family homes like Zineb's, husband and wife rarely spend time alone, as a couple.

What Zineb wants and doesn't see in the rural husband-wife relationship is, then, a type of privacy and togetherness that she and other young women describe as being *dyal brra* (of [the] outside). She says, for example, that she wants to have her first child just after the wedding and then wait a long time before having other children, so she can enjoy her time with her husband and get to know him well before becoming a full-time mother with two or three children (but no more) to take care of. I have often sensed a strong resemblance between my young Tadla interlocutors' conjugal imagination and the marital scenarios I have encountered in Moroccan upper-middle-class urban couples. However, it would be reductive to conceptualize these imaginings as merely upward mobility aspirations—if anything, outward mobility is at stake here. This does not mean that class and other aspirations are not involved in these conjugal expectations, but *l-brra* remains a fundamental, generative, and distinctive component. Although the French term *modern*—something that is often associated with the urban upper classes of Rabat and Casablanca—figures at times in the women's discourses, it is never a modernity devoid of *l-brra*. Zineb is imagining a relationship of the outside, not solely an upper-class Moroccan one.

Similarly, it would be mistaken, I think, to frame young women's aspirations for an *'alaqa dyal brra* as being simply a desire for all things "Western." Nor would it be accurate to conceive of the young women's conjugal aspirations as being solely a result of globalization and the accompanying transnational movement of ideas of romantic (and modern) love, as some of the recent anthropological research on the subject of love and intimacy seems to suggest (Hirsch and Wardlow 2006; Padilla et al. 2007). Young women's proclivity for *brra*-infused relationships is deeply rooted not only in the specific local conceptualizations of "the outside" but also in their specific personal, historical, and generational positionality. As Laura Menin (2015) argues in her work on the expectations and experiences of love in a Tadla town, the comparison the young women make with their own mothers' life trajectories, the Egyptian romantic comedies followed just as eagerly as Hollywood dramas, the theological imagination that shapes their conceptualization of the future, and their pioneering educational trajectory all must be taken into account when gauging the relational landscape young women imagine for themselves. Indeed, I would argue that *l-brra*, far from signifying a simplistic longing for the West or a mere absorption of a globalized ideal of modern love, becomes here a subtle idiom through which the young women carve out a unique space for their conjugal desires and gendered selves in the here and now of the Tadla. I return to this subtly carved-out space below. Before I do this, let me turn to young women's discussion of the unavoidable coprotagonists of their desired relationships "of the outside": migrant men.

A Suitable Boy

Only certain kinds of men are seen as being even remotely able to sustain *brra*-infused relationships. Contact with *l-brra* is seen as a key prerequisite for the kinds of marital lives young women are imagining for their future. This is not only because migrants embody the possibility of *l-brra* itself. It is also because young women conceptualize migrants' contact with *l-brra* as an intangible process of absorption, which somehow positions these men a step closer to the kind of *brra*-infused life they desire. Perhaps by virtue of having *l-brra f l-dakhel* (the outside inside—see chap. 2), migrants are seen by young women as being more likely to offer the possibility of an *'alaqa dyal brra* compared to men who stay put. I often discuss with my young interlocutors the negative discourses circulating in the Tadla about migrants, which frequently focus precisely on their crass and vulgar behaviors (inauspicious for the kinds of refined *brra*-infused conjugal futures women describe) as well as the sometimes difficult situations of migrants' wives in the area. Women are clear in these conversations that their migrant husbands will be different from the rest: "*huwa maghadish ikun bhalhom*" (he's not going to be like them).

Some young women offer me a bleaker explanation of why migrant men are the husbands to aim for, stating that "anything is better than what's here." They argue that all men are the same deep down, that education doesn't necessarily mean a different life for a highly educated man's wife (referring here to the accusation often leveled at migrants of being illiterate peasants, as we saw in chap. 2) and that a woman might as well concentrate on migrants, as they offer more possibilities than a man "stuck in Morocco." Asmee, a woman in her midtwenties who has dropped out of university but still lives in the student area of Zafiah, has always been very vocal on this aspect. Asmee is in fact very vocal on any issue regarding men and is well known in the neighborhood for her not-exactly-holy interactions with the opposite sex. She has always been a compellingly irreverent guide for me through the spoken and unspoken gender and moral rules of the area, often providing me with refined critiques of gendered (and class—cf. Cheikh 2017, 2018) expectations of women like herself and openly defying these expectations through her actions—particularly her actions with men. Asmee regularly goes off on car rides with migrant men when they visit town. She is constantly receiving presents from *l-brra*—perfumes, shoes, bags, pajamas—and always has the odd extra coin to buy herself a new face cream or expensive fruit at the market. The link between the car rides and the presents is an easy one to make for my other interlocutors. They tell me that with Moroccan men in particular, "*hatta haja fabour*" (nothing comes for free), implying that Asmee is paying a price for her perfumes and money. As for Asmee, she will say that "the girls" (*le-bnat*) are just envious, that she is doing nothing wrong, and that she is just more honest than the rest about her plans to reach *l-brra*. Asmee is categorical about the fact that she will have romantic encounters only with migrant men. This way, she explains to me, she has a better chance of leaving. When the right man comes along, she tells me, he is going to marry her, get her a visa, and "*besslama*" (goodbye!). In no time she'll be sending a postcard *dyal ruma* (of Rome) to her envious roommates.

Although she says it in a defiant way, Asmee is referring to something that is common knowledge in the Tadla: it is migrant men who often create the conditions of possibility of *l-brra* for women. As described in previous chapters, although it is not unknown for unmarried women to leave for *l-brra*, marriage both makes possible and legitimizes women's migratory movements. It is interesting to note here that while the male-dominated character of Tadla migration is everything but universal in global migration—countless historical and contemporary migratory movements are women-led—the majority of the literature on youths' imagination of and desire for a migratory elsewhere is in fact based on young men (Ali 2007; Capello 2008; Gaibazzi 2015; Jónsson 2008; Pandolfo 2007; Schielke 2012; Vigh 2009). One of the reasons for this male-centered analysis is that in many of the ethnographic settings studied, as in the Tadla, the migration of young unmarried men is acceptable, desirable, and at times even expected while that of young unmarried women is more controversial and rarer. In the Tadla, not only is the migration of men more acceptable, but it is also conceptualized, in many cases, as a route to marriage by providing the young man with the social maturity and economic resources required for the wedding and for starting a family. In a way, from a young woman's point of view, the logical sequence from *l-brra* to marriage is inverted, and it is marriage that can hopefully provide *l-brra*. The desire for and conceptualizations of *l-brra* thus have different connotations for young women, as it is often through migrant men that *l-brra* is imagined as a possibility.[6]

But while all young women acknowledge that marriage to *huma lli kaimshiw* (those who go) can lead to migration, rarely do they speak of their orientation toward migrant men solely in terms of a pragmatic move toward *l-brra*. As we have seen, young women have complex expectations about their *brra*-cum-conjugal futures, in which the possibility of reaching *l-brra* is intertwined with specific expectations about the conjugal bond itself. The young women see men who have left their villages, survived the perilous journey across the Mediterranean Sea, reached Europe, and successfully established themselves there as being more likely to sustain their desired conjugal futures. In short, from my interlocutors' point of view, a suitable conjugal future requires a migrant man. The bustling emigrant town of Zafiah provides a unique site for such migratory futures to potentially materialize. And it is in this multilayered setting, made of migratory aspirations and pioneering educational trajectories, filled with unique possibility and fraught responsibility, that young women strive to realize their destined conjugal future in specific, hopeful ways.

Prospective Beauty

As we do nearly every evening, we are getting ready for our stroll in Zafiah's lively medina, the old part of town with fruit and vegetable stalls, clothes and hardware shops, street vendors, and loud music. The small room I share with Aisha and Amira, two university students in their twenties, is bustling with young women. Music is playing from someone's phone, a student hints at sensual dance moves to roars of laughter, news is exchanged, tea is drunk, clothes are swapped and tried on, insolent jokes are made about common male acquaintances, and perfume is passed around and generously sprayed in the crowded room. A few women are congregated around the thin shelf where cosmetic products of varying quality and origin are gathered, to give a last touch to their makeup in front of a small plastic mirror. As always in these moments of preparation preceding the evening outing, the mirror becomes a much sought-out object, around which there unfold subtle power relations among roommates, as each maintains careful timekeeping and endures joking but stern exhortations to "get a move on." I am usually excluded from this struggle for the mirror—mainly because when I do manage to get to it, I am considered to spend such a small amount of time with it that the young women consider it pointless to count me in for my turn in the first place. When I do get to the mirror, students will regularly comment, with a mixture of interest and pity, that I don't really care about being beautiful. They will quickly add, "You're a *gauriya* [Western, white foreigner]. . . . You'll get a husband in no time anyway. . . . *'Endek zin u le-wraq*"—meaning you have beauty (*zin*, in this case referring to pale, European skin) and papers (*le-wraq*—i.e., European documents).

As described in my opening passage, the young women begin a careful process of beautification once they have the mirror. The result is checked many times, and if it is not just right, the process may start all over again. Their preparation in front of the mirror before leaving the house is careful, methodical, and lengthy. Indeed, a considerable amount of my fieldwork in Zafiah has always been spent hovering around beautifying areas of houses, waiting for friends and interlocutors to get ready. Despite the absorbingly boisterous atmosphere often surrounding this preparation, when I first began my research in Zafiah, I felt frustrated during these long waits, eager to get out in the streets and observe social life as I felt I was meant to do, and also somewhat irritated—if rather guiltily so—by what I felt was my friends' extreme concern with makeup and physical appearance. With time, I have come to realize that there is much more to preparation and makeup than I could initially see.

Young women like Amira and Aisha maintain the possibility that their destined husband is among the eclectic mix of people that an emigrant town like Zafiah attracts. During an evening stroll in Zafiah's medina, a man may see a young woman, notice her beauty and her demure posture and style, and approach her. A conversation may start, a romantic relationship may begin, and, *ila mektab* (if it is written), the man may one day be knocking at the girl's family door asking for her hand. The possibility of a destined husband's presence in Zafiah's streets places considerable responsibility on the young women. "If you look scruffy, ugly, untidy, he's not even going to look at you, he's not even going to know you exist in this world. . . . His eyes are going to pass by you and not see you," says Saliha, Aisha's fellow student in the history degree program. She sees it as her responsibility to be appropriately prepared for a destined man's gaze. "You can't go out there looking like a village peasant just arrived in town and then complain about your fate. You have to be ready, prepared."

It is mainly through the cultivation of physical beauty that women make themselves ready and prepared for a destined man's gaze. They describe beauty as both a necessity and a duty and as requiring specific skills and abilities, which they continually share, compare, and reinvent (cf. Ossman 2002). Saliha explains to me that beauty requires balance and taste. "If you are too dressed up," she says, "if you have too much makeup, if it's just all too much and *bla qias* [without measure], men will see you but quickly look away, or keep looking at you, but for the wrong reasons."

Beauty also requires the ability to classify and distinguish between different products and practices. Knowledge about natural beauty treatments on the one hand, and the ability to retrieve European cosmetics on the other, are revered qualities within the women's student community. Aisha, my roommate during my first period of fieldwork in Zafiah, is particularly renowned for her skill in acquiring products from Europe through various channels. At one stage during my stay in town, she had found a way to buy Swedish beauty products through a string of mediators. For about two months, our room became a highway of young women coming to study the torn, expertly read product catalog and order creams, soaps, lipsticks, and face masks. When I asked why the students did not simply go to the local corner shop and buy very similar but cheaper products, they would answer that cosmetics in corner shops are "*mashi qualité*" (not [Arabic] [good] quality [French]) or "*shinwa*"(Chinese), a term used to indicate low quality.

"If you want to be beautiful, you have to use good-quality stuff!" Aisha often says when criticizing my choice of cheaper products. This is particularly important for unmarried women like Aisha, since for her, working toward beauty also means asserting her will to find a husband. "An ugly man always finds a wife. An ugly woman rarely gets a husband. You can't change that," she sighs while turning the pages of an expensive beauty-products catalog.

Taking control of the mirror before leaving the house is thus no small matter for unmarried women like Aisha. Leaving the house looking beautiful, clean, tidy, and attractive but nevertheless modest and discreet means increasing one's chances of finding (or, better, being found by) one's husband. And if beauty opens one to the possibility of finding a husband, mastering the skills of beauty also means being able to master, at least in part, one's future. The beauty practices young women perform in front of the mirror are in this sense anticipatory actions that inscribe in the present a specific orientation toward the future (Miyazaki 2004; Nielsen 2011; Reed 2011).

Crucially, however, these careful anticipatory actions are not discussed as operating in relation to a future that is limitless in its possibilities and open in its outcome. On the contrary, the conjugal future that beauty is hopefully oriented toward is repeatedly described by young women as fixed: determined by God before any action is conceived of, let alone staged. The ways in which young women imagine and work toward a future of the outside is inextricably linked to a specifically theological understanding of the possibilities and limits of human freedom, action, choice, and responsibility. This is not because *l-brra* itself has any kind of divine property (at least not in any straightforward way—see chap. 6) but because *l-brra* is enmeshed in dimensions of young women's lives—hope, the future, conjugality, and even love and desire—that are underpinned by a religious imagination and, more specifically, by conceptions of divine destiny. In short, it is impossible to engage with my young interlocutors' prospective actions toward *l-brra* without also attending to some of the key properties of divine destiny itself.

The Makeup of Destiny

Young women in the Tadla posit divine predestination as a dimension of their conjugal future that is neither negotiable nor avoidable. "You can run away from home [if unhappy with a marriage arrangement], but your destiny will run with you," they say. It is considered self-evident that the shape and content of their future, including their married future, has been already determined and that no human action or intention—be it beauty techniques or pressure from kin—can interfere with these divinely preordained trajectories. Zineb tries to spell this out for me:

Listen, it's simple. Before you are born, when your soul is infused in your body, God writes your life [ktab hayatek]. He writes down everything that will happen to you. Who you'll marry, how many children you'll have, when you'll die. He knows every-thing before you even think it. Of course he does, because he's the one who wrote it! Everything is written, even what you're going to have for breakfast tomorrow, I think, is written somewhere [she laughs]. . . . But, much more important, your

husband is also there, written before you were even born. God has already decided,
he already knows who your husband is, his name, his personality . . . even if he's
handsome. It's all written!

When I was first confronted with this explicitly theological imagination of the future, one that poses divine will as the ultimate determinant of a life course, I struggled to reconcile it with my young friends' and interlocutors' cosmetic techniques oriented toward *l-brra*, described above, and the premarital migrant romances we will encounter shortly. I was aware of the copresence in the Islamic scriptures of notions of God's supreme knowledge and power over all things and notions of human free will and responsibility—as well as of the centuries of debates about their complex relationship (De Cillis 2013).[7] However, I was still confused by the ways in which my interlocutors were stating that everything in their lives has been determined in advance by God while at the same time actively orienting themselves toward *l-brra*—even more so because in doing so, they were also engaging in anticipatory actions (use of makeup, attention to the male gaze) that seemed to run against the kind of pious behavior one may link to such a deeply religious imagination.

Crucially, however, my young interlocutors do not discuss their premarital actions as contradicting the precept of destiny. Rather, they frame these actions as an integral part of realizing a divinely determined life: "I'm just helping destiny," Zineb says as she looks at me in the mirror with one eye while applying eyeliner to the other. "What if he is out there today and doesn't see me because I look bad, huh? What if I'm not ready for him? Oh Lord, I have studied too many years to be so stupid." She winks at me in the mirror. Zineb is telling me that the inevitability of divine plans does not imply human inactivity. More specifically, she is telling me that if one desires a decent conjugal future of the outside, one has the responsibility to be open to it—and this openness requires work. "God doesn't like lazy people," my friends often comment with their invariable evasive irony when I ask why they even bother making themselves beautiful if everything has already been written.

My struggle to grasp the refined relationship between divine destiny and intimate action has always prompted absorbing exchanges with (and warm mocking from) my interlocutors—as well as a mutual realization, and sometimes challenging mutual explorations, of our different assumptions about causality, possibility, and more (cf. de la Cadena 2015). What follows, then, is my attempt to come to grips with the idea and practice of destiny through what Marisol de la Cadena (2015, 31–34) calls the "partially connected conversations" of ethnographic encounters. My engagement here, as throughout this book, is not a claim to explanation—be it of Islamic destiny or of my young interlocutors' lives—but rather, as de la Cadena argues, a translation of what I am told into what I can (inevitably incompletely and imperfectly) understand—with a little help, as we shall see, from Max Weber and Ash'ari theology.

Fixity and Hopeful Ignorance

Throughout my years of partially connected conversations with friends and interlocutors in the Tadla, two qualities of destiny have emerged as key to beginning to understand the relationship between divine destiny and intimate action toward *l-brra* and its futures: fixity and unknowability. People in the Tadla invariably describe destiny as both fixed and unknowable. Although they do endeavor in different ways to discern God's will and elicit divine guidance, divine plans are considered to be ultimately obscure to mere humans. This is particularly the case when it comes to the identity of a destined husband: young women are adamant that there is no way of knowing for sure who one's destined husband may be.

Rather than being overwhelmed by a sense of fatalistic doom in the face of such mysterious fixity, young women in Zafiah actively and thoughtfully engage with it. Confirming anthropological arguments on the social and religious traction of uncertainty and lack of knowledge (e.g., Carey 2012; Dilley and Kirsch 2015; Johnson-Hanks 2005), destiny's unknowability has "a productive side" (Højer 2009, 577), becoming "a powerful presence gaining effects exactly by not being fully known" (576). Not knowing what the future may bring makes destiny a compelling kind of entity for my interlocutors, ripe with possibilities: "the future is unknown/uncanny [*ghrib*]," students often say. Crucially, this sense of a compellingly inscrutable future is coupled with a deep awareness that the future has already been determined— destiny's indefinite quality of unknowability is coupled with its definite quality of fixity.

My sense is that the coupling of these two qualities—unknowability and fixity—makes destiny a peculiar kind of engine for and presence in social action, prompting women to act in specific, hopeful ways in view of their marital lives to come. My suggestion here relates directly to Max Weber's classic insight on the relationship between earthly conduct and faith in divine predestination. In Weber's famous account, the Calvinist doctrine of predestination fueled a deeply this-worldly ethic of work and capital accumulation. Although God's plans are unknowable and unintelligible to humans, it became almost irresistible to obey the imperative to act *as if* one were among the elect by striving to be successful in one's earthly calling. Despite the obvious differences between the two cases, one insight in particular from Weber's analysis offers a useful way to reflect on the explicit relationship my young interlocutors establish between faith in divinely determined futures and (seemingly irreverent) anticipatory action. This insight resides in the idea that the precept of predestination, by virtue of its fixity and opacity, may fuel forms of earthly action directed toward a future one hopes is one's own.

My understanding is that my young interlocutors, faced with a destiny that is both fixed and unknowable, are acting in view of a future they hope is their own—not because they conceive of action as having the agentive power to determine the future but because, in a thoroughly Weberian way, action opens the possibility that a hoped for future may indeed be one's written path. The fact that anything that happens in one's life is seen as simply revealing what was already there but unknown places a peculiar kind of responsibility on young women, as the outcome of conjugal action (or inaction) is read, albeit tentatively, as a materialization of God's plans.

It may seem unorthodox to posit Weber's theory of early Protestantism as good to think within the context of contemporary Muslim Morocco, not least because Weber himself explicitly contrasts the Calvinist logic of predestination with what he sees, together with a string of Western social theorists, as Islam's inherent fatalism (Acevedo 2008, 1741)—as well as because he seems to get so many things wrong about Muslim life and Islamic theology more generally.[8] But in a sense this is what makes the Weberian lens even more interesting, as my young interlocutors seem to turn the stereotype of "Muslim fatalism" on its head precisely through the kind of proactive labor of hope that Weber theorized for Protestants. Here, young women's preoccupation with a written but unknown fate, far from hindering action, powerfully propels it in hopeful directions.

The fact that transcendental forces are conceived as being implicated in worldly events such as marriage further heightens the necessity of human action, as action here does not represent so much a testimony of one's destiny—for example, signs, in Weber's analysis, of afterlife salvation—but rather constitutes a tentative actualization of it. While Weber's Calvinists understood actions in this world (doing good works, the accumulation of capital, being morally upright) as proof but never a cause of salvation in the next, here human actions such as the use of makeup carry the concrete potential to actualize desirable earthly futures. If for Weber action was a sign of but never a means for the realization of a hoped-for destiny, here it is very much a means as much as a sign.

Interestingly, what emerges from this comparative engagement with Weber—per above, my own imperfect route to begin to grasp what my friends and interlocutors have told me about destiny and action all along—is very much in line with the currently mainstream Ash'ari theology of destiny, where actualization, or more correctly acquisition (*kasb*), is at the heart of the relationship between divine will and human action. For this school of Sunni philosophy, God alone is the creator of the predestined course of events, but humans have the responsibility to "acquire" God's predestined decree through their own actions: "any act such as the mere raising of the hand is created by God but acquired by the creature who thus takes responsibility for it" (Glassé 2002:62). As Islamic studies scholar Abdur Rashid Bhat argues, the concept of *kasb*/acquisition, while reserving the absolute power of producing an act with God, also ascribes a responsibility to act to individuals: "man has no real effective power but has the derived power to share in the production of an act" (Bhat 2006, 11).

Such derivative power and responsibility to "acquire" a predetermined future through action resonates powerfully with the ways in which Zafiah students discuss their *brra*-oriented practices. Women know that care of the body can attract the attention of men in town, and thus that beautifying actions can precipitate encounters with possible migrant husbands. While they don't know whether marriage, and marriage to a migrant man, has been written for them by God, they do know what actions are required in the human world to actualize, or acquire, such a future, were this future written for them. In the space left open by the unknowability of destiny, the least (and most) women can do is act in a way that, in line with their knowledge of how the world actually works (and more specifically how *rjal*, men, work), will open the possibility to bring about a hoped-for future. To do otherwise, for the young Tadla women I know, is simply, to put it mildly, stupid (*mkellekh*): not only because it is seen as illogical to "share in the production," as Bhat (2006, 11) puts it, of a destiny one strongly hopes is not one's own but also, I would argue, because such actions—for example, behaving as if one's destiny were to remain unmarried, or as if one's destiny were *not* to marry a migrant—dangerously materialize the possibility that this may indeed be one's written path.

Young women are very clear that the outcome of this hopeful actualization or acquisition of the future is not in their hands. Only what has already been written will emerge from such actions. As Amira Mittermaier (2012, 252) has argued with regard to divine dreams in Egypt and the "incubation practices" they require, here actions are to be understood more as acts of openness and receptivity than as acts of creation and determination. Women do not see it as being within their power to determine the future, which has been fixed in advance by God. However, they do see it as their responsibility to open themselves to what is already there but unknown in specific, hopeful ways.[9]

It is in this openness and receptivity that *l-brra* emerges in all its might. Young women in the Tadla are imagining for themselves *brra*-infused futures with *brra*-infused men, and it is toward this specific kind of future and men that their practice of destiny, as I would call it, is oriented. Such a practice of destiny becomes particularly important once women exit their cramped student rooms and enter Zafiah's medina, where they need to recognize desirable futures in the men they encounter. But as the stakes of actualizing one's written conjugal life become higher, the possibility becomes greater that one might get something wrong.

Recognizing the Future

The boisterous atmosphere of the student rooms preceding the evening outings quickly dissipates once women close the house doors behind them. In the street, voices are lowered, gazes are oriented mostly toward the ground, comments and gossip are exchanged through knowing nods and whispered words, and stride and posture become controlled and measured.

Groups of young women quickly attract the attention of the men who populate Zafiah's medina. Some whistle or make loud comments at the women walking by, others observe silently, and others still might make the brave/arrogant move (judgments vary) to approach one of the women in the group, asking for a minute of her time, her phone number, or her name. Aisha warns me, "They all give you stupid smiles and say sweet words and swear they want to marry you on the spot. But you have to be careful. Only one is your destiny [*ghir wahed mektabk*]. The rest are just fooling around with you." As with the preparation of the self in front of the mirror, the fact that one's future has already been written does not let young women off the hook—if anything, it increases their responsibility.

"All men look the same if you don't know how to see," another student tells me. In the streets of Zafiah, young women are very alert to visual signs of future possibility and attempt to ascertain the kinds of futures contained within the men who surround them. This evaluation often needs to be quite rapid, because once a woman responds to the attentions of a man, numbers may be exchanged, phone calls may be received, and meetings may be arranged. In short, a romantic relationship can be and often is established following an encounter in the street. But the only relationships that the young women are ready to recognize as acceptable, at least explicitly, are the ones that lead to marriage. This is not only because of the (fragile) respectability the discourse of marriage confers to morally questionable premarital interactions but also, I would argue, because of the specific moment in their lives at which these encounters are taking place. Khadija, a student in her last year of university, comments, "Look . . . if you're my age and you're playing around with men instead of looking for your destiny, you're either bad or stupid . . . or both. Back home they are already saying 'bent Hassan fat 'liha l-kar' [Hassan's daughter has missed the bus—i.e., she is too old to marry]. . . . I've got no time to play around, even if I wanted to . . . which of course I don't." She winks.

Whether because it's considered morally appropriate or pragmatically sensible, interaction with men on the streets is generally enacted within a framework of a possible future marriage. So, if a young woman is to interact with a man on the streets of Zafiah, this man has to be someone with at least the likelihood of being a predestined husband. This likelihood needs to be somehow recognized in the man himself. Khadija's friend and coursemate tells me, "It's not written on their foreheads, you know. . . . There's no writing saying 'I'm your destiny [ana mektabek], speak to me!'" She laughs. "You have to take a good look at him/in him [shuf mazyan fih], feel it here [she taps her head], and here [she points to the heart] that he is right. . . . You can't go off with the first bastard [weld le-hram] who smiles at you and then cry about your fate."

In the streets, as in their rooms, young women are confronted with a very tangible problem: their husband may well have been determined by God, but who he is, and indeed where and when they will encounter him, is unknown to them. As argued above, my sense is that young women's way of dealing with this fixed opacity is to actively open up the possibility that what they hope for is indeed there, written in their destiny. While women do not know what awaits them, they do know which types of men wandering Zafiah's medina may offer the kinds of livable futures they hope for, and it is precisely among these men that they actively search for, and through them tentatively actualize, their destiny.

As we have seen, the men in question are mostly migrant men. Students place their expectations of a migratory conjugal life at the pragmatic heart of the process of actualizing their predestined future. *L-brra* becomes an important lens through which men encountered in the streets are observed and a way to selectively contain the many potential conjugal futures a town such as Zafiah offers. This containment is realized, *in primis*, through a refined ability to see.

My young friends and interlocutors possess remarkable observational skills when it comes to Zafiah's men. With a quick, barely perceptible glance, they are able to tell at a distance whether a man is from the countryside or from the city, whether he is Amazigh or Arab, and, most importantly, whether he is a migrant. As we have already seen in previous chapters, migration is often treated in the Tadla as a recognizable bodily attribute, and young women point out to me that signs of *l-brra* are clear in men's eyes, posture, and stride. Importantly, together with the recognition of migrants generally, women cultivate the ability to identify the specific country a man has emigrated to. This is an essential skill because, as they often remind me, "*l-brra* is not all the same"—and, thus, the futures it offers are not all equal.

Men who have migrated to countries like Norway and the United States, for example, are invariably seen as offering different kinds of futures from those who have left for the more standard Tadla destination countries of Italy and Spain. This is not only because of my interlocutors' knowledge about the economic differences between northern and southern Europe or between Europe and North America but also because of the qualities considered inherent in the migrants themselves. Young women often classify Moroccan men who have migrated to southern Europe as *harraga* (undocumented migrants), *'rubiya* (peasants), or *wlad l-ghobra* (drug dealers, literally sons of the powder). They contend that migrants who make it to New York or Oslo are, generally speaking, more educated and modern (*moderne* [French]) and thus more likely to instantiate the kinds of conjugal futures they imagine for themselves.

I have always been impressed by the skilled vision of my young interlocutors when it comes to judging, from a distance, which country a man has migrated to (cf. Grasseni 2009). On their part, friends and acquaintances in Zafiah have always been amused by my own remarkable inability to distinguish between a Moroccan man who has migrated to Italy and one who lives in Canada, and our evening strolls often become an engrossing tutoring session, where the young women provide me with basic information on how to recognize a man's personhood, past, and future.

"This man on the left, the fat one with glasses, the one walking toward us with that silly smile. France. Look at his jeans! Look at his hair! Look at his skin. . . . It's France!" With one quick, barely visible look, so concealed in her bodily posture I can hardly notice it, my friend Myriam knows not only whether the man is a migrant but also where he has migrated to. Myriam, like other young women, is able to know in such detail that her response is ready if the man in question were to approach her. Like beauty techniques, the cultivation of a skilled vision becomes, in this sense, a crucial future-nurturing practice. The response to a French migrant (a Moroccan man who has emigrated to France) will be different to one given to an Italian migrant, for example. Distinctions are, however, even more subtle and comprise complex situational exceptions, some of which are whispered to me during our evening promenades: "You see that one, the one speaking on the phone. He's in Italy [*kayn f talyan*]. You see his shoes and his shirt? Italy, my sister! Look at the other one over there, leaning on the scooter. He's in Germany. He's got dark skin because he's been sunbathing, not because of the fields."

Women know that life as the wife of a fruit picker in southern Italy will be different from that of a waiter's wife in Germany, and their observations and interactions with men are imbued with a careful search for embodied future potentiality (cf. Herzfeld 1995; Vigh 2011). But this search for desirable conjugal potentiality, and the skilled vision it requires, is constituted by distinctive understandings of temporality, causality, and agency. As we have seen with makeup, the ultimate outcome of a future-oriented gaze is not conceived as being in the young women's hands.

"*L-mektab huwa l-mektab* [fate is fate]. All you can do is try to find it," Myriam tells me while composing a text message to a migrant man she has recently met. Like the technique of beauty, the technique of seeing is understood as a way of actualizing a future that is predetermined, not open-ended. Choice and agency lie not in the outcome of one's actions, invariably defined by my interlocutors as divinely fixed, but in the ways in which possibilities for desirable (written) futures are carefully opened. The texture of this participation in divine plans is unavoidably and explicitly human, oriented as it is toward the hopeful actualization of this-worldly futures: lipstick is never framed as containing some kind of godly essence, nor is the ability to see migration classified as containing some kind of piety. Such human participation in divine plans has its own very human implications. For if fixity and unknowability pull destiny into the complex web of the human world, it is also unavoidably the case that the practice of destiny also becomes embroiled in the human world—embroiled, as Gregory Simon argues in his analysis of Islamic prayer in Indonesia, "in larger social and cultural systems, their contradictions, and the experiences of individuals employing and embodying them" (2009, 259).

Practice Makes Imperfect

Destiny, by virtue of its fixed opacity, leaves open a space for human practice, and this is not without consequence. The ways young women hopefully participate in predestined plans are far from flawless: this is unavoidable, my interlocutors tell me, since predestined futures are of divine making, but the actions they are performing to actualize them are *ghir dyalna* (just ours—i.e., only human).

Young women point out, for example, that they do not always correctly "read" the men about town. Indeed, most encounters and romantic relationships of this type I have witnessed in Zafiah have not resulted in marriage. Very often, migrant boyfriends suddenly disappear—"*msha*" (he went), women tell me—or cut off all communications after a few months back in *l-brra*. Young women are remarkably unsurprised by the fate of their friends' relationships, since it is common knowledge that those who go, and men in general, are not keen to marry women who are ready to engage in premarital relationships (see also Davis and Davis 1989). This common knowledge tends to be suspended when young women speak about their own cases, however. The only reason they had entered the relationship, they say, is because they *hessit* (felt) that the man in question may have been *huwa* (the one). His disappearing is attributable to the woman's mistaken judgment; she misread God's signs, erroneously seeing predestination in a *weld le-hram* (bastard) and seeking her destiny with and through the wrong person. In other words, the mistakes made are generally in perception rather than intention, and a young woman will make it clear to whoever cares to listen that the intention behind her now-shattered relationship was marriage with someone she erroneously identified as her potential destiny.

The way my interlocutors frame the imperfection of their premarital actions is perhaps where the role and traction of hope in the practice of destiny emerge most clearly. Young women rarely frame a failed relationship or a lousy boyfriend as their final conjugal destiny—rather, these are discussed as unfortunate temporary hurdles in the way of actualizing one's lifelong marital future *dyal brra* (of [the] outside) still to come. In other words, one's conjugal destiny is generally discussed in positive terms, and the possibility of a desirable future is not necessarily disproved by negative events and encounters in the present. Women do acknowledge that one's destiny may be to marry an undesirable man (e.g., a nonmigrant peasant) or even to not marry at all. Indeed, the work of hope is intimately linked with the awareness that undesirable futures are a possible (ever closer) horizon just as much as desirable ones (cf. Reed 2011). Khadija's bleak comment on "missing the bus" testifies to my interlocutors' positioning at a critical moment in their lives, when the possibility that marriage may not be written for them is increasingly tangible but when, also, the possibility is still open that one's destiny may be otherwise and desirable. This makes it crucial for young women to treat failed relationships and disappeared migrant boyfriends as intermediate mistakes and hurdles rather than as manifestations of their definitive conjugal destiny, and thus to continue probing their written lives in view of a more desirable "future of the outside" (hopefully) still to come.

The way young women discuss such intermediary mistakes also reveals the tricky moral questions that lie at the heart of their practice of destiny. By opening up a space for human action, circumstantial choice, personal preference, and instinct, destiny makes hazy the distinction between actions performed in view of a (hoped) predestined future and actions performed in view of, say, romantic infatuation or pragmatic migratory calculation—indeed, the logic of destiny itself never allows the two to be completely distinguishable. This haziness can be socially and emotionally productive (see Carey 2012), since it allows women to maneuver the opacity of destiny, and the human participation it requires, in ways they consider most personally appealing, or at least most livable according to their own human judgment. The practice of destiny can be seen in this sense as a practice that by definition straddles a thin and shifting line between personal aspirations and tentative abidance of divine will—this cautious straddling, constantly prone to error and shot through with moral judgment, is the work that destiny and *l-brra* require.

To confirm this, one need only consider how students in Zafiah relentlessly question each other's moral intentions and religious integrity when it comes to premarital interactions with migrant men. There is a thin line between obeying and defying divine plans, both in one's own life and when judging others, and negotiating predestination in everyday life is far from an unflinching religious ethic. At times, women openly discuss their doubts, second thoughts, and mistakes in their pursuit of a divinely preordained future as well as the difficulties entailed in this multilayered responsibility they feel they must assume. The imperative to participate in actualizing a predetermined life does not always play out in the expected way, nor is it always possible to avoid other "grand schemes" that intercede in their lives (Schielke 2015). Secret passionate love for a man whom a young woman senses is not her predestined husband, for example, or the irrevocable mistake of judgment in pursuing an intimate, compromising encounter with a migrant who then disappears, is an integral part of how women in Zafiah experience a future that is at the same time *pre*determined and demanding human participation. Always lurking in the background is the nagging knowledge that a premarital encounter, relationship, or even platonic exchange of texts is, fundamentally, morally doubtful—unlicensed by more traditional understandings of Islam, unspeakable for most women with their parents and acquaintances, and only precariously positioned within a conceptual frame of assenting to one's destiny.

These complexities do not dampen the religious configurations through which my young interlocutors understand subjectivity, future, and the possibility of *l-brra*. Quite the contrary, in fact—it is precisely because human practice is imperfect that divine destiny is such an important, embroiling entity in these young women's work toward a future of the outside.

Outside Selves

Young women in the Tadla are preparing for a future that has *l-brra* at its very heart. In many ways, *l-brra* is the future for my interlocutors, as a future devoid of "the outside" is not worth engaging—at least not for the time being. This labor of hope for *l-brra* permeates young women's lives in multiple complex ways—from the ways they take care of their bodies to the ways they reckon with the Islamic principle of divine predestination. Focusing on this at once intimate and cosmological "labor of hope," my aim in this chapter has been to give a sense of the complex and deep entanglements of theological, migratory, and conjugal imaginations fueling young women's actions in the Tadla. Here, the technologies of the self that young women are mastering in view of their conjugal futures—from skillful makeup tricks to refined migratory vision—are distinctly oriented toward a future that is both God's and, hopefully, *l-brra*'s. *L-brra* emerges here as a complex space where theological precepts and personal aspirations meet—moving between religious duties, educational trajectories, and conjugal expectations, young women are imagining, and prospectively acquiring, specific kinds of outside futures and, at the same time, specific kinds of outside selves. These carefully crafted selves are emerging in a very unique context—the young women I know in Zafiah are moving on an unprecedented trajectory when compared to the previous generations in their families. University educated, still unmarried at an age when their own mothers already had two or three children, living away from home in a bustling emigrant town—my interlocutors have an uncharted life trajectory that gives substance and meaning to their encounters with and reflections and actions on *l-brra*. Young women in Zafiah are having to delineate for themselves novel life trajectories, and in this setting, made up of possibility and indeterminacy, divine will and unknowable paths, they are skillfully preparing for *l-brra* to become their future.

Just as for the "women of the outside" we encountered in the previous chapter, migrants play a fundamental role in these processes of self-formation and future orientation. Indeed, throughout my discussion so far, the figure of the migrant has emerged time and again as *l-brra*'s most powerful conduit in gendered processes of subject formation—be it of married women, unmarried students, or expectant parents-in-law. In the following chapter, I return to the controversial figure of the migrant introduced at the beginning of the book and address the role *l-brra* plays in making and unmaking migrants' masculinity and trace what this may tell us about the constitutive relationship between migration and gender in the Tadla.

Notes

1. The academic system in Morocco bears important traces of the country's colonial past and the role France has traditionally played in its intellectual life (Boutieri 2016). The university teaching calendar is mostly based on the French model as well as the subjects taught in most non-Islamic universities. Until relatively recently, French was the main teaching language. Modern Standard Arabic (MSA) has now become the official language at all school levels, and some space is being accorded to Tamazight, although French is still a fundamental component of university-level studies and a central marker of academic knowledge more generally. For an overview of the language ideologies underpinning the French colonial policies in Morocco, see Katherine Hoffman (2008); see Charis Boutieri (2016) for a close study of the Arabization policy characterizing the contemporary Moroccan schooling system.

2. Of course it would be mistaken to claim that education is entirely noninstrumental for young women in the Tadla. One just needs to consider the kinds of distinctions educated women make between themselves and their illiterate peers and relatives to realize that the uses of *l-qraya* (education/study) are multifaceted (cf. Bourdieu 1991; see also Adely 2012; Eickelman 1992; Wagner 1993). What I am trying to illustrate here, however, is the way in which education is considered important in and of itself, rather than as an instrument that is seen as necessarily enhancing, say, the young women's working careers.

3. On the relationship between class, education, and women's employment in Morocco see Laetitia Cairoli (2007); Katja Zvan Elliott (2015); Rachel Newcomb (2017).

4. Though, as we shall see in chapter 5, in more rural households there may also be a stronger gendered expectation of men to exist outside domestic spaces in the daytime.

5. For a classic description of the gendered division of space in Moroccan upper-class urban households, see Fatima Mernissi's (1994) memoir *Dreams of Trespass* on girlhood and adolescence in a Fez home during the 1940s.

6. The conjugal flavor of *brra* imaginaries is reinforced (if not, at least in part, generated) by restrictive European migration laws that tend to accord visas and permits to stay mainly on the basis of the aspiring migrant's kin and conjugal ties (see Salih 2003; Alpes 2014; cf. Piot with Batema 2019).

7. Islamic scriptures explicitly refer to God's omniscience and omnipotence as well as to humans' responsibility to act and choose between good and evil. The tension between divine predestination and human free will is a pivotal topic in both ancient and contemporary Islamic thought, encompassing different historical traditions and scriptural interpretations with distinct philosophical, theological, and political genealogies (Belo 2006; De Cillis 2013; Hourani 1966; Watt 1946; for anthropological discussions of this tension, see, e.g., Elliot and Menin 2018; Gaibazzi 2012; Menin 2015; Schielke 2015).

8. Although Weber never completed his intended opus on Islam, he made comparative reference to Islamic predestination in a number of his writings (e.g., Weber 2010, 1978, 1993). Interestingly for the present discussion, Weber locates the root of what he frames as Islamic fatalism in the fact that, in his understanding, predestination in Islam determines everyday, this-worldly events: "not the fate of the individual in the world beyond [adequately secured by faith in Allah and the prophets], but rather the uncommon events of this world" (Weber 1978, 574). Stripped of "the most important thing" (Weber 2010, 185) that veered Calvinists away from fatalism—the concerned search for signs in this world of salvation in the next—for Weber the "Islamic belief in predestination easily assumed fatalistic characteristics in the beliefs of the masses" (Weber 1993, 205). Weber's analysis of Islam is incomplete and even incorrect in a number of ways. For example, it has been shown ethnographically that the search for divine signs as well as a preoccupation with afterlife salvation are crucial aspects of Muslim life, contrary to Weber's assumption (e.g., Mittermaier 2013; Smid 2010; see also Rustomji 2013). Judging from my own ethnographic material at least, Weber is, however, correct in identifying Islamic predestination as a precept directly implicated in "events of this world"—though crucially, as I argue in this chapter, this implication seems to generate rather than hinder, as Weber argued, action.

9. Dale Eickelman makes a similar point in his early analysis of the concept of predestination in Morocco, arguing that "God reveals his will through what happens in the world, and men of reason constantly modify their own course of action to accommodate this will" (1981, 126). When it comes to their conjugal futures, my interlocutors accommodate God's will preemptively, in hopeful anticipation of, rather than solely in subsequent adjustment to, what God has written for them.

5

THE GENDER OF THE CROSSING

"He sits like a woman," Rashida mutters bitterly, nodding in the direction of her husband, Samir, who is watching TV in the opposite room. Samir, a migrant in Italy for many years, has been back in the Tadla since the beginning of the summer, and the atmosphere in the Ghzaouli family is getting increasingly tense. His first few days back home were marked by intense family activity—receiving guests, visiting relatives, distributing gifts and money *men l-brra* (from the outside), telling stories about *temma* (there). Following this short burst of activity, Samir has now started spending increasing amounts of time at home, watching TV, mending little things around the house, playing with his two children, drawing sketches of the extra story he is planning to build on the family home, and taking long naps. The whole household, after a festive interlude for Samir's return, has gone back to its daily rhythms of cooking, going to school and the marketplace, and working on night shifts and building sites. In the midst of this web of activities and routines, Samir is increasingly still, "sitting"—doing nothing.

Samir is unemployed in Italy and does not have the resources to "move" (act, plan, buy, busy himself) as a migrant man is expected to do when he returns to Morocco for a visit. Samir cannot build a new house, cannot plan and pay for the wedding of one of his younger brothers, and cannot sponsor the building of a new mosque in the neighborhood. He does not have the resources to engage in any of the activities that would lift him from the precarious stasis his wife identified with her acerbic comment "he sits like a woman."

His prolonged "sitting" in a domestic space—a space that, in the working-class neighborhood where the Ghzaouli live, is considered a female sphere in the daytime—is creating palpable tensions in the household.

Samir's children (a girl age ten and a boy age twelve), after a period of obeying their father to the letter and taking pains to show him their loving respect, have gone back to their usual way of behaving. This includes treating their two uncles—their father's brothers—as the figures of authority in the house, as if Samir's presence is quickly fading to the point of becoming invisible. Samir's wife has started complaining about how he hovers around her in the house, telling her how to do her chores and interfering with her domestic routine—something she finds both highly annoying and thoroughly inappropriate for a man. Samir's "sitting" seems to be bringing into question his qualities not only as a migrant man but also as a man.

Taking Samir Ghzaouli's tense homecoming as an ethnographic starting point, this chapter focuses on the ways in which *l-brra* simultaneously shapes and calls into question—or, makes and *un*makes—men in the Tadla. The link between *l-brra* and gender has emerged in different ways and in different forms throughout the book: through *l-brra*'s effects on local temporality and tempos of kinship and care (chap. 1), through *l-brra*'s implication in migrants' wives' "paused personhood" (chap. 3), and through young women's imagination of their future conjugal lives (chap. 4). In the preceding chapters, migrants emerged as key conduits through which *l-brra* comes to inflect the formation of gendered persons in the Tadla. Here, I want to shift my ethnographic thinking to the conduits themselves and trace the ways in which *l-brra* intersects their gendered selves. In particular, I wish to address how migration becomes a fundamental component of masculinity for Tadla men and how gendered expectations intersect with expectations of *l-brra*, setting complex performative requirements for migrant men when they return home. Rather than focusing on the ways in which migration is a gendered act and often instantiates a passage from boyhood to manhood, a topic dealt with extensively in the migration literature (e.g., Ali 2007; Jónsson 2008; Menin 2016; Pandolfo 2007; Vacchiano 2018), I want to focus here on the work required of migrant men to *remain men* despite all odds and trace the specific ways in which *l-brra* makes gender a particularly precarious achievement. Indeed, while the migration scholarship tends to frame migration as a strategic move to acquire locally idealized masculinities, here I want to trace the key role *l-brra* plays in what Farha Ghannam (2013) terms the "materialization of masculinity" and the continual reiteration this materialization requires—a reiteration that is not without (gendered) risks (Butler 1990).

I address this complex gendered reiteration by tracing the kinds of idealized, at times even stylized, expectations that are put on those identified and who identify themselves as migrant men when they return home to the Tadla. My sense is that only by taking the intersection of gendered and migratory expectations seriously can we begin to understand why Rashida's comment about her husband—"he sits like a woman"—is so important and effective. As we shall see, taking normative models of femininity and masculinity seriously does not mean assuming that life in the Tadla—or anywhere else for that matter—is straightforwardly lived as and by these gendered ideals or in any straightforward sense looks like them. Rather, it means attending to the complex workings of gendered ideals and abstractions on specific people, bodies, and relations, as well as to the ways in which, as Ghannam (2013, 3) writes, masculinity is a "collective project," deeply connected "to the recognition granted by others." As we have already seen in previous chapters, the fact that these are ideal types and abstract expectations of "men" and "women" does not diminish their purchase and power in everyday life—if anything it heightens it, particularly when migration is involved.

The Gender of Sitting

"Sleeping in the house," or "sitting," these terms were expressive of lack of activity, activity which in the world of "being a murafiq*" [honored companions of feudal lords] was so central and took such different and esteemed forms. Every value with which the young* aghas *[families of small landholders] had been inculcated said that a man had to act. "Sitting" represented a kind of limbo, without dignity and without any arena in which one might either confront or collaborate with others. "Sleeping in the house" confined one to the woman's sphere as a dormant figure, a doubly anomalous position. Some men tried to pass it off, saying that a given job "didn't suit them, they didn't need it," but this was socially unconvincing and taken to be mere empty words.*[1]

By accusing her husband, Samir, of "sitting like a woman," Rashida is drawing on a specific gendered understanding of "sitting," especially domestic sitting, and using it to frame her migrant husband's behavior in explicitly gendered terms. The house is not a place where men are expected to spend excessive amounts of time in the rural Tadla—as Pierre Bourdieu (1977, 91) wrote in his classic essay "The Kabyle House," "a man who spends too much time at home in the daytime is suspect." In his analysis of the symbolic and embodied social and spatial division between men and women in 1960s rural Algeria, Bourdieu argued that women learned to move through their bodies and throughout their lives in a centripetal fashion with respect to the domestic, intimate sphere while men learned to move in a centrifugal way: "for the man the house is not so much a place he enters as a place he comes out of, movement inward properly benefits the woman. A man who spends too much time at home in the daytime is suspect. [A] man affirms his manliness by turning his back to the house" (91).

Bourdieu's analysis of gender, space, and embodiment has been meticulously dissected both by anthropologists of the Middle East (e.g., Silverstein 2004b) and anthropologists of gender (e.g., Moore 1986), and the classic homologies man-woman, public-private, and outside-inside, particularly prevalent in mainstream analyses of the Muslim world, have been carefully interrogated and subverted by generations of scholars of the Middle East and North Africa. In her work on the gendered inhabitation of space in urban Yemen, Gabriele vom Bruck (1997b) engages in a direct dialogue with Bourdieu's analysis, highlighting how the "Kabyle House model" and the man-woman, public-private, outside-inside homologies are rarely so straightforward. Vom Bruck points out that "the house" in a Yemeni context is never unambiguously private, as "privacy" and "insidedness" are nested and relative concepts, dependent on which categories of people are inhabiting a specific space at a specific time. She brings the key factor of status into her analysis of the gendering of public and private space, arguing that "the embodiment of socio-spatial divisions is contingent on both gender and non-gender-based principles such as age and status differentiation" (vom Bruck 1997b, 139; see also Ghannam 2002) and emphasizing that both women and men of Yemeni elites have historically excluded themselves from the public/market space, and the inhabitation of the domestic space becomes a sign of privileged distinction.

In an ethnographic context closer to that of the Ghzaouli family, Deborah Kapchan (1996) also highlights the fundamental role that status plays in the gendered inhabitation of domestic and nondomestic space in Béni Mellal, one of the major towns of the Tadla region. In particular, she shows how it is mainly peasant/urbanizing poor women who, increasingly, are occupying the traditionally male arena of the marketplace, whereas the privatization and interiorization of public life (installation of private ovens and baths, enclosing of domestic and leisure spaces within apartments and high-rise buildings, and so on) becomes a marker of middle-class status—an analysis that strongly also recalls Fatima Mernissi's (1994) autobiographical account of gender and space in a Fez upper-class home.

The neighborhood on the outskirts of Zafiah where the Ghzaouli family live, however, is populated neither by the elite intellectuals of vom Bruck's work nor by the middle classes mentioned by Kapchan nor by the urban upper classes of Mernissi's classic memoir. Although the gendering and inhabiting of space is, as we shall see, unquestionably more complex than Bourdieu's analysis of the Algerian "Kabyle house" of the 1970s, there is no doubt in the Ghzaouli's neighborhood about the fact that *d-dar* (the house) is predominantly women's space in the daytime. In contrast to the more urban Tadla middle classes described by Kapchan in the 1990s, daily life here is not interiorized, nuclearized, and closed off "from a more interactive and visible community" (Kapchan 1996, 15). The streets of the Ghzaoulis' neighborhood are constantly populated by informal gatherings of neighbors and relatives. When not at school or sleeping, children play in the unpaved alleyways throughout the day, and men and older boys are also out of the house most of the day—working in the surrounding fields or on building sites, looking for jobs, sitting in coffeehouses, dealing with bureaucratic issues, sorting out some other unspecified business, secretively meeting girlfriends, hanging around with friends, and so on.

In the Ghzaoulis' neighborhood, then, men are generally "moving," whereas "sitting" is, ideally, a woman's affair. As I mentioned in chapter 3, *galsa* (sitting, f.) is a term that refers to a particular gendered positionality and predisposition at various levels of abstraction. *Galsa* implies that a woman is not involved in activities such as employment or formal education but that she has a proper position within the gendered moral economy, meaning, for example, that she is not considered to be roaming around without a purpose (*bla sabab*) and that her center of gravity resides, so to speak, in the home. In this sense, then, *galsa* is not the description of a static, nonworking body—indeed, women never actually sit idle for long periods in the Tadla and are generally occupied with arduous domestic and nondomestic activities throughout the day (cf. Mernissi 1988). *Galsa* refers to a certain type of (female) person, implying a moral disposition rather than an actual immobile body.

Gales (sitting, m.) has different connotations for men. *Gales* can mean that the man in question is unemployed or that he has recently lost his job and/or is looking for one. But in a context where paid labor is not a totalizing norm, and where men's subsistence activities can also include working on the family land or busying oneself in other ways to generate an income—from selling old bicycles at the weekly market to transporting villagers on a horse and cart—*gales* implies more than simply being unlucky on the job market. It also conveys a sense of someone not making, not doing, not busying himself in a range of different areas of social life.

Indeed, *gales* (sitting) can indicate, just as for women but in the opposite sense, a specific kind of (gendered) positionality and predisposition. "*Dima gales*" (he always sits/he's always sitting around) is a telling comment that refers not only to the inactivity of a body but also to the sort of person someone is. In this sense, then, *not* to sit—and thus to work, do, search, and generally busy oneself—is considered a proper state of being for a man. Importantly, *gales* acquires different meanings in different contexts. While a man sitting at a café for too long can be directly and indirectly criticized for his inactivity, laziness, or irresponsibility toward *daru* (his house/family), the stakes become significantly higher for a man who sits in the house for too long—something that is not only ridiculed but also calls into question one's claim to male adulthood. Contingency, then, is crucial in the gendered evaluation of "sitting." The older the man, for example, the more he is expected to spend time *fe d-dar* (in the house), looked after by the younger members of the family, leaving the house just for short strolls or to visit the local mosque.

Another crucial element that affects the evaluation of (domestic and nondomestic) "sitting" in the Tadla is, as we have seen with vom Bruck (1997b) and Kapchan (1996), status and position in a social hierarchy. A man may "sit" for longer periods than others because he can afford more idle time: he may have the money to pay someone to work his land, he may be receiving a generous pension after early retirement from state employment, or he may be simply part of a wealthier (and luckier) lineage. In his ethnography of descent groups in Tadrar, an Amazigh village of the High Atlas Mountains, David Crawford (2008) brilliantly illustrates the gendered values of "empty time" (155). He traces how, in Tadrar, "despite an egalitarian ethic among lineages, material conditions vary" (Crawford 2008, 89), and some household heads have at their disposal both more land and more labor (i.e., adult sons) than others.[2] Having more land and more able-bodied adult sons to work it means having more time at one's disposal, as one is not compelled to dedicate all one's time to rural labor. Crawford argues that "sitting," in this context, directly translates into power, as it means having time for social and political "work" in the village, time to "gather information . . . cement friendships, trade gossip, express political views, comprehend and comment upon political dynamics beyond the village" (110). "Sitting," in this context, becomes a source of prestige and power (cf. Gaibazzi 2015).

However, sitting because one can afford to—for example, having the resources to delegate physical labor to others or being part of an intellectual elite—differs fundamentally from sitting because one cannot afford or is unable to "move." And while the Amazigh men described by Crawford are "sitting" in the sense that they are not involved in physical labor, they are intensely active in many other spheres of local life and definitely not "just sitting" in the house.

Within this context, it may become clearer why Samir's "sitting" in the Ghzaouli household is problematic, for his wife at least, in a gendered sense. Samir is not of the right sex, status, or age to be spending prolonged amounts of time "sitting and doing nothing" at home. Most importantly, Samir is the wrong type of man. His connection with *l-brra*, the fact that he is a man *lli kaimshi* (who goes), makes his domestic stillness all the more problematic, as this defining connection is expected to actualize itself back home in the Tadla through specific gendered movements and doings.

Moving Like a Migrant

When migrants return home from *l-brra*, they are expected to "move," and in a sense excessively so. If "doing" and "not sitting" are expected of all men, these expectations are infinitely multiplied when it comes to migrant men. Movement to *l-brra* becomes a quality of one's personhood (chap. 2), and this quality is observed and evaluated in specific ways when migrants return home. Energetic "doings" in areas ranging from construction to social relations are seen as the inevitable consequence of one's contact with *l-brra*. In a way, a man becomes a *rajel lli kaimshi* (man who goes) through his behavior and attitudes during his visits home: the way he walks confidently down the street, the way he beckons the waiter from across the bar, the way he approaches a young woman in a shop, the choice of decoration on his newly built house. Recalling Michael Herzfeld's point about the value placed on the "conventionalized unconventionality" (1985, 25) of male behavior in the Cretan village of Glendi, migrant men in the Tadla are expected not simply to stick to conventional male behaviors but to embody them with originality, excess, and even eccentricity. As Herzfeld shows for Glendi men, the essential thing for an action is that it both confirms stereotypical expectations of manhood and skillfully and inventively manipulates these expectations.

My sense is that the "conventionalized unconventionality" expected of migrant men is intimately linked to the fact that for a migrant, to be a man means being a migrant man. This is more than a simple play on words. The fact that the social personhood of migrants is rooted in their movement to *l-brra* means that people's expectations of migrants are inseparable from their expectations of *l-brra* itself. *L-brra* contributes to the production of specific kinds of men, and these men, in turn, respond to specific kinds of requirements and expectations. With this I do not mean to imply that the expectations are static, nor that adherence to them is expected to be mechanistic (Herzfeld 1985). As work on Arab and Muslim masculinities has richly argued—in an explicit effort to subvert the scholarly trend to depict the figure of the "Arab Man" (whoever and whatever that may be) as "rigid, inflexible, and defined within unchanging codes of honor and systems of 'patriarchy'" (Marsden 2007, 475; see also, e.g., Amar 2011; Ghannam 2013; Ghoussoub and Sinclair-Webb 2000; Ismail 2006; Inhorn and Naguib 2018; Khalaf and Gagnon 2006; Schielke 2015)—the gendered expectations of migrants returning to Morocco are extremely varied, sometimes profoundly contradictory, and continually reconfigured.

These continual reconfigurations are related not only to the social changes taking place in Morocco itself—most notably, perhaps, the steadily increasing schooling and employment of women and its gendered implications (see chap. 4)—but also to the complex, shifting, and contradicting perceptions of what *l-brra* is, does, and has to offer. Indeed, the conundrum facing many migrant returnees is the indeterminacy and boundlessness that characterizes people's imagination of *l-brra*. These imaginations translate into a complex set of expectations and requests, often expressed, crucially so, through a normative gendered language of male worth and male duties.

This makes migrants' return visits fundamental moments of gender performativity—or indeed fundamental moments of "materialization of masculinity," as Ghannam (2013, 33) defines the struggles, challenges, and emotional and physical pressures of becoming a man in her work on masculinity in urban Egypt. Whether a man is "good at being a man," as Herzfeld (1985, 16) puts it, is subject to close scrutiny during return visits. It is through migrants' performative ability in the Tadla that gendered assertions, expectations, and reconfigurations are played out, and the peculiar intersections between *l-brra* and masculinity emerge.

One crucial area where these intersections are played out and crystallized is in the construction of houses. Migrants' house building is a classic topic in the migration literature and has been variedly associated with the assertion and reinvention of status and materialization of success in "the outside" and as testimony to one's (hopeful) relationship with "home." Crucially, "house-making" (Dalakoglou 2010) in the Tadla is also a fundamental way in which migrant men actualize their ability to move and thus instantiate their *brra*-infused gendered selves.

To illustrate this, let me return to Samir's "domestic sitting" and trace the relationship between migrant house-making and gendered personhood.

Building Masculinity

Samir fills the many hours he spends "sitting" at home sketching the extra story he is planning to build on the Ghzaouli house. This extra story, Samir tells me, has always been in his imagination of "*dari*" (my house), from the very day he bought the land where his one-story house now stands. The plan for the extra story is evident in the material nature of the house itself. Its upper part stands visibly unfinished and unpainted, rebars are still sticking out vertically from the main walls, and Samir has often walked me through the geography of future rooms on the house's flat roof and floor-to-be—currently used, as is normal practice in the area, for washing clothes, grilling meat, fixing domestic and other appliances, Eid proceedings, and, in the case of the Ghzaouli family at least, keeping chickens.

For over ten years, the Ghzaouli family has lived in a house that incorporates the visible and material intention of its expansion. This expansion has yet to be actualized, but Samir dedicates most of his energy to it during his returns and probably many of his thoughts when he is in Italy. After dinner, while watching TV, while waiting for tea to be served, when sitting on a plastic chair outside the house in the evening breeze, Samir often takes out a pen and a worn piece of paper from the pocket of his jeans and starts sketching over older sketches of his planned house-to-be. He changes the size of the rooms, calculates the height of the walls, plans where the various members of the family will have their bedrooms, and makes other little alterations. After sketching and thinking for a while, he folds up the piece of paper and puts it back in his jeans pocket. This ritual is repeated several times in the course of the day, and Samir always keeps this ever-evolving plan of the house with him and on him.

The first time I noticed this carefully stored piece of paper it reminded me of a *hjuba*, the tiny piece of paper with phrases from the Quran written by a *fqih* (local Muslim cleric), kept in an amulet or tucked into clothes for protection—for example, during a dangerous crossing of the Mediterranean. And this piece of scribbled-on paper is, in many ways, a protection for Samir. First of all, it is a protection against insanity. Samir tells me, when I sit next to him observing his architectural diagrams, that if he doesn't plan his house he will go mad: "*gha nwalli hmeq khti*" (I'm going to go mad, sister). It is difficult for me to discern whether he is referring to the tensions

I can sense rising in the household, to the sense of unmet expectation emanating from those around him, or to a more subtle existential need to have something to aim toward. Whatever the reason, Samir pats the jeans pocket where he stores his house plan and tells me, "Without this, I'm going to implode [*ntartaq*]."

My sense is that together with insanity and implosion, and strongly linked to these, the piece of paper also protects Samir against stillness and inactivity. Drawing, planning, and talking about the extra story of the house are what anchors Samir to a migrant, gendered personhood. It is what protects him, from his perspective at least, against inactive stasis in his own home. Indeed, Samir sees this extra story as his main commitment when he is in Morocco: drawing, planning, reimagining, and discussing the house is, in fact, what he does most during his visits.

By immersing himself in sketching out the future development of his house, Samir is paralleling what most migrant men do, and are expected to do, when they return to Morocco: house-making. As observed time and again in a variety of ethnographic settings (see, e.g., Chu 2010 on China; Dalakoglou 2010 on Albania; Lopez 2015 on Mexico), one of the main activities that occupy migrants during their visits to Morocco is the building of a house. In many ways, the whole migratory project is oriented toward "doing a house" back home, with the physical building of a house becoming the material expression of a fundamental commitment to "the construction and maintenance of an economically stable and emotionally nurturing household in the . . . homeland" (McMurray 2001, 21). "Doing a house" goes beyond the tangible function of providing a shelter and acquires specific significance and meaning in the context of migration. In Morocco, this is not only linked to the socio-economy of symbols and the need to have tangible signs of both success in the outside and enduring belonging to *le-blad* (one's country/land) (McMurray 2001). It is also, as I have suggested, linked to the fact that migrant men, when they return home, are expected to actualize their precious connection with *l-brra* through constant doings. "Doing a house" is in many senses the most fundamental of all doings, the generative matrix for other subject-defining activities, such as "doing a wedding" (*dir 'ers*) and having children.

In this sense, building a house is inextricably linked to the building and display of a (specific type of) person. As Janet Carsten and Stephen Hugh-Jones (1995, 2–3) write in one of the classic anthropological engagements with "the home," "the house is an extension of the person. . . .Like an extra skin, carapace or an extra layer of clothes it serves as much to reveal and display as it does to hide and protect. . . . If people construct houses and make them in their own image, so also do they use their houses and house-images to construct themselves as individuals and as groups." The role of self-display played by migrants' houses, together with their role as conduits for upward mobility, has been addressed by a number of scholars of Morocco (Capello 2008; Geertz 1995; McMurray 2001; Salih 2003).[3] To these analyzes I would add that in the Tadla, the display of a *brra*-infused self is to be found not only in the finished, lavish, and grandiose product but also, and perhaps more fundamentally, in the actual process of "doing a house"—the evidence, expression, and performance of a particular type of active, "nonsitting" person, of a man *lli kaimshi* (who goes) rather than *igles fe l-meghrib* (sits in Morocco).

Indeed, the actions involved in the process of building a house are as important as the end product: thinking up a plan, paying an architect, finding the builders, buying the materials, negotiating a building permit with the local *caid* (district representative of the central government) and then negotiating with the local *muqaddem* (neighborhood representative of the city administration) to stretch the permit obtained, mixing the cement, working on the construction site and/or supervising the works as they unfold, and so on. The whole process of "doing a house" is in this sense tangible testimony to migrant men's personhood, characterized by the ability to "move" and "do" and fundamentally distanced from the personhood of those who "sit" and "wait."

The fact that the building process never really comes to a halt confirms that the process of construction and related multiple doings is as essential as the final built house itself. Houses are continually expanded, embellished, and changed every time migrants return. Extra stories and new rooms are added, internal furnishings are upgraded, new covers for the long couches are bought and fitted. Depending on the migrant's financial and other possibilities, the foundations for a completely new house—and, in some cases, even for a mosque—can be laid. A person's quality as someone who *kaimshi brra* (goes [to the] outside) is thus always based on something above and beyond a first completed house, and so the process of building or thinking about building never really comes to a halt. Indeed, I would say that this process can't stop: if this movement ever does cease, the ability of a migrant man to "move" rapidly begins to be questioned. And this is precisely what is happening with Samir.

From Samir's perspective, by sketching the future development of his house, he is doing what other migrants do when they return home: he is building. For the time being, he is building on a piece of paper, but it is the building of an indisputable future reality rather than daydreaming or a fantasy. It couldn't be otherwise, as he conceives of himself as someone who "moves" and "does," not someone who "sits" and "waits." He doesn't have enough money, for the time being, to add the new story to the house. But the preparatory work for its building (planning, imagining, sketching, worrying, fixing) is taking place constantly. Its execution is, for Samir, imminent.

His wife, Rashida, out of earshot of her in-laws, tells me that the only thing that is imminent is Samir's madness: "he's been scribbling on that piece of paper for years, Alice. . . . Don't believe him when he says he'll build on the top. *Makaynsh la flus la walu* [there is no money no nothing], and he's just going mad." What Samir does in order to avoid madness, building on paper, is seen by his wife precisely as the sign of his impeding madness. And while his architectural imaginings keep Samir anchored to the conceptualization he has of himself as a moral male subject who provides for his family, these imaginings are clearly not enough to prove to those around him that he is worthy of such personhood. For those around him, starting with his own wife, Samir is awkwardly inactive and problematically behaving *bhal shi mra* (like some woman). Indeed, the fact that the house stands unfinished is material proof, for Rashida, of Samir's failure to act as a man when he returns home.

Leaky Crisis

Samir's returns home have not always been typified by "sitting" and the absence of house-making activities. Throughout the first ten years of his migration to Italy, Samir in many ways successfully complied with the complex expectations placed on "men who go." He married a young woman the first time he returned to the Tadla, and a son was born about a year later. On his second visit, he bought a piece of land on the outskirts of Zafiah and paid laborers to lay the foundation and put up the supporting pillars for a house. On his third visit, the walls and roof of the first floor of the house were built, and his wife, his two children, his mother, his father, his two brothers, and his sister moved in. In the years that followed, he continued "doing" the house, and every time he returned home, he picked up from where he had left off on his previous visit. He painted the internal walls and decorated the exterior ones, fitted the kitchen appliances he bought in Italy and bought long divans for the rooms, tiled the bathroom and built a provisional shed on the flat roof of the house.

It is only since the early 2010s that Samir's house doings have decelerated. Samir's problematic stasis in Morocco coincides, temporally, with his unemployment in Italy. I was told about Samir's bleak work situation long before the return described in this chapter. As I discussed in chapter 2, people in the Tadla tend to be particularly and often intentionally vague about migrants' doings in *l-brra*, and migrant men tend to be simply inserted into one of two master categories: *kheddam* (working, employed) or *gales* (sitting, out of work). Samir, his relatives told me before his arrival, has been "sitting" in Italy for a while. The Italian factory where he used to work closed down in the midst of the European financial crisis, and the opportunities for manual labor in the fields, where he worked in the past to subsidize his factory income, are now all taken by *l-romaniyin* (the Romanians), Samir's older brother explained to me once with a grave tone in his voice—politely ignoring my protestation that he seemed to be rehearsing a typical Italian anti-immigrant motto.

People in the Tadla generally acknowledge that life is difficult *f l-brra* (in the outside), and since the 2009 European financial crisis, stories about the effects of *l-azma* (the crisis) on Moroccan migrants have been increasingly circulating in the area, and both national media and local word of mouth often report how migrants are "sitting" in *l-brra*. Importantly, however, this factual and often strikingly accurate knowledge of *l-brra*'s economic situation does not tend to translate into decreased expectations put on returnee migrants, nor does it transform the gendered and moral scales through which migrants' ability (or not) to "move" is evaluated. While Rashida and other family members acknowledge and even discuss openly Samir's unemployment in Italy, Samir's stillness back home is still read in gendered terms and related directly to his standing as a man. In other words, knowledge of economic realities and events in "the outside" does not eclipse or erase other regimes of value and evaluation through which individual persons are understood and expected to be, indeed, persons when they return home. This may well be linked to the resilience of the local understanding of *l-brra* as a space of possibility, where economic crisis not only may well be different from what it is *hna* (here) but also does not necessarily extinguish the possibility of possibility that *l-brra* represents and that migrants should or even must be able to somehow capture (cf. Sayad 1999; see also the book's conclusion for further reflection on the relationship between imagination and crisis as the latter persists). Either way, the gendered conceptualization of "sitting" effectively trumps economic rationalizations about *l-brra*. "Sitting" remains about gendered personhood, even if the reasons for such "sitting" may be understood to be also economic.

The fact that gendered expectations of migrant men are resilient to economic considerations about *l-brra* has particular tangible and even physical effects on those caught up, for good or worse, in such intersecting regimes of value and valuation. The fact that Samir does not have the resources (material but not only) to move as someone *lli kaimshi* (who goes) further entrenches him—before the eyes of his family, his neighbors, regular customers at the coffeehouse, and even fellow worshippers at the local mosque—in what is seen as the female space of the house. It is not just that Samir does not have the resources to engage in house-doing. He also does not have enough money to leave extravagant tips or enough foreign-bought cigarettes to pass around to his friends at the café, and he does not possess a new *brra*-bought garment to wear for Friday prayer. Samir's sense of unease in the neighborhood manifests itself quite clearly in his bodily posture on those rare occasions when he does leave the house. In his increasingly rare outings, Samir walks in a stooped fashion, his head lowered toward the ground, his feet dragging on the street. This is a very different picture from the man who arrived from Italy confident and radiant at the beginning of the summer. "*Mabaynsh rajel meskin*" (he doesn't appear/look like a man, poor thing), Samir's mother once told me when we were looking out of the window one evening and noticed Samir slowly walking toward the house. She was suggesting, perhaps, that the very weight of expectations positioned on her son inside and outside the home were compromising his gendered self and body (though this interpretation of her words may come more from my own instinctive sympathy with Samir's position whenever I visit the Ghzaouli family, a sympathy that his wife, Rashida, always grounds with sobering perspective: "at least he's not stuck here like me," she will say, nodding to a pile of dishes, clothes, or—more surreptitiously—her in-laws).

So, it isn't only through his inability to build that Samir's gendered standing is coming under scrutiny in the Tadla. His building stasis—visible in the unfinished house itself—is the palpable manifestation of his inability to move in a variety of other realms, including his own neighborhood. And the longer Samir stays in Morocco, the more problematic this stillness becomes. This is also because the passing of time is somehow measured differently when it comes to migrants, and while there is no direct, explicit relationship, there is a sense in which idle time in the Tadla means time lost in *l-brra*. This is an observation Crawford (2008) also makes in the Amazigh village of Tadrar, where he argues that, for the migrants coming up from the city to their family homes in the High Atlas Mountains, the period of relative inactivity of "the visit" has come to be conceptualized as lost wages:

"time lost when paying work could have been done" (156; see also Gilsenan 1996, 281–97). In the Tadla, just as in the High Atlas, a specific philosophy of measurement is applied to the days, afternoons, and hours of "sitting" for migrants like Samir.

It is probably also for this reason that when Samir one day announces "*ana ghadi*" (I'm going—i.e., I'm returning to Italy), there is a palpable sense of relief in the Ghzaouli household. Let me consider for a moment the significance of this departure to show how, for men like Samir, returning to *l-brra* becomes a fundamental way to counterbalance their precarious standing in the Tadla.

Gendered Crossings

Like the whistling of pressure cookers full of meat, vegetables, and spices that can be heard at lunchtime in any Tadla alleyway, Samir's exclamation "*ana ghadi*" (I'm going) seems to finally release the pressure from the Ghzaouli household. His mother and wife start baking sweets for Samir to take back to Italy, his brothers rush to the weekly market to buy mint, olive oil, and olives, and his children start spending more time indoors with their father. The whole household gets involved in the prolonged process of packing Samir's bag. His mother takes his passport out of the drawer in the kitchen where it has been locked away throughout his stay, the key dangling safely from her apron. Rashida washes his favorite shirts, his son helps him fold his clothes, and his daughter stacks items for the trip in a corner of the bedroom where the suitcase lies for a few days as objects, clothes, and foods are inserted, rearranged, taken out, and vigorously pushed back in. Both children sit on the suitcase when it is eventually time to close it, laughing hard with their father as the three of them undertake the seemingly impossible task of zippering it. The whole family ends up joining them in the bedroom, everyone with different advice on how to get the bag to close, and everyone, by the end, is crying tears of laughter.

Samir's imminent departure has the effect of clicking a switch—the Ghzaouli household is once again bustling with preparations, laughter, and special foods. Friends and relatives call in to say goodbye, and the house becomes, for about three days, full of people, tea, big meals, children running in and out the front door, and music. The festive, special atmosphere of Samir's arrival reappears for his imminent departure. On both occasions, arrival and departure, Samir's position in the household is strikingly unambiguous and clear-cut. He busies himself to make sure his guests have enough to eat and that his bag is being packed correctly, has boisterous conversations with his friends, and makes witty appreciative comments about his wife's beauty when she serves them tea. Samir becomes transformed on these occasions. He is the proud head of the household, and all the activities and movements of food and goods and guests are now centered around him. When his departure is imminent, Samir appears firmly in his place. In these moments, neither his wife nor his mother, nor indeed any onlooker, would accuse him of being *mashi rajel* (not a man).

Once Samir leaves for Europe, the household changes again—the children are noisier, the arguments between mother and daughter-in-law grow harsher, the brothers take longer naps, less meat is served at mealtimes, and so on. And as the household resumes its normal daily activities, the language surrounding Samir also shifts: stories about Samir *f l-brra* (in the outside) gradually reemerge in family conversations, and "*gal Samir*" (Samir said) becomes once again the standard opening of a story or the introduction to a remark (cf. Kapchan 1996). In his absence, Samir is mentioned constantly, and the Ghzaouli family is somehow structured around his figure: Samir is the household head, the owner of the house, the breadwinner despite his prolonged unemployment in Italy, and the one who is consulted, transnationally, for any important family decision. Samir's structural place in the household is indisputable, and it is clear to all. It is the place for his physical presence when he returns home that feels unclear—Samir's "sitting" at home, his stooped gait in the neighborhood, and his inability to "move" in the (undefined) ways expected of migrant men makes his positioning in the Tadla particularly awkward, unjustified, and, above all, threatening to his gendered standing. My sense is that his departure—his crossing into *l-brra* that reiterates his original crossing as an unmarried boy—somehow "restores" his positioning as a migrant man and thus as a man tout court. By leaving once again for *l-brra*, Samir is also reiterating the personhood of "someone who goes," eschewing the stillness that marks his visits to the Tadla.

The whole family knows that what Samir is returning to in *l-brra* is also stillness—the stillness of unemployment. But just as it does not affect (at least not in immediately obvious ways) the gendered expectations positioned on Samir when he visits home, this awareness does not seem to affect the value people around Samir attach to his crossing back into Europe. The fact that he still has the ability (and, indeed, quality) to move in and out of *l-brra* makes Samir's "sitting" in Italy virtually irrelevant. And while in "the outside" *gales* (sitting) is about lack of employment, bad luck, laziness, racism of the *nsara* (Christians/Westerners), in Morocco *gales* is about personhood and, more specifically, gendered personhood.

It is in this sense that I am suggesting the gendered personhood of people like Samir is attached—by a thin, precarious thread—to their ability to move between Morocco and "the outside." As long as his visit remains a visit and not a stay, Samir's temporary "sitting" in Morocco is tense and odd but just about acceptable. If this movement between home and abroad were to be indefinitely interrupted, this would have fundamental consequences on Samir's position. In this case, "sitting like a woman" would become definite and definitive rather than temporary and transient. The conceptualization of *l-brra* as a place of possibility, part of a cosmos where cause and effect, work and money, movement and sitting follow different logics, makes Samir's inexorable return to *l-brra,* despite his recent bad luck there, a fundamental, undeniable quality of his personhood. Indeed, this is what anchors him to the position of being an adult man (*rajel*) despite his sporadic appearance back home recently resembling more that of an unmarried girl (*bent*) "sitting at home." Samir's gendered self could be seen as being continually reformed and reinstated through the repetition of the crossing into "the outside."

I would suggest that this process of continual reformation and reinstatement of gendered selves through the repetition of the crossing can be considered applicable to Tadla migration more broadly Indeed, my sense is that even in the case of very successful migrants, masculinity remains deeply tied to movements to and from *l-brra.* Samir's wealthy migrant neighbor, Hajj Khalid, provides a good example of this. I do not have the kind of close interactions with Hajj Khalid as I have with the Ghzaoulis, so I am unable to provide a comparable picture, but I mention him here because I have always been struck by the way in which commentators in the neighborhood dissect his migrant riches in explicitly gendered terms.

Hajj Khalid's five-story detached house is just a few streets away from the Ghzaouli home, and the imposing house reflects the success of his migratory biography. He left for Italy in the mid-1980s and has always found a way of making money abroad. Throughout his years as a migrant, Hajj Khalid has built five houses in his native town and on its outskirts, each containing several apartments. He has also been on two Mecca pilgrimages (a costly and prestigious venture), married three women and divorced one, and had seven children, all but one now living in Italy. Every time he returns to Morocco, Hajj Khalid engages in multiple doings: he starts building a new house, enriches the decorations of his older houses, pays for a lavish wedding for one of his relatives, and organizes big meals to celebrate the victory of one of the local politicians he sponsors. When I first met him in the summer of 2009, Hajj Khalid was in the middle of prolonged and animated negotiations about the price of a piece of land behind one of his houses. His plan was to build a mosque on the land. It would be, he told me, an offering to God and a present to the neighborhood where he had grown up.

To my surprise, the neighborhood was not as enthusiastic as Hajj Khalid about the building of the mosque. Indeed, the people I know in the neighborhood are not particularly enthusiastic about anything that Hajj Khalid does or has done throughout his decades of migration. Most people in the neighborhood speak of Hajj Khalid with contempt. Although I am accustomed to the constant criticism and mocking of migrants (see chap. 2), what surprises me in the case of Hajj Khalid is that the criticism is directed specifically at his masculinity (or lack thereof) when, to a naïve observer like myself, everything he does seems to abide by the unwritten rules of masculinity expected of migrant men. This points to the fact that gendered scrutiny in the Tadla is directed not only toward those men who fail to "move" in the expected ways like Samir, but also to other more successful and definitely more active migrants. "He's not a man; he's a princess [*princesse* (French)]," people tell me when I ask about Hajj Khalid. "He just wants, wants, wants [*bgha, bgha, bgha*] and buys everything, without measure [*bla qyas*]."

These comments could be read simply as an expression of envy on the part of Hajj Khalid's less wealthy neighbors, and they probably do contain elements of this. However, they are also referring, just as importantly, to another key element: the lack of measure in Hajj Khalid's behavior. As Caroline Osella and Filippo Osella (2000) observe in their study of Kerala migration, where men who use the money they accumulated in the Gulf states without measure back home are not accorded adult manhood, Hajj Khalid's excessiveness in things that signify and generate "men" in the area (marriage, pilgrimage, house-making) seems to call into question rather than enhance his gendered standing. In fact, in the eyes of neighbors and even relatives, this excess risks becoming a parody of manhood rather than an inventive reiteration of it.[4] A *rajel bla qyas* (man without measure) is not necessarily more of a man than one who does not have the resources to move at all. By failing to attune his migrant success to neighborhood requirements, Hajj Khalid, just like Samir, has made the place he occupies back home controversial. His repeated crossings to *l-brra* and his prolonged absences somehow counterbalance the tensions and questioning that his brief and intense appearances produce. If men like Samir and men like Hajj Khalid are somehow to protect the gendered personhood they have acquired through migration, it is not acceptable for either of them to spend extensive amounts of time back home. The condition of "double absence" of the migrant discussed by Abdelmalek Sayad (1999) here takes on palpable, even necessary properties.

Indeed, I have come across very few cases of men who have made one initial crossing into *l-brra* and then settled indefinitely back in the Tadla being spoken of with respect and admiration. Those who are thus spoken of are men who have somehow found a way to live up to the persona of "someone who goes" without having to reiterate the actual physical movements to and from *l-brra*. They are generally older men who, in their doings, incorporate their contact with *l-brra* without needing to periodically return to it: they have built a number of houses through the years, regularly expand the family-run shop they originally opened in the first years of migration, have been on Mecca pilgrimages, and perhaps have even remarried. These are men who have somehow established a grounding in the Tadla through their contact with *l-brra* but who also have the ability and resources to calibrate their *brra*-qualities to local requirements—they are successful (any lack of success would call into question why they are "staying" rather than "going") but not excessively so. Their behaviors, bodily posture, even tone of voice mirror the confidence and expertise of a "man who goes" but stop short of being arrogant, the trait most commonly identified in temporary returnees.

However, most of the men I know or know about who have settled back in the Tadla after migrating to *l-brra* are not shown such respect and admiration. Rather, I would say that a parallel is drawn between their interrupted interaction with "the outside" and a precarious interruption of their *rejla* (masculinity/manhood). Many of the younger men who have returned to live in the Tadla have not come back of their own free will but because they have been deported—put on a boat or plane by the Spanish or Italian border police and handed over to the Moroccan authorities. "*Kharjouh*" (they exited him), someone will mutter quietly to me, nodding toward a man passing in the street. Deportation often takes place when men have not yet accumulated (or have lost) resources and status to embody the kinds of migratory and gendered qualities expected back home—in Italy especially, policies of *rimpatrio* (deportation) generally target migrants who are most socially and economically vulnerable (Del Grande 2010). This makes those men who have been to "the outside" but can no longer return a particular type of person whose behaviors and attitudes are often described by onlookers as being woman-like: they spend most hours of the day in the house; walk quickly in the street, keeping their eyes to the ground; rarely show their faces in coffee bars; and stop to talk mostly with older women from the neighborhood. It takes a lot of resources, guts, and inventiveness to convey a sense of complete manhood when the migrant component has disappeared from one's personhood. This means that most men who have been to *l-brra*, if they can, keep repeating the crossing throughout their life.

Repeating Difference

Movement to *l-brra* engenders specific types of men in the Tadla. Migrants' constitutive relationship with *l-brra* described in chapter 2 comes to form specific kinds of gendered subjects, *l-brra* becoming a fundamental and inescapable ingredient of the masculinity of "those who go." This means that the dimming of *l-brra* in one's person—the interruption of one's movements toward it, for example, or becoming unable to actualize it in the appropriate ways when at home—risks bringing into question not only one's standing as a migrant but also one's standing as a man. These *brra*-infused masculinities find themselves embroiled in multiple and at times competing local expectations and evaluations, which draw both on peoples' imagination of *l-brra* and on complex and ever-shifting gendered scripts. Men's "materialization of masculinity" (Ghannam 2013) requires a particular kind of performative finesse here, one that is able to carefully balance *brra*-qualities with recognizable gendered traits. Samir's "performative failure" (Schieffelin 1996) reveals how such materialization of *brra*-infused masculinities is, perhaps in the same way as any gender materialization (Butler 1990), deeply precarious because, as we have seen, it can be called into question at any time—when a house is left "undone" for too long, when a body sits idle at the wrong time and in the wrong place, or even when a global financial crisis curtails a migrant's "doing" abilities. But migrants' materialization of masculinity is also precarious in the sense that it is not permanent and instead needs to be reiterated and reinstated throughout a migrant's life. In other words, for men like Samir, gender trajectories are not settled, as it were, with their original crossing into Europe. As much of the migration scholarship testifies, one's first crossing—generally a clandestine and perilous passage—is undoubtedly framed as a gendered act and often as an explicit passage into male adulthood: "*wulla rajel temma*" (he became a man there), mothers tell me of their migrant sons. But in order to *remain* men, migrants need to sustain, in time and in space, their constitutive relationship with *l-brra*, inaugurated with their first crossing. This sustainment pivots around different kinds of movements at different kinds of scales, from intimate movements of the body in the domestic sphere to the transnational movement of money, but my sense is that it is the repetition of the crossing between home and abroad that anchors migrant men most firmly to a recognized and recognizable gendered existence. This repetition is what keeps making a migrant man a man or a man a migrant man—here, crucially, one and the same.

Such repetition is not without consequences. In the summer of 2014, I was sitting with my friend Zahra in front of her Zafiah house enjoying the evening breeze. Zahra was telling me a story I have heard time and again from migrants' wives in Tadla—she was describing to me how her husband looks worse, different, changed every time he returns home from Italy. In this particular visit, she said, he looked worse than ever: "it's as if he isn't here," she whispered to me. "His head and his spirit are broken/ruined [*khessru*]." While speaking, she gestured toward me for a coin and started rubbing it on a paper tissue she had opened on her lap. After a few strokes, the tissue tore. Zahra lifted the tissue to look through the rip in the dimming evening light. "Repeat [*'awed*], repeat too many times, and it will tear," she murmured.

Zahra's evocative gesture exposes a crucial tension lying at the heart of migration in the Tadla—and, my sense is, migration more generally. While repetitive contact with *l-brra* makes certain strands of social and gendered existence possible, it also fundamentally threatens others. As we have seen throughout the book, contact with *l-brra* ultimately produces deep, nonnegotiable difference—different kinds of people, different kinds of expectations, different modes of life, different ways to succeeded and fail. This difference is at once enthralling and tragic. It is enthralling because *l-brra* adds *shi haja* (something) to one's person, and this something puts migrants on a different scale. Whether it is because of the economic success that at times results from their venture or because of *l-brra*'s cosmological, quasi-magical qualities spilling over onto them, or even because they embody the legal as well as imaginative possibility of transnational movement for others, *l-brra* makes migrants special kinds of subjects in the Tadla.

Specialness, however, contains within it the potential for strangeness and, indeed, estrangement, and often migrant men return home only to be treated, one might say, as awkward subjects. I identify this as the tragic side of migration's involvement in the formations of subjects because, if on the one hand migration in the Tadla is grounded in a desire for difference, *l-brra*'s constitutive feature being its ontological distinctiveness from the here and now of the Tadla, on the other it is grounded in a desire for what could be conceived as a form of sameness.

In his analysis of Mongol nomads, Morten Pedersen (2007, 317) writes how "people are in one sense moving and yet they are in another sense not moving at all, for the whole point about nomadic migration is for the world to repeat itself: one moves to be the same." In the Tadla, too, while on the one hand one migrates to change, on the other one migrates to stay (also) the same. One leaves to become different, independent, special. Yet there is often also a deep desire for repetition underlining the movement of young men especially: one moves also to become the man one is expected to be, to be the father one's father was, to have the means and the possibilities to offer sameness to one's family. However, something goes wrong with movement in this context. Or, maybe, something goes too right, if we consider that successful migrants like Hajj Khalid can also be treated with suspicion back home. Either way, repetitive crossing into *l-brra* throughout one's lifetime makes repetition at other scales difficult, if not impossible. So, while the repeated movement between home and abroad is what enables migrant men to remain men, this repetitive contact is also what ultimately risks eroding the very gendered and relational projects that migration is imagined to nurture. As Zahra showed me with a coin, repetition of the crossing can wear someone out—physically, emotionally, and relationally—until they may even tear.

This paradox starkly exposes what I believe defines the overall ambivalent experience of *l-brra* in Morocco and the delicate balancing, or perhaps juxtaposing, acts it continually and relentlessly requires. It is to this ambivalence that I turn to in my next and closing chapter, where I attend to the elusive ethnographic and conceptual textures of *l-brra* itself.

Notes

1. Michael Gilsenan, *Lords of the Lebanese Marches: Violence and Narrative in an Arab Society* (London: I.B. Tauris, 1996), 282. © Michael Gilsenan, used by permission of Bloomsbury Publishing Plc.

2. The fact that unequal material resources may exist within the same segment of a lineage is connected, according to Crawford (2008), both to demography (a household may have more

adult men than another and thus more available labor) and to indirect inheritance (more women with inherited land may have married into one household compared to other households).

3. See also Susan Ossman (1994) for a historical analysis of the "display of the self" and the search of prestige and symbolic capital in the context of competitive relations between European colonists and Moroccan bourgeoisie.

4. It may be interesting to think of the gendered criticism of migrants' excesses in light of the classic literature on Moroccan egalitarianism (e.g., Gellner 1969; Hart 1981) and consider whether migrants' "lack of measure" and conspicuous consumption are also judged on the basis of an ethos of male egalitarianism and suspicion toward individuals who raise their heads above the rest. From this perspective, the whole project of migration becomes a deeply problematic endeavor—though not, perhaps, if considered from the perspective of another body of classic anthropological literature, that on "Moroccan authoritarianism" (e.g., Hammoudi 1997; Bourqia and Miller 1999), which explicitly contrasts the idea of "Moroccan egalitarianism" by positioning hierarchy and domination at the heart of Moroccan social life.

6

THE OUTSIDE

In Tangier, in the winter, the Café Hafa becomes an observatory for dreams and their aftermath. . . . Leaning back against the walls, customers sit on mats and stare at the horizon as if seeking to read their fate. They look at the sea, at the clouds that blend into the mountains, and they wait for the twinkling lights of Spain to appear. They watch them without seeing them, and sometimes, even when the lights are lost in fog and bad weather, they see them anyway. Everyone is quiet. Everyone listens. Perhaps *she* will show up this evening. She'll talk to them, sing them the song of the drowned man who became a sea star suspended over the straits. They have agreed never to speak her name: that would destroy her, and provide a whole series of further misfortunes. So the men watch one another and say nothing. Each one enters his dream and clenches his fists. . . . Even Azel has come to believe in the story of she who will appear and help them cross, one by one, that distance separating them from life, the good life, or death.

Tahar Ben Jelloun, *Leaving Tangiers*

People in the Tadla often refer to the perilous clandestine crossing of the Mediterranean as a thin dividing line between life and death: life if the other side is reached, death if the sea swallows you up and drags you down. In this book I have traced how this delicate balancing act permeates not only the migratory move itself but also the very places where its impulse originates. Because of its pervasive character, and because it involves crucial elements around which not only life but also the very (self) definition of subjects is grounded, migration engenders a perpetual balancing act where the stakes are as high as can be: differences between life and death, achieved and failed manhood, future and futility. The lives of migrants' wives come to be defined by a precarious proportioning between their relations with blood and acquired kin, between the Tadla and *l-brra*, and between womanhood and *walu* (nothing) while they wait for their future movement to *l-brra*, when they will finally become complete subjects—or, in their own, always clearer words, "*mra dyal bessah*" (real women). Young women strive to subtly harmonize transcendental will with *brra*-infused desires, where the line between piety and its transgression and between livable and unlivable futures is extremely thin. Migrant men find themselves involved in a balancing act between signifiers of excess and of failure and between multiple scales of magnitude, including those of *l-brra* and *le-blad* (land/home), a balancing act where what is at stake is their very gendered personhood.

At the heart of these delicate and perilous balancing acts lies *l-brra*— the beguiling place/concept/power that permeates lives, bodies, and imaginations in the Tadla. But what exactly is "the outside"? The unrivaled protagonist of this book, *l-brra* has been left somewhat undefined in my discussion so far. This palpable indeterminacy stems directly from the distinct challenges, indeed resistance, *l-brra* poses to any simple and singular ethnographic or theoretical framing. In closing the book, I want to address explicitly the problem of definition of the indigenous concept of *l-brra*—and, in doing so, begin to address the problem of a general and generalized definition of *migration*. The positioning of this discussion at the very end of the book may strike some readers as odd—why does the effort to define *l-brra* appear only in the closing passages of the work, given its prominence, even dominance, throughout? The architecture of the book reflects a realization I had very early on in Morocco: it is impossible to speak of *l-brra* as such, to define or frame it in any way, without engaging first with the complex, enigmatic, multiscalar textures it acquires in the intimacy of everyday life. This is true of *l-brra*, but my sense is that it may be also true of migration more generally. This chapter, then, works both backward: sifting through the multiple definitions and presences of *l-brra* of previous chapters; and forward: preparing the ground for the conclusion, where I push the Moroccan experience of *l-brra* into broader conversations and assumptions about migration itself.

Topographies of Possibility

If you ask for a definition of *l-brra* in the Tadla, the answer is often a quick geographical one: "*urobba*" (Europe), or "*'amrika*" (United States). However, these geographical answers vary according to the speaker. University students in Zafiah will probably list a number of European countries—as will young children in the Tadla countryside, although not necessarily with the same geographical rigor and probably with the names of a few extra cities thrown in. Older women, asked about *l-brra*, often simply say, "*L-brra l-kharij, benti!*" (the outside is the outside, my daughter/dear!), *kharij* being another Arabic term for "outside," also meaning abroad, overseas. Others still refer to *l-brra* as the place where their sons and daughters live. Thus *l-brra* is *talyan* (Italy) for some, *fransa* (France), *calabria* (southern region of Italy), or *prato* (city in Tuscany) for others. For others still, *l-brra* is about places difficult to identify on a map, either because they are too small to be marked or because the names of cities, towns, and boroughs of "the outside" have been gradually modified as they have entered everyday Tadla parlance. Even as a geographical space, then—generally the most immediate way of describing it—*l-brra* varies substantially according to whom you are speaking to in the area and is positioned differently on different geographical and imagined maps drawn from personal experience and migrant husbands or kin, TV channels and academic knowledge, bleak frustration and migratory hope.

The concept of *l-brra* opens a number of challenging ethnographic, methodological, and theoretical questions for any study of Moroccan migration. If *l-brra* is first and foremost a geographical space, not only does the location and description of this space vary according to the speaker and the context in which it is invoked but it also acquires characteristics and manners of being and being described that, although always rooted in a geographical imagination, go beyond those generally ascribed to geographical places. *L-brra* carries connotations of hope and threat, beauty and loss, order and democracy, hygiene and respect, and money and love. But as well as being a peculiar repository for the imagination, one that strongly resembles the "outsides" and "elsewhere(s)" anthropologists have found in a variety of ethnographic settings, *l-brra* is also characterized by a peculiar type of power, force, and essence—one that pervades core dimensions of life in the Tadla. As we have seen throughout the chapters, *l-brra* is conceptualized as having its sui generis ontological characteristics in the Tadla: it has its own temporality and a peculiar power to transform people and things; it can seduce and be married; it gets under people's skin and nests in people's brains. *L-brra* is not just a place "out there" to be longed for—it is also an entity to be reckoned with in the here and now of everyday life. In a fluid dialectic between its imagination and the direct experience of its effects and powers, *l-brra* emerges in the Tadla as being a force as much as a concept, a thought as much as a destination, and a quality as much as a place.

Crucially, however, although *l-brra* has characteristics and ways of behaving that go beyond those ascribed to mere geographical places, it is not described as an especially remarkable entity as such. Indeed, *l-brra* lacks any kind of elaborate cosmological framing in the Tadla—as opposed, say, to the striking Congolese cosmological rendering of "the West" described in Wyatt MacGaffey's classic works (1968, 1972), where there is a complex symmetry, for example, between Europe and the land of the dead, or otherworld. In the Tadla, it is rare to encounter an elaborate discourse that qualifies *l-brra* as an extraordinary, let alone otherworldly, kind of place, substance, or presence. As we saw in chapter 4, ideas of *l-brra* and theological imaginations overlap in deep and complex ways, but I have never heard those young friends and interlocutors, or anyone else in Zafiah, concerned about destined migratory futures describe or engage with *l-brra* as a theological entity in its own right. *L-brra* seems to require a conceptual space of its own in the anthropological understanding of places and forces, one that recognizes not only its peculiar and at times quasi-metaphysical qualities but also its rather ordinary geographical ones. In the first sections of this chapter, then, I trace how *l-brra* is less than a metaphysical or otherworldly entity, as no elaborate theological or cosmological content is ascribed to it, and yet is more than a geographical place or an imaginary elsewhere, since *l-brra* operates as a force and is reified as such quasi-metaphysically. I then move to consider how—to begin to grasp this liminal conceptual space occupied by *l-brra*—one needs to trace its intimate action in everyday life, as I have tried to do in this book.

Topographies of Possibility

What is l-brra, *you said?* L-brra *is everything, everything that you can't see here, is* l-brra, *Alice . . . respect, courage, roads . . . women!*
   [I interject: "But I can see all this in Morocco!"]
   You can't see anything [walu]. *. . . If you live here all your life you learn that these things aren't here . . . not for real . . . like, women here they aren't real . . . you can just look at them, because you will never have the money to marry them. . . . They are just photographs/images* [tsawer]. *. . . The government puts them there [laughs], on the streets, in the cafes, so you think one day you will be able to have her in your life. . . . So you work, you study, you pay bribes . . . because you are thinking that one day the photograph will become real, you understand me* [fhem-tini]? *. . . But you never have enough in Morocco. . . . They remain images. . . . So you leave for* l-brra, *where women are not photographs, they are real. . . . I told you . . .* l-brra *is everything.*

   The excerpt above is taken from one of the many conversations I have had over the years with Younes, a young unemployed graduate living in Zafiah who has been planning his departure to *l-brra* for a very long time—or, as he would put it, "*men dima*" (since always). Younes's words express what many young men in the Tadla explicitly or implicitly refer to when speaking of *l-brra*. *L-brra* is a mixture of geography, marital expectations, political frustration, fantasies, projects, irony, and bitterness. It is not only a space for the imagination but also a place of the imagination, in the sense that imagination plays a fundamental role in its constitution.

As well as being a geographical place with very specific locations—Europe, New York, Rome—*l-brra* is thus also a classic illustration of what Alexei Yurchak (2005) defines an "imaginary elsewhere," an elsewhere that is "not necessarily about any real place" (Yurchak 2005, 159). *L-brra* is in fact in many ways akin to Yurchak's (2005) description of the Russian imaginary elsewhere of *zagranitsa*. Meaning "beyond the border," or "that which is abroad," Yurchak argues that the concept of *zagranitsa* played a key role in the social and cultural imagination of the late Soviet Union: "[*Zagranitsa,*] an imaginary place that was simultaneously knowable and unattainable, tangible and abstract, mundane and exotic. This concept was disconnected from any 'real' abroad and located in some unspecified place—over there (*tam*), with them (*u nikh*), as opposed to with us (*u nas*)—and although references to it were ubiquitous, its real existence became dubious" (2005, 159).

While *l-brra*'s "real existence" is never in doubt in the Tadla—as we have seen, contact with it is constant—*l-brra* is often talked about, just as the concept *zagranitsa* was in the late Soviet Union, as an unspecified, at times intangibly nebulous place of possibility on the other side of the Mediterranean. Importantly, its imagination is deeply rooted in what is seen as lacking in contemporary Morocco, with *l-brra* often operating as what Mounia Bennani-Chraïbi (1994) defines as a reversed mirror (*miroir inversé*). In her pioneering study of Moroccan youths, Bennani-Chraïbi traces how *l'ailleurs* (the elsewhere) functions as a reversed mirror for everything that is perceived by her young interlocutors as being wrong, corrupt, and degrading in Morocco. On all levels, from the individual to that of national politics, *l'ailleurs* emerges as an imaginary space where one can be free from the weight of kin and religious groups, where scientific development is ubiquitous, and where people are tolerant, open, and modest. Like *l'ailleurs* in Bennani-Chraïbi's work, *l-brra* is often conceptualized as a double negative space: anything non-Moroccan (a space of negativity) is *l-brra*. Often talked about in terms of backwardness and underdevelopment, the contrast between Morocco and *l-brra* sometimes emerges as stark, harsh, and hierarchical: "what's here is *zbel* [trash]. What's there is just better," Younes once told me. Acquiring qualities similar to those of Michel Foucault's concept of heterotopia, *l-brra* emerges as "a space that is other, another real space, as perfect, as meticulous, as well arranged as ours is messy, ill constructed, and jumbled" (Foucault 1968, 26). Different people in the Tadla identify different problems *hna* (here), which, in turn, are translated into different properties of *temma* (there). So, my younger acquaintances, for example, often refer to factors that are also identified in scholarly analyses of structural poverty and inequality in Morocco (e.g., Cohen 2003; Miller 2013; Tozy 1999), some referring to the number of unemployed in the area, for example, while others to the corruption and bribery that characterize their daily encounters with public officials and private institutions. Others tend to dwell on the more sociological aspects of their country, describing how, for example, *n-nas hnaia mashi nishan* (people here aren't "straight"—i.e., honest, frank), or *rjal huma zero* (men are "zero"—i.e., nothing/worth nothing). In an elegant, if bleak, exercise of structuralist binary oppositions, negative features identified in Morocco are contrasted to their imagined structural positive opposites in *l-brra*.

But characterizations of both "here" and "the outside" vary substantially in the Tadla. Not everyone talks in such negative terms about Morocco or in such positive ones about *l-brra*. The same person, almost in the same breath, can switch from highlighting all the reasons why "*l-brra hsen men hna*" (the outside is better than here) to being boisterously proud of *bladna* (our land/Morocco) and explaining how, in "the outside," there is no respect for key things such as family, God, and elderly people. The qualities people associate with *l-brra* are constantly shifting, and, from one moment to the next, *l-brra* can change from a place of existential possibility into, say, a threat to morality or a metaphor for crippling, deadly loneliness. Indeed, references to *l-brra* do not oscillate solely between negative and positive qualities, good and bad descriptions. The kind of entity invoked with the concept of *l-brra* also shifts incessantly.

Cosmology and Geography

As we have seen throughout the book, people in the Tadla fluctuate between different scales when describing and reckoning with *l-brra*—at times using the term as a metaphor for an imagined future that is contrasted starkly with everyday life in Morocco, at times making explicit reference to *l-brra*'s power to *dkhel f bnadem* (enter people/humans) and discussing it as a quasi-metaphysical force, and at times simply treating it as a geographical destination with desirable employment rights. In the same conversation *l-brra* can move seamlessly from being an assortment of different elements (immigration laws, face creams, money, well-being, tourists) to being a totality greater than the sum of its parts, a future you aspire to, an entity you wait for your husband to be released from, a yardstick by which you gauge a potential boyfriend.

Notwithstanding the striking variations in the ways the outside is conceptualized and experienced and, with this, the variations in the kinds of knowledge produced and reproduced about it and through it, it is significant that people in the Tadla refer to *l-brra* as a single and obvious entity. In the Tadla, and in Morocco more generally, the meaning of *l-brra* is self-evident—it requires no explanation or discussion. Despite acquiring strikingly different meanings for different people and in different contexts, *l-brra* is a shared concept in the Tadla, and there is no general confusion or contradiction when *l-brra* is invoked in social life: everyone knows what *l-brra* means.

Such striking polysemy-cum-singularity strongly evokes the classic notion of "floating signifier," developed by Claude Lévi-Strauss in order to solve, analytically, the kinds of complexities encountered in the anthropological conceptualization of magical and life forces such as the Oceanian *mana* and its cousin concepts *wakan*, *orenda*, and *ache*: "Force and action; quality and state; substantive, adjective and verb at once; abstract and concrete; omnipresent and localized. And, indeed, *mana* is all those things together; but is that not precisely because it is none of those things, but a simple form, or to be more accurate, a symbol in its pure state, therefore liable to take on any symbolic content whatever?" (Lévi-Strauss 1987, 64)

I am hesitant to define *l-brra* as a "simple form" or as a symbol in its pure state—as we have seen, *l-brra* has very real, palpable power over people and things in the Tadla. However, *l-brra* seems to pose precisely the kinds of questions Lévi-Strauss was trying to solve analytically in his discussion of *mana* as "floating signifier." Just as in classic anthropological descriptions *mana* avoids easy categorizations, *l-brra* also eludes simple description and classification—*l-brra* is at times described as a force, at times as a geographical destination, at times as a seductive spirit, and at others as frustrating bureaucratic machinery. In its haziness, "the outside" is both referential and has specific, palpable, and powerful qualities. However, the comparison with metaphysical forces and entities, be they Moroccan traditional Islamic forces or those extrapolated from other ethnographic contexts such as the classic anthropological accounts of Melanesia, should not be overstated. Let me briefly consider works that do make the comparison between a geographical elsewhere and otherworldly entities explicit, and show how *l-brra* somehow differs—but only partially so—from these.

No Heaven

As mentioned already, an important theme in the anthropology of West and Central Africa is the overlapping of divine/otherworldly/ancestral maps with geopolitical maps, where the West and its inhabitants are structurally if not also formally equivalent to the otherworld and its spirits—see, for example, MacGaffey (1968) on Congo; Sasha Newell (2012) on Côte d'Ivoire; Francis Nyamnjoh (2011) on Cameroon.

In a piece that recalls this classic Africanist theme, Joel Robbins (2009), making reference to his fieldwork in Papua New Guinea, explores the complex connections between the cosmological map of the sacred and the hierarchical global map of political economy. Robbins describes how his interlocutors, in a similar way to my acquaintances in the Tadla, speak of the centers of globalization and their associated forces such as "development" and "modernity" with a "profound sense that real power and real economic success and real health are elsewhere. . . . The most highly valued places— the places where work is plentiful and food and medicine are easy to acquire—are far away and maximally different from home" (Robbins 2009, 63). It is in this awareness of an overpowering difference and distance from global centers that Robbins sees a parallel with his interlocutors' religious cosmology: "And just as their social maps recognize great distance between places and put the highest value on those places most distant from where they live, so too do the Pentecostal and Charismatic cosmological maps they have adopted devalue their earthly dwelling places and tell them that the place they really want to be is a heaven that is nothing like home" (63).

Robbins argues that we must attend to the ways in which the fundamental split between the mundane and transcendental realms, greatly emphasized in Pentecostal and Charismatic Christianity, mirrors "the split globalization opens up between the local and the more highly valued central or 'global' places in the social landscape" (2009, 63). Although Robbins deals with the parallel between sacred and global centers at the level of idiom, arguing that Pentecostal and Charismatic Christianity is "good to think with" (64) for people living at the global margins, his analysis infers strongly that the two dimensions overlap for his interlocutors, despite the fact that earthly global centers are kept in a subordinate position to heavenly ones. After all, Robbins's argument is grounded precisely in the fact that in Pentecostal and Charismatic Christianity, there is no qualitative difference between the nature of global centers and that of heaven (both characterized by radical alterity and distant positioning), which is why one is good to think about with the other.

I have often considered, following the work by Robbins and others, the possibility of a parallel—if not ethnographic, at least conceptual—between the meaning, value, and powers associated with *l-brra* in Morocco and those associated with a divine space such as heaven, or to supernatural entities such as *jnun* (spirits). However, my own material on *l-brra* is somewhat resistant to a parallel of the kind Robbins makes between divine and this-worldly entities. The main problem lies in the fact that *l-brra* occupies a qualitatively different space from theological entities such as paradise (*jenna*). Although Robbins is not suggesting that Europe or other centers of power and capital are entirely equivalent to the Christian heaven for his Papuan interlocutors, there is a sense in which, within specific theological imaginations, these spaces/places/entities may not be too different from what heaven either represents or is imagined to be.[1] Although this intuition is appealing, I would argue that what qualifies *l-brra* is precisely the fact that it is not a transcendental entity in the way my Moroccan interlocutors conceptualize heaven or other metaphysical domains, and this is what makes its powers so peculiar—and its theorization so challenging.

"*L-brra mashi jenna, ya khti!*" (the outside isn't paradise, sister!), people often tell me in the Tadla. In saying this, they are directly referring to a discourse they know is popular among city dwellers in Rabat and elsewhere, a discourse that casts fellow Moroccans living in rural emigrant areas such as the Tadla as gullible peasants who believe they will find paradise on the other side of the Mediterranean Sea. Their comment is a direct response to this scornful *mdini* (city/urban) discourse and states that they are all too aware of the fact that *l-brra* is neither perfect nor sacred and constituted also of human flaws and cramped rented rooms, violent police and racist thugs, hardship and loneliness. These observations, made especially by young men waiting to leave, are not only a response to explicit and implicit accusations of peasant ignorance but also a testimony to the fact that *l-brra* is positioned on a this-worldly scale, imagined as an imperfect entity that has little to do with the perfection of the Islamic heaven (Rustomji 2008). If anything, *l-brra* is explicitly devoid of the sacredness of other mystical and holy places in my interlocutors' religious geography. After all, "the sacred" very much revolves around an Arab-infused geography: it is about the Mecca in Saudi Arabia, about the shrines of Muslim saints in different parts of Morocco, and about an Islamic heaven.

As we saw in chapter 4, this in no way implies that theological entities, or indeed other metaphysical concepts, are not mobilized in and indeed constitutive of people's discourses and practices surrounding *l-brra*. As Stefania Pandolfo (2007) shows in her compelling analysis of Moroccan youths' imaginaries of clandestine migration to Europe, political theology and Islamic eschatology are often mobilized in people's discourses about their uninhabitable life in Morocco and the possibility of life in "the outside." Pandolfo concentrates in particular on the theological underpinnings of the actual act of crossing the sea, with both the physical and religious risks it entails, including heresy, suicide, and severing genealogical ties. Islamic conceptual configurations— as well as other otherworldly forces and entities sanctioned and unsanctioned by mainstream Islamic morality—also underpin a number of practices surrounding *l-brra* in the Tadla and are very much part of the local economy of migration. The inscrutable temporalities of divine predestination, for example, are often invoked when discussing the timing of migratory ventures as well as, as we have seen, conjugal projects with migrants. Visits are often paid to a *majduba* (a seller of remedies for removing magic spells)[2]—or even, in certain circumstances, to a *fqih* (local Muslim cleric)—to obtain concoctions, blessings, or protection for a son's imminent crossing of the Mediterranean, for the rapid arrival of *le-wraq* (the papers—i.e., foreign travel documents), or for a cure for a peculiar illness *dyal brra* (of [the] outside). However, although the realms of magic and religion are implicated in the conceptualization of and interactions with *l-brra*, nobody I know in the Tadla is inclined to come up with an elaborate idiom about *l-brra*'s essence in cosmological or transcendental terms.

In short, in the Tadla at least, there is no explicit formulation of *l-brra* as a cosmological entity in its own right. This presents the anthropologist with an analytical—indeed theoretical—conundrum, similar perhaps to the kinds of conundrums faced by classic anthropological engagements with secular master-concepts such as development (e.g., Ferguson 1994), modernity (e.g., Meyer and Pels 2003), or the state (e.g., Taussig 1997). After all, although *l-brra* is not altogether commensurate with heavenly entities or metaphysical forces, people do invariably reckon with it, both pragmatically and imaginatively, in terms going well beyond those used to refer to more ordinary geographical places. This emerges most clearly when one considers how my acquaintances in the Tadla attribute to *l-brra* the power, for example, to permeate migrants' bodies (chap. 2, chap. 5), a power that is not satisfactorily theorized by the description of *l-brra* as an ordinary place, lacking qualities of a more metaphysical order.

Indeed, when compared to MacGaffey's or Robbins's work, the problem with more secular/mundane analyses of *brra*-like spaces is precisely the fact that they tend to stop short of theorizing how these spaces may have forces and powers that affect both those who leave and those who stay. Anthropologists such as Yurchak (2005), Henrik Vigh (2009), and Samuli Schielke (2012), for example, who have written, respectively, about "the Imaginary West" in Russia, "the elsewhere" in Guinea Bissau, and "the other side" in Egypt, have concentrated their efforts on theorizing these "other places" as, broadly speaking, spaces for the imagination, where the characteristics of the places in themselves are not accorded as much analytical significance as the opportunity they offer to imagine better lives, recognition, manhood, modernity, and so on. "The elsewhere" in these works is not always a pure floating signifier in the Lévi-Strauss sense— Schielke shows how "the other side" in Egypt, for example, has a clear geographical grounding between Europe, North America, and the Gulf— however, attention is mainly focused on its mirroring effects and qualities.

In many ways, this is the kind of characterization that emerges also from my conversations with people like Younes, where *l-brra* appears as an inverse mirror of everything seen as lacking in their everyday surroundings in Morocco. Nevertheless, theorizing *l-brra* as mainly a place of and for the imagination poses an ethnographic problem. *L-brra* may be a Foucaultian heterotopia, a place of and for the imagining of multifarious possibilities, but it is also a place/space/entity that strikes back, with very concrete effects, on personhood, temporality, intimacies, and more. Throughout the book we have seen how *l-brra* can impact people's lives and appearance, temporality and sanity, genealogy and health. Framing *l-brra* simply as an imaginary place—or a Lévi-Straussian floating signifier for that matter—does not exhaust all of its qualities, including, above all, the effects it is conceptualized and experienced as having in Morocco.

It is for this reason that I suggest that *l-brra* may require a category of its own in our theoretical imagination of forces, places, and entities, one that is able to capture the peculiar middle ground (or, the ambiguous, complex, paradoxical *non*ground) it occupies between, if you will, cosmology and geography. My sense here is that it is precisely this liminal positioning that qualifies and defines *l-brra*: it is a quasi-cosmological force that has no elaborated theology to accompany it, and it is a geographic (or secular, or nonmetaphysical) "elsewhere" that is deemed to have tangible, even quasi-magical effects. One key consequence of *l-brra*'s ambiguous, liminal positioning is that its qualities seem to reside not in its content but, rather, in its action.

Operative Force

In my discussion so far, I have traced how any attempt to frame *l-brra* as something that goes beyond a merely geographical designation is foiled by the fact that *l-brra*, per se, does not have the cosmological content, so to speak, that allows it to be paralleled to entities such as heaven or forces such as magic. This makes *l-brra* rather a flat entity to describe, as reflected in the somewhat flat descriptions people in the Tadla generally provide when I ask them to explain it as such. Indeed, when I ask what *l-brra* is as an entity, people tend to have very little to say. *L-brra* is considered so obvious and self-evident that the answers I receive, typically, are brief, noncommittal, and ordinary. My question is often dismissed with a gesture of the hand indicating a geographical place, something faraway, or with a vague reference to money or a migrant brother. Even the more vivid depictions given by young people like Younes are very much linked to a critical contraposition to the here and now, rather than to the description of *l-brra* as an entity in its own right.

The limited things people have to say about *l-brra* as such stand in striking contrast to *l-brra*'s ubiquitous and vivid presence in everyday life, and to the references people make on a daily basis to *l-brra*'s powers to do, change, and actualize things, people, and lives. The question to be asked in the Tadla seems to be not what "the outside" is, this being a self-evident fact in Morocco, but rather what "the outside" does. It is indeed very difficult to extrapolate *l-brra* as an entity in its own right from its embeddedness in the life of the Tadla and almost impossible to frame *l-brra*'s properties without also delving into the ethnographic details surrounding the emergence of these properties. This descriptive/conceptual difficulty may be telling with regard to the very nature of *l-brra*.

In the Tadla, it is not *l-brra*'s content that is striking (a place of imagined "betterness," as destinations of migration arguably tend to be) but its action. *L-brra*'s constitutive properties emerge in the ways it makes itself operative in the Tadla, rather than by virtue of what could be called its cosmological or metaphysical content. One can deduce what it is by what it does: by the ways it intrudes in the temporality of intimacy by regulating the tempo of migrant husbands' visits home (chap. 1), by the ways it affects the performance and content of gender and kinship (chap. 3), and by the ways it makes migrants' skin lighter and eyes brighter (chap. 2). In short, it is *l-brra*'s modus operandi that makes it more than just a desired geographical place.

This point can be developed with reference to Herzfeld's (1985) opening discussion, in *The Poetics of Manhood*, of the concept of *simasia* (meaning) in the Cretan community of Glendi, where he also explicitly makes reference to the concept's operative principle:

> Simasia *is not a lexicographical abstraction. On the contrary, it is something that Glendiots recognize in* action, *a term that includes speech but that does not necessarily give linguistic meaning any special priority. It is an essentially* poetic *notion, in the technical sense that it concerns the means in which significance is conveyed through actual performance. . . . Meaning is found in all spheres of social action, the commonplace as much as the ritualistic or artistic. At the same time, the key concept here is* action. *The Glendiot concept of meaning gives short shrift to any text, be it a song, a raid, or a malicious remark, unless it is drawn from specific and lived experience. (Herzfeld 1985, xiv)*

Despite the obvious differences between Herzfeld's discussion of a native concept and my consideration of the conceptualization of a place/idea/power, Herzfeld's focus on the way *simasia* is grounded in and comes into being through action and specific lived experiences sheds light on the definition of *l-brra* as an operative entity. As I have mentioned, when asked to define *l-brra*'s properties per se, my interlocutors have little to say and respond by locating it in a geographical "outside"—they provide me, to borrow Herzfeld's terminology, with its lexicographical coordinates. Like *simasia*, *l-brra* is recognized as such "in action." When it is not operative, there is no cosmological or transcendental idiom or model to frame it— *l-brra* is, simply, a place on the other side of the Mediterranean Sea. Action, just as Herzfeld argues, is the key. It is through its complex lived experience that *l-brra* appears in all its force—through the ways it emanates laws and rejects visas, changes migrants' behavior and physical appearance, affects pregnancies and structures relations of kinship and love.

Because of this, the only way to access *l-brra*'s complex and multilayered meanings is to observe it "in action" in the Tadla. Looking ethnographically at how "the outside" is operative, both in the Tadla and on those who leave for it, inevitably involves unveiling what "the outside" is—and vice versa. This is precisely the kind of dialectical analytics that has guided my exploration of *l-brra* in this book. However, my sense is that *l-brra*'s peculiar mode of revealing itself in action—that is, in the ways in which it operates and is operated upon in daily existence, and the kind of dialectical method this demands of analysis tells us something about migration as a social, historical, anthropological entity more generally. It is to the learning about migration we may gain from *l-brra* that I turn in my conclusion.

Notes

1. Indeed, the equivalence between the otherworld and the West is instead literal in some of the West and Central African work (see, e.g., MacGaffey 1968).

2. See Deborah Kapchan's (1996) study of women herbalists and healers in the Tadla town of Béni Mellal.

CONCLUSION

MIGRATION AS LIFE

In his pioneering work on the Algerian migration to France, Abdelmalek Sayad mounts a sophisticated and unforgiving critique of the "discourse and science" (2004, 119) of the study of migration. At the heart of his critique lies what he sees as a failure, even resistance to recognize migration as a *fait social global* (Sayad 1991, 15)—a whole entity, an entire social system, that implicates at once the historical, the political, the cultural, and the personal (cf. Mauss 2002). As I mentioned in the introduction to this book, Sayad develops this observation most powerfully, and most famously, by insisting on the simple but deeply significant fact that "one country's immigration is another country's emigration" (Sayad 2004, 1). He rejects the caesura at the heart of dominant studies of migration, one that arbitrarily separates the process of immigration from the process of emigration. It is this separation, Sayad argues, that allows migration studies to be grounded and guided only by the (self) perceptions, needs, and concerns of the country of *im*migration—the receiving or "host" society. This ends up reproducing— more or (often) less innocently (see Sayad 1984)—migration as an isolated phenomenon that starts and ends in, say, France, extracted from its geographical, cultural, historical, and colonial roots and understood in terms of a list of disconnected social problems to be solved. For Sayad, to speak of migration must be to speak "about the migratory phenomenon in its totality" (2004, 63), and to begin to capture this "totality" one needs to trace the steps of migrants themselves and start, "logically and chronologically" (1976, 12), from the places of origin.

Following Sayad's insight, this book is grounded in a place where and with people among whom migration begins. As Sayad argues throughout his writings, this decentering of the traditional location of migration studies unavoidably becomes more than a mere geographical move—it produces and demands a conceptual decentering of the modes of thinking about migration. This conceptual decentering happens first and foremost because the analytical tools at the heart of migration studies come to be interrogated when migration is thought through departure rather than (solely) arrival. So, for example, the prism of and concern about migrant "adaption" or "assimilation," still as dominant in the production of knowledge about migration as they were (to his deep exasperation) in Sayad's time, are suddenly parochialized when the theoretical imagination of migration is expanded to include its origins, and, as we have seen in this book, a multitude of other conceptual prisms and social concerns powerfully erupt on the scene. Similarly, the dominant economistic understanding of migration, one that postulates migratory movement as being ultimately about economic disadvantage, is suddenly revealed to be "no more than an exercise in accountancy" (Sayad 2004, 127) if extricated from the multiple conceptualizations of what migration (and indeed "the economic") is, should, and might be about in spaces of departure such as the Tadla.

But the conceptual decentering that happens when one begins to observe migration in its "totality" and from its origins is not only at the level of tools, modes, or models of analysis. It also concerns the conceptualization of migration itself, the very object these tools, modes, and models aim to analyze. What *l-brra* reveals is that the constitutive texture of migration, the thing migration is imagined to be in migration studies and beyond, emerges as something new and different when observed at its origins. What I have tried to show in this book is how migration reveals itself, just as Sayad suggests, as a *fait social global*, in the Maussian sense of a "total social fact" that implicates the totality of social and intimate (and religious, and esthetic, and economic, and linguistic) life. With this I do not mean to simply say that migration affects and is affected by life—arguably an uncontroversial statement, at least in the social sciences (though not necessarily in migration policy making and thinking, where life is often disregarded, if not actively dispelled [De León 2015; Smythe 2018]). What I have tried to show in this book is that migration cannot be analytically extricated from life—that is, imagined and conceptualized as an entity/phenomenon separate from the life that makes it and is made through it, and thus something external to life that can be observed and understood in terms of its causes in and effects on life.

The anthropology of migration has often implicitly and explicitly unpacked dominant theories about the causes and effects of migration—

starting from the incredibly resilient push/pull model, which is rooted in neoclassical economics that conceptualizes migratory movement in terms of labor supply and demand, global wage differentials, and individual migratory decisions based on cost-benefit calculations. Anthropology has a long tradition of actively shifting the understanding of migration away from (crude) economics and the kind of "exercise in accountancy" that Sayad laments, drawing attention to other complex causes and effects of migration in local life: hope, history, kinship, imagination, colonialism, personhood, love, empire, and the divine, to name but a few. But throughout the work of deepening, expanding, and subverting recognized causes and effects of contemporary migrations, the conceptualization of migration itself generally remains that of an entity/phenomenon that is, at some scale at least, external to its causes and effects; and it exists, and can be known, independently of them—indeed, it is by virtue of this conceptual independence between migration and life (be it hope, history, or kinship) that one can be imagined as affecting or affected by the other.

In my attempt to understand *l-brra*, I have encountered a different kind of relationship between migration and life. As I argued in the closing chapter, what is significant about *l-brra* is its social and intimate action in and through life, which is—in all its complexity, ambiguity, and contingency—both *l-brra*'s operative ground and its constitutive texture. Extricated from this (specific) life—the bodies, households, imaginations, relationships, words, and gestures that actualize it and are actualized through it—*l-brra* is merely a flat place of vague betterness, as most destinations of migration probably reveal themselves to be when extricated from the specific lives that actualize and are actualized through them. In other words, it makes little sense to conceptualize *l-brra* as an entity/phenomenon independently and independent from its action in life—to conceptualize, that is, "what is it" independently from "what it does"—as it is the action that makes it.

The kind of constitutive relationship *l-brra* instantiates between migration and life in the Tadla offers a different way of thinking about migration and the dominant "discourse and science" (Sayad 2004, 119) that accompanies it. It suggests that the conceptual labor migration requires may not be so much at the level of identifying more—and developing a more refined analysis—of its causes and effects in local life. Rather, it may be about tracing, as I have tried to do in this book, how migration emerges through life. This does not mean ignoring the obvious fact that migration has both causes and effects—be they historical, economic, or divine. But it does mean shifting the conceptual imagination of the relationship between life and migration, which also underpins the understanding of migration's causes/effects, from one of causation to one of coconstitution.

This relational shift also shifts the imagination of what the study of migration should look like—or, better and less prescriptively, where the study of migration might begin, conceptually as much as geographically (as Sayad shows, geographical and conceptual shifts are inextricably linked when it comes to migration). If migration is sometimes inextricable—conceptually, ethnographically, experientially—from the life through which it emerges, then this constitutive relationship must be contained within, rather than considered extrinsic to, the unit of analysis of migration studies—imminent in the very thing migration is conceptualized to be. This Stratherninan move—that is, one that takes, as Marilyn Strathern (1988, 2004) teaches, the relation rather than the objects/persons/things being related as its unit of analysis—means making the subject of migration studies not an insulated and a priori definition of migration but rather the multiple constitutive relationships between migration and life that emerge in different migratory realities. But this relational move in the study of migration also means working with a resolutely humble and expansive conceptual imagination of migration—humble because if the texture and definition of migration is inextricable from (specific) life, then the entity/phenomenon of migration can never be treated as something that is already known prior to close ethnographic and conceptual work, and expansive because the conceptual imagination of migration must be one that is able to hold as much multiplicity and complexity as life itself.

A humble and expansive understanding of migration also requires a specific kind of thinking that is, as Martin Holbraad (2012) defines it, "motile"—transforming itself even as the constitutive relationships between migration and life themselves transform. As I discuss in the introduction, this book is mostly a synchronic engagement with *l-brra*—an attempt to capture the contingent constitution of *l-brra* by tracing its intimate workings at a specific historical and ethnographic moment. But the constitutive relationship between migration and life revealed by this synchronic focus on *l-brra* also implies a fundamentally contingent and therefore changing nature of migration, and thus the need for an equally contingent and changing conceptualization of it. To give a sense of this ethnographic and conceptual contingency, let me return to *l-brra* one final time and trace, with reference to my return visits to the Tadla throughout the 2010s, how (historical, social, intimate) change may require humble and expansive rethinking.

Contingent Horizons of Possibility

In the summer of 2015, I visited Zafiah for an old friend's wedding. On my way back to Mohammed V Airport in Casablanca, I started chatting with the young woman sitting next me on the rattling bus. "Italy is just country now," she commented when she found out where I am from. The young woman was on her way to the Italian consulate in Casablanca to file her third and, she was confident, finally successful visa application. "Soon I'll be living in Italy," she told me. Her older sister, her younger sister's husband, her paternal cousin, her maternal uncle, his two grandchildren—"*kollhom f l-brra*" (they are all in the outside), she said. Now, it is her turn to leave: "*besslama ciao ciao*" (bye-bye, bye-bye [Italian]) she whispered with a wide smile. She then looked out of the window and sighed: "the truth is, though . . . Italy is just country now [*ghir 'rubiya*] . . . country and crisis . . . that's all the outside has become, sister."

My travel companion's words surprised me. Many times before, I had heard negative, sarcastic, disillusioned comments about Italy, Europe, and "the outside" more broadly. These comments, however, were generally made with the shared understanding that, despite all its flaws, irrational bureaucratic systems, and racist police, *l-brra* was anyway better than *hna* (here). The young woman's words on the bus slightly jarred the picture of *l-brra* I had become accustomed to—a place of hope and possibility, of escape and wealth, of power and prestige. Referring to Italy as countryside (*'rubiya*) casts *l-brra* in a very different light indeed. *'Rubiya*, as we have seen throughout this book, can be a loaded term in Morocco, one that holds deep connotations of backwardness, illiteracy, and coarseness. *'Rubi* (peasant, or from the country) can be used disparagingly and immediately classifies someone as vulgar, ignorant, even animallike. And *'rubiya* is precisely the term used by the Moroccan urban middle and upper classes to refer to areas like the rural Tadla and its inhabitants, often portrayed as uneducated, gullible, and desperate to reach Europe even by way of rickety, overcrowded boats. By defining Italy as *'rubiya*, the young woman was knowingly turning such venomous images on their head. But she was also positioning *l-brra* not only in the realm of backwardness and hardship but also in the realm of the vulgarly familiar and miserably unimpressive.

During my 2015 visit, I noticed a change in tone and language in the ways my Moroccan friends and acquaintances referred to *l-brra*. In the Tadla in particular, I noticed an increasing sense of bafflement, disillusionment, and skepticism toward the opposite shore and its tangible signs of deterioration.

My interlocutors tended to explain such troubling developments in terms of *l-azma* (the crisis), the expression used to refer to the European (and particularly southern European) financial crisis of the 2000s. As we saw with the Ghzaouli household in chapter 5, signs of the crisis were already very palpable in the Tadla in my doctoral fieldwork; however, by 2015, references to *l-azma* had increased and become more prevalent. The crisis seemed to be everything but an event of the past and continued erupting in different areas of personal and relational life.

For example, an old acquaintance from Zafiah showed me to her bedroom and pointed to two big suitcases on the floor, filled to the brim with food. "These are going to Italy tomorrow," she told me. "My son can't afford to eat [over] there [*temma*]." I had often witnessed families in the Tadla sending food to their migrant relatives living in Europe: mint rolled up in damp newspaper, homemade bread and biscuits, olive oil, sometimes even pieces of frozen sacrificial ram, dutifully preserved since the last Eid. Rarely, however, had I seen such basic staple foods as the ones I saw packed in this woman's suitcases: packs of pasta, bags of rice, onions. And rarely had I heard the sending of food to migrant relatives living in *l-brra* framed as a question of necessity and emergency rather than as a question of comfort, a way of maintaining a faraway husband's, daughter's, or cousin's ties to home. The woman told me that every Thursday, a man from the neighborhood left with his car packed full of food and drove the goods to his neighbors' relatives living in Italy. "We used to pay him to carry over clothes and washing machines from the outside. . . . Now we pay to send food to the outside," the woman muttered to me. "I'm telling you, the whole world is turning upside-down," she concluded grimly.

I heard these comments frequently during this visit to the Tadla. People commented on how the world was behaving in unpredictable, "upside-down" ways—and, in particular, on the fact that relationships between "here" and the opposite shore were gradually turning wild. News circulated in the area about fit young men losing their jobs on construction sites in Italy, about water being cut off in flats in southern Spain where Moroccan relatives had lived for decades, about money being sent to husbands in France to pay electricity bills, and about phone calls asking for help received from, rather than made to, *l-brra*. My sense is that *l-azma* was subtly permeating not only people's remittances and economic possibilities but also people's very imagination of *l-brra* and the horizons of possibility it has for decades constituted and sustained.

The sense of a shifting horizon of possibility I encountered in the Tadla at that time is linked not only to *l-azma* of the opposite shore. Other equally grand events have erupted in the region since the end of my fieldwork, and these have also been interacting in complex, often unpredictable ways with people's imagination of the possible. First among these are *t-turat* (the revolutions)—the revolutionary upheavals in the Middle East and North Africa that have been called, by some, the Arab Spring. Crucially, for many living in emigrant areas of Morocco such as the Tadla, economic crisis and political revolutions overlapped, both temporally and experientially. When I spoke with Moroccan friends at the height of the revolutionary events in North Africa in early 2011, they were gazing over the sea with angst toward a Europe showing increasing signs of crisis and gazing to the East with thrilled and stunned curiosity. The aftermath of this peculiar historical conjecture continues to be palpable in the Tadla—just as the financial crisis is still very much the stuff of the present for people in the area, so would it be mistaken to define the Arab revolutions as the ineffectual and settled stuff of the past.

"Did you see us on TV?" Fatima, an elderly acquaintance from an Amazigh village of the Middle Atlas, asked me when I visited her in 2015. "We can do things too, if we really want to." She smiled at me. She was making reference to *t-turat*: we hadn't met or spoken since their outset. Her question surprised me at first, and not only for the time lag between the events she was referring to and our conversation. Never before had I heard her referring to the rest of the Middle East, or North Africa, let alone to the rest of Morocco as "us." Most importantly, maybe, never before had I heard her contemplating the possibility that it would be *l-brra* watching, rather than the other way around. As is the case also in the bus conversation I recounted earlier, it feels as if both *l-azma* and *t-turat* afforded a fundamental change of perspective, where who was observing, and the quality of what was being observed, suddenly switched, even if perhaps only fleetingly so. When Mustafa, Fatima's son, heard his mother mention the revolutions, he told me that shortly after the outset of the Tunisian (2010) and Egyptian (2011) revolutions, there had been a peaceful revolt in a Tadla village market, resulting in small vendors like himself finally obtaining the right to move their unlicensed stalls from the tiny backstreets to the main square, where most of the bigger, more established stalls stand on market day. Mustafa explained to me that the move had finally succeeded (and in fact still remains in place to this day) because "*ikhafu*" (they are frightened). The police, local officials and other local emissaries of the central government that are ever present in Moroccan rural life were watching the news too, Mustafa explained to me. "And now they know what can happen," he added, pointing his thumb to the right, to the east of his country. Interestingly and crucially, at no point in his story did Mustafa refer to the possibility of a Moroccan revolution, nor did he (or his mother for that matter) express any particular desire for it. However, the nearby revolutions—together with their complex, multidirectional aftermaths and afterlives—unexpectedly emerged at the horizons of his actions in the narration and suddenly seemed to contribute in fundamental ways to what Mustafa considered possible to do and think in the immediacy of his own life.

What might these ethnographic moments tell us about this book's engagement with *l-brra* and the kind of constitutive relationship between migration and life I outlined earlier? In recounting episodes from just one of my many return visits to the Tadla since the end of my doctoral fieldwork, I want to provide a sense of the deeply contingent nature of *l-brra* and its deep, complex relationship with the transformation of life itself. My aim in doing so is to show how the contingency of *l-brra*'s constitution in the minutiae of life, which I have tracked in this book mostly on the synchronic scale of the ethnographic present of my fieldwork of 2009–10, plays itself out also diachronically, with conceptions, experiences, and practices relating to *l-brra* shifting through their contingent constitution in changing historical processes. I have chosen my 2015 visit because it testifies to how grand historical events such as revolution and crisis may reverberate in both expected and unexpected ways in the imagination of and action on the possible. But I could equally evoke transformations at other scales of life, both less grand and more intimate, to explore *l-brra*'s contingency—the sudden 2013 death of the migrant son of an old Tadla acquaintance and the acquaintance's decision to cross into Italy and live with his fatherless grandchildren after a lifetime of vowing, to me and whoever else cared to listen, he would never set foot in *l-brra*. The 2016 marriage with a Moroccan man with no links to *l-brra* of one of my student roommates in Zafiah during my doctoral fieldwork, and the abandonment of her *brra* plans—"*per adesso*" (for now [Italian]), as she whispered to me when I sat next to her for my customary wedding photo with bride and groom, in the Italian I taught her when we lived together. The 2019 return to Spain of a friend from the outskirts of Zafiah, who had left shortly after the closure in 2011 of the Spanish tiles factory he worked for; he told me over the phone that his body (*dati*) and his head/mind (*rasi*) couldn't survive, after all, away from *l-brra*. The list of ethnographic examples or evocations of the continually transforming nature of *l-brra* is potentially boundless—as boundless as the possible transformations of the relationship between migration and life and the horizons of possibility this relationship continually opens and closes. My argument throughout this book has been that close attention to, and care for, the intimate detail of life reveal this contingency most powerfully, infusing our understanding of migration at large with new forms of conceptual imagination. Humble and expansive in the sense I have outlined above, this imagination of migration is informed by a deep awareness, as the Tadla continues to teach, that hope and bleakness are conditions ever latent on all shores.

BIBLIOGRAPHY

Abu-Lughod, Janet. 1980. *Rabat: Urban Apartheid in Morocco*. Princeton: Princeton University Press.

Abu-Lughod, Lila. 1991. "Writing against Culture." In *Recapturing Anthropology: Working in the Present*, edited by Richard G. Fox, 137–62. Santa Fe: School of American Research Press.

Abu-Shams, Leila, and Araceli González-Vázquez. 2014. "Juxtaposing Time: An Anthropology of Multiple Temporalities in Morocco." *Revue des Mondes Musulmans et de la Méditerranée* 136: 33–48. http://Remmm.Revues.Org/8817.

Acevedo, Gabriel A. 2008. "Islamic Fatalism and the Clash of Civilizations: An Appraisal of a Contentious and Dubious Theory." *Social Forces* 86(4): 1711–52.

Adely, Fida. 2012. *Gendered Paradoxes: Educating Jordanian Women in Nation, State and Progress*. Chicago: Chicago University Press.

Agamben, Giorgio. 1999. *Potentiality: Collected Essays in Philosophy*. Stanford: Stanford University Press.

Agnaou, Fatima. 2012. *Gender, Literacy, and Empowerment in Morocco*. New York: Routledge.

Ait Ben Lmadani, Fatima. 2018. *La Vieillesse Illégtime? Migrantes Marocaines Âgées ou les Chemins Sinueux de la Reconnaissance*. Rabat: Editions et Impression Bouregreg.

Aït Hamza, Mohammed. 1995. "Les Femmes d'Emigrés dans les Sociétés Oasiennes." *Le Maroc et La Hollande. Une Approche Comparative des Grands Interêts Communs*, Colloques et séminaire, no. 39, 159–69. Rabat: Faculté des Lettres et des Sciences Humaines, Université Mohammed V.

Akesson, Lisa. 2009. "Remittances and Inequality in Cape Verde: The Impact of Changing Family Organization." *Global Networks* 9(3): 381–98.

Akesson, Lisa, and Jørgen Carling. 2009. "Mobility at the Heart of a Nation: Patterns and Meanings of Cape Verdean Migration." *International Migration* 47(3): 123–55.

Ali, Syed. 2007. "'Go West Young Man': The Culture of Migration Among Muslims in Hyderabad, India." *Journal of Ethnic and Migration Studies* 33(1): 37–58.

Allan, Diana. 2014. *Refugees of the Revolution: Experiences of Palestinian Exile*. Stanford: Stanford University Press.

Alpes, Maybritt Jill. 2012. "Bushfalling at All Cost: The Economy of Migratory Knowledge in Anglophone Cameroon." *African Diaspora* 5(1): 90–115.

———. 2014. "Female Spouses at the Doors of Fortress Europe: Migration and Security at Consulate Offices in Cameroon." *Tijdschrift voor Genderstudies* 17(3): 245–58.

Alzetta, Roberto. 2006. "Diversity in Diversity: Exploring Moroccan Migrants' Livelihood in Genoa." *Fondazione Eni Enrico Mattei Working Paper*, 66.

Amahan, Ali. 1988. "Le Temps dans un Village du Haut Atlas." *Signes du Présent* 4: 1–29.

Amar, Paul. 2011. "Middle East Masculinity Studies: Discourses of 'Men in Crisis,' Industries of Gender in Revolution." *Journal of Middle East Women's Studies* 6(3): 36–70.

Andersson, Ruben. 2014. *Illegality Inc.: Clandestine Migration and the Business of Bordering Europe*. Berkeley: University of California Press.

Atekmangoh, Christina. 2017. *Les Mbengis: Migration, Gender, and Family. The Moral Economy of Transnational Cameroonian Migrants' Remittances*. Bamenda: Langaa RPCIG.

Bachelet, Sebastien. 2019. "'Wasting *mbeng*:' Adventure and Trust Amongst Sub-Saharan Migrants in Morocco." *Ethnos* 84(5): 849–66.

Barak, On. 2013. *On Time: Technology and Temporality in Modern Egypt*. Berkeley: University of California Press

Barlow, Tani E. 1994. "Theorising Woman: Funu, Guojia, Jiating." In *Body, Subject and Power in China*, edited by Angela Zito and Tani E. Barlow, 253–90. Chicago: University of Chicago Press.

Barnard, Alan, and Jonathan Spencer. 2010. *The Routledge Encyclopedia of Social and Cultural Anthropology*. New York: Routledge.

Bassi, Marie, and Farida Souiah, eds. 2019. "Corps Migrants aux Frontières Méditerranéennes de l'Europe." *Critique Internationale* 83(2): 9–123.

Bellagamba, Alice, ed. 2011. *Migrazioni dal Lato dell'Africa*. Lungavilla: Edizoni Altravista.

Belo, Catarina. 2006. "Ibn Rushd on God's Decree and Determination (Qaḍā' Wa-Qadar)." *Al Qantara* 27(2): 245–64.

Ben Jelloun, Tahar. 2009. *Leaving Tangier*. Translated by Linda Coverdale. London: Arcadia Books.

Bennani-Chraïbi, Mounia. 1994. *Soumis et Rebelles: Les Jeunes au Maroc*. Paris: Editions Le Fennec.

Berque, Jacques. (1955) 1978. *Structures Sociales du Haut-Atlas*. Paris: Presses Universitaires de France.

Berriane, Mohammed, Hein De Haas, and Katharina Natter. 2015. "Introduction: Revisiting Moroccan Migrations." *The Journal of North African Studies* 20(4): 503–21.

Bhat, Abdul Rahman. 2006. "Free Will and Determinism in Islamic Philosophy." *Journal of Islamic Philosophy* 2: 7–25.

Boum, Aomar. 2013. *Memories of Absence: How Muslims Remember Jews in Morocco*. Stanford: Stanford University Press.

Bourdieu, Pierre. (1972) 1977. *Outline of a Theory of Practice*. Cambridge: Cambridge University Press.

———. (1980) 1990. *The Logic of Practice*. Translated by Richard Nice. Cambridge: Polity.

———. 1991. *Language and Symbolic Power*. Cambridge: Polity Press.

Bourdieu, Pierre, and Loïc Wacquant. 2000. "The Organic Ethnologist of Algerian Migration." *Ethnography* 1(2): 173–82.

Bourqia, Rahma, and Susan Gilson Miller, eds. 1999. *In the Shadow of the Sultan: Culture, Power and Politics in Morocco*. Cambridge: Harvard University Press.

Boutieri, Charis. 2016. *Learning in Morocco: Language Politics and the Abandoned Educational Dream*. Bloomington: Indiana University Press.

Brettell, Caroline. 1986. *Men Who Migrate, Women Who Wait: Population and History in a Portuguese Parish*. Princeton: Princeton University Press.

———. 2003. *Anthropology and Migration: Essays on Transnationalism, Ethnicity and Identity*. Oxford: AltaMira Press.

Brink, Judy H. 1991. "The Effect of Emigration of Husbands on the Status of Their Wives: An Egyptian Case." *International Journal of Middle East Studies* 23(2): 201–11.

Brown, Kenneth L. 1976. *People of Salé: Tradition and Change in a Moroccan City, 1830–1930.* Manchester: Manchester University Press.

Bryant, Rebecca, and Daniel M. Knight. 2019. *The Anthropology of the Future.* Cambridge: Cambridge University Press.

Buch Segal, Lotte. 2013. "Enduring Presents: Living a Prison Sentence as the Wife of a Detainee in Israel." In *Times of Security: Ethnographies of Fear, Protest and the Future,* edited by Martin Holbraad and Morten Axel Pedersen, 122–40. New York: Routledge.

———. 2016. *No Place for Grief: Martyrs, Prisoners and Mourning in Contemporary Palestine.* Philadelphia: University of Pennsylvania Press.

Burke, Edmond III. 2014. *The Ethnographic State: France and the Invention of Moroccan Islam.* Berkeley: University of California Press.

Butler, Judith. 1990. *Gender Trouble: Gender and the Subversion of Identity.* London: Routledge

Cairoli, Laetitia M. 2007. Girl but Not Woman: Garment Factory Workers in Fez, Morocco. In *From Patriarchy to Empowerment: Women's Participation, Movements, and Rights in the Middle East, North Africa, and South Asia,* edited by Valentine M. Moghadam, 160–79. Syracuse: Syracuse University Press.

Calvo, Janet M. 2000. "Spouse-Based Immigration Laws: The Legacy of Coverture." In *Global Critical Race Feminism: An International Reader,* edited by Adriene Katherine Wing, 380–86. New York: New York University Press.

Candea, Matei. 2007. "Arbitrary Locations: In Defence of the Bounded Field-Site." *Journal of the Royal Anthropological Institute* 13: 167–84.

Candea, Matei, and Giovanni da Col, eds. 2012. "Special Issue: The Return to Hospitality: Strangers, Guests, and Ambiguous Encounters." *Journal of the Royal Anthropological Institute* 18(s1).

Capello, Carlo. 2008. *Le Prigioni Invisibili: Etnografia Multisituata della Migrazione Marocchina.* Milan: Franco Angeli Edizioni.

Carey, Matthew. 2012. "'The Rules' in Morocco? Pragmatic Approaches to Flirtation and Lying." *HAU: Journal of Ethnographic Theory* 2(2): 188–204.

Carling, Jørgen. 2002. "Migration in the Age of Involuntary Immobility: Theoretical Reflections and Cape Verdean Experiences." *Journal of Ethnic and Migration Studies* 28(1): 5–42.

Carsten, Janet, ed. 2000. *Cultures of Relatedness: New Approaches to the Study of Kinship.* Cambridge: Cambridge University Press.

Carsten, Janet, and Stephen Hugh-Jones, eds. 1995. *About the House: Lévi-Strauss and Beyond.* Cambridge: Cambridge University Press.

Cheikh, Mériam. 2017. "De l'Ordre Moral à l'Ordre Social: L'Application des Lois Pénalisant la Sexualité Prémaritale Selon des Lignes de Classe." *L'Année du Maghreb* 17: 49–67.

———. 2018. "De L'amour Tarifé au Don D'amour: Intimité et Sexualité Entre Filles Qui 'Sortent' et Garçons de la Diaspora Marocaine." *Migrations Société* 173(3): 51–64.

Cheikh, Mériam, and Michel Péraldi. 2009. *Des Femmes Sur les Routes, Voyages Au Féminin Entre Afrique et Méditerranée.* Casablanca: Le Fennec; Paris: Khartala.

Chu, Julie Y. 2010. *Cosmologies of Credit: Transnational Mobility and the Politics of Destination in China.* Durham: Duke University Press.

Clancy-Smith, Julia A. 2012. *Mediterraneans: North Africa and Europe in an Age of Migration, C. 1800–1900.* Berkeley: University of California Press.

Cohen, Jeffrey H. 2004. *The Culture of Migration in Southern Mexico.* Austin: University of Texas Press.

Cohen, Shana. 2003. "Alienation and Globalization in Morocco: Addressing the Social and Political Impact of Market Integration." *Comparative Studies in Society and History* 45(1): 168–89.

Cole, Jennifer, and Lynn M. Thomas, eds. 2009. *Love in Africa*. Chicago: University of Chicago Press.

Comaroff, Jean, and John Comaroff, eds. 1999. *Civil Society and the Political Imagination in Africa: Critical Perspectives*. Chicago: University of Chicago Press.

Corsín Jiménez, Alberto. 2008. "Well-Being in Anthropological Balance: Remarks on Proportionality as Political Imagination." In *Culture and Well-being: Anthropological Approaches to Freedom and Political Ethics*, edited by Alberto Corsín Jiménez, 180–97. London: Pluto Press.

Covington-Ward, Yolanda. 2016. *Gesture and Power: Religion, Nationalism, and Everyday Performance in Congo*. Durham: Duke University Press.

Crapanzano, Vincent. 1973. *The Hamadsha*. Berkeley: University of California Press.

———. 1980. *Tuhami: Portrait of a Moroccan*. Chicago: University of Chicago Press.

———. 2004. *Imaginative Horizons: An Essay in Literary-Philosophical Anthropology*. Chicago: University of Chicago Press.

Crawford, David. 2008. *Moroccan Households in the World Economy: Labour and Inequality in a Berber Village*. Baton Rouge: Louisiana State University Press.

———. 2010. "Globalization Begins at Home: Children's Wage Labor and the High Atlas Household." In *Berbers and Others: Beyond Tribe and Nation in the Maghrib*, edited by Katherine E. Hoffman and Susan Gilson Miller, 127–50. Bloomington: Indiana University Press.

———. 2013. "The Power of Babies." In *Encountering Morocco: Fieldwork and Cultural Understanding*, edited by David Crawford and Rachel Newcomb, 195–212. Bloomington: Indiana University Press.

Crawford, David, and Rachel Newcomb, eds. 2013. *Encountering Morocco: Fieldwork and Cultural Understanding*. Bloomington: Indiana University Press.

Dalakoglou, Dimitris. 2010. "Migrating-Remitting-'Building'-Dwelling: House Making as 'Proxy' Presence in Postsocialist Albania." *Journal of the Royal Anthropological Institute* 16: 761–77.

Dal Lago, Alessandro. 1999. *Non-Persone: L'Esclusione dei Migranti in una Societá Globale*. Milan: Feltrinelli.

Das, Veena. 1995. *Critical Events: An Anthropological Perspective on Contemporary India*. Delhi: Oxford University Press.

David, Rosalind. 1995. *Changing Places? Women, Resource Management and Migration in the Sahel: Case Studies from Senegal, Burkina Faso, Mali and Sudan*. Oxford: SOS Sahel International.

Davis, Susan Schaefer. 1983. *Patience and Power: Women's Lives in a Moroccan Village*. Cambridge: Schenkman Books.

Davis, Susan Schaefer, and Douglas A. Davis. 1989. *Adolescence in a Moroccan Town. Making Social Sense*. New Brunswick: Rutgers University Press.

Day, Lincoln H., and Ahmet Içduygu. 1997. "The Consequences of International Migration for the Status of Women: A Turkish Study." *International Migration* 35(3): 337–72.

De Cillis, Maria. 2013. *Free Will and Predestination in Islamic Thought: Theoretical Compromises in the Works of Avicenna, Al-Ghazali and Ibn 'Arabi*. Abingdon: Routledge.

De Haas, Hein. 2007a. "Remittances, Migration and Social Development: A Conceptual Review of the Literature." *Social Policy and Development Programme Paper* No. 34, United Nations Research Institute for Social Development, October 2007.

———. 2007b. "Morocco's Migration Experience: A Transitional Perspective." *International Migration* 45: 39–70.

———. 2014. *Morocco: Setting the Stage for Becoming a Migration Transition Country?* Washington, DC: Migration Information Source.

De Haas, Hein, and Aleida Van Rooij. 2010. "Migration as Emancipation? The Impact of Internal and International Migration on the Position of Women in Rural Morocco." *Oxford Development Studies* 38(1): 43–62.

De la Cadena, Marisol. 2015. *Earth Beings: Ecologies of Practice across Andean Worlds.* Durham: Duke University Press.

De León, Jason. 2015. *The Land of Open Graves: Living and Dying on the Migrant Trail.* Oakland: University of California Press.

De Genova, Nicholas. 2002. "Migrant 'Illegality' and Deportability in Everyday Life." *Annual Review of Anthropology* 31(1): 419–47.

———. 2018. "The 'Migrant Crisis' as Racial Crisis: Do *Black Lives Matter* in Europe?" *Ethnic and Racial Studies* 41(10): 1765–82.

Del Grande, Gabriele. 2010. *Il Mare di Mezzo al Tempo dei Respingimenti.* Formigine: Infinito Edizioni.

Derrida, Jacques. 1976. *Of Grammatology.* Translated by Gayatri Chakravorty Spivak. Baltimore: Johns Hopkins University Press.

Dilley, Roy, and Thomas G. Kirsch, eds. 2015. *Regimes of Ignorance: Anthropological Perspectives on the Production and Reproduction of Non-knowledge.* New York: Berghahn.

Donner, Henrike. 2003. "The Place of Birth: Childbearing and Kinship in Calcutta Middle-Class Families." *Medical Anthropology* 22(4): 303–41.

D'Onofrio, Alexandra. 2017. "Reaching for the Horizon: Exploring Existential Possibilities of Migration and Movement within the Past-Present-Future through Participatory Animation." In *Anthropologies and Futures: Researching Emerging and Uncertain Worlds*, edited by Juan Francisco Salazar, Sarah Pink, Andrew Irving, and Johannes Sjöberg, 189–207. London: Bloomsbury.

Dresch, Paul. 2000. "Wilderness of Mirrors: Truth and Vulnerability in Middle Eastern Fieldwork." In *Anthropologists in a Wider World: Essays on Field Research*, edited by Paul Dresch, Wendy James, and Andy Parkin, 109–27. Oxford: Berghahn.

Dusenbery, Verne A., and Tatla S. Darsham. 2010. *Sikh Diaspora Philanthropy in Punjab: Global Giving for Local Good.* New Delhi: Oxford University Press.

Eickelman, Dale. 1977. "Time in a Complex Society: A Moroccan Example." *Ethnology* 16(1): 39–55.

———. (1976) 1981. *Moroccan Islam: Tradition and Society in a Pilgrimage Center.* Austin: University of Texas Press.

———. 1992. "Mass Higher Education and the Religious Imagination in Contemporary Arab Societies." *American Ethnologist* 19(4): 643–55.

El Ghali, Kenza. 2005. *Casos de Mujeres Immigrantes Marroquies en España: Identicación de Causas, Proyectos y Realidades.* Rabat: Fundation Hassan II pour les Marocains Résidant à l'Etranger.

Elder, Joseph W. 1966. "Fatalism in India: A Comparison between Hindus and Muslims." *Anthropological Quarterly* 39(3): 227–43.

Elliot, Alice. 2016. 2020. "Mediterranean Distinctions: Forced Migration, Forceful Hope, and the Analytics of Desperation." In *Refuge in a Moving World: Tracing Refugee and Migrant Journeys Across Disciplines*, edited by Elena Fiddian-Qasmiyeh, 111–122. London: UCL Press.

———. 2020. "Trickster Hospitality: A Moroccan Escalation Act." *History and Anthropology.* https://doi.org/10.1080/02757206.2020.1817002

Elliot, Alice, and Laura Menin. 2018. "For an Anthropology of Destiny." *HAU Journal of Ethnographic Theory* 8(1/2): 292–99.

Elliott, Katja Zvan. 2015. *Modernizing Patriarchy: The Politics of Women's Rights in Morocco.* Austin: University of Texas Press.

Empson, Rebecca. 2011. *Harnessing Fortune: Personhood, Memory, and Place in Mongolia.* Oxford: Oxford University Press.

Ennaji, Moha, and Fatima Sadiqi. 2008. *Migration and Gender in Morocco: The Impact of Migration on the Women Left Behind.* Trenton: Red Sea Press.

Fadloullah, Abdellatif, Abdallah Berrada, and Mohamed Khachani. 2000. *Facteurs d'Attraction et de Répulsion des flux Migratoires Internationaux. Rapport National: Le Maroc.* Rabat: Commission Européenne.

Ferguson, James. 1994. *The Anti-politics Machine: "Development," Depoliticization, and Bureaucratic Power in Lesotho.* Minneapolis: University of Minnesota Press.

Fortes, Meyer. 1936. "Culture Contact as a Dynamic Process. An Investigation in the Northern Territories of the Gold Coast." *Africa: Journal of the International African Institute* 9(1): 24–55.

———. 1978. "Parenthood, Marriage, and Fertility in West Africa." *Journal of Development Studies* 14(4): 121–48.

Foucault, Michel. 1968. "Of Other Spaces." Translated by Jay Miskowiec. *Diacritics* 16(1): 22–27.

Gabaccia, Donna. 2006. "When the Migrants Are Men: Italy's Women and Transnationalism as a Working-Class Way of Life." In *American Dreaming, Global Realities: Rethinking U.S. Immigration History,* edited by Donna R. Gabaccia and Vicki L. Ruiz, 190–206. Urbana: University of Illinois Press.

Gaibazzi, Paolo. 2012. "God's Time Is the Best: Religious Imagination and the Wait for Emigration in the Gambia." In *Global Horizon: Expectation of Migration in Africa and the Middle East,* edited by Knut Graw and Samuli Schielke, 121–35. Leuven: Leuven University Press.

———. 2015. *Bush Bound: Young Men and Rural Permanence in Migrant West Africa.* London: Berghahn.

Gardner, Katy. 1993a. "Desh-Bidesh: Sylheti Images of Home and Away." *Man* 28(1): 1–15.

———. 1993b. "Mullahs, Miracles, and Migration." *Contributions to Indian Sociology* 27: 213–35.

———. 1995. *Global Migrants, Local Lives: Travel and Transformation in Rural Bangladesh.* New York: Oxford University Press.

Gardner, Katy, and Ralph Grillo. 2002. "Transnational Households and Ritual: An Overview." *Global Networks* 2(3): 179–90.

Gay Y Blasco, Paloma, and Liria Hernández. 2020. *Writing Friendship: A Reciprocal Ethnography.* Cham: Palgrave Macmillan.

Geertz, Clifford. 1995. *After the Fact: Two Countries, Four Decades, One Anthropologist.* Cambridge: Harvard University Press.

Geertz, Clifford, Hildred Geertz, and Lawrence Rosen, eds. 1979. *Meaning and Order in Moroccan Society: Three Essays in Cultural Analysis.* Cambridge: Cambridge University Press.

Gellner, Ernest. 1969. *Saints of the Atlas.* Chicago: University of Chicago Press.

Ghannam, Farha. 1998. "Keeping Him Connected: Labor and Migration in the Production of Locality in Cairo." *City and Society* 10(1): 65–82.

———. 2002. *Remaking the Modern: Space Relocation and the Politics of Identity in a Global Cairo.* Berkeley: University of California Press.

———. 2013. *Live and Die Like a Man: Gender Dynamics in Urban Egypt.* Stanford: Stanford University Press.

Ghoussoub, Mai, and Emma Sinclair-Webb, eds. 2000. *Imagined Masculinities: Male Identity and Culture in the Modern Middle East*. London: Saqi Books.

Gilsenan, Michael. 1996. *Lords of the Lebanese Marches: Violence and Narrative in an Arab Society*. London: I.B. Tauris.

Glassé, Cyril. 2002. *The New Encyclopedia of Islam*. Walnut Creek: AltaMira.

Gottreich, Emily. 2020. *Jewish Morocco: A History from Pre-Islamic to Postcolonial Times*. London: I.B. Tauris.

Grasseni, Cristina. 2009. *Developing Skill, Developing Vision: Practices of Locality at the Foot of the Alps*. New York: Berghahn.

Graw, Knut, and Samuli Schielke, eds. 2012. *The Global Horizon. Expectations of Migration in Africa and the Middle East*. Leuven: Leuven University Press.

Guessous, Soumaya Naamane. 2007. *Au-delà de Toute Pudeur: La Sexualité Féminine au Maroc*. Casablanca: Editions Eddif.

Guyer, Jane. 2007. "Prophecy and the Near Future: Thoughts on Macroeconomic, Evangelical and Punctuated Time." *American Ethnologist* 34(3): 409–21.

Hage, Ghassan. 2009. "Waiting Out the Crisis: On Stuckedness and Governmentality." In *Waiting*, edited by Ghassan Hage, 97–106. Carlton: Melbourne University Press.

Hammoudi, Abdellah. 1980. "Segmentarity, Social Stratification, Political Power and Sainthood: Reflections on Gellner's Theses." *Economy and Society* 9(3): 279–303.

———. 1997. *Master and Discipline: The Cultural Foundations of Moroccan Authoritarianism*. Chicago: University of Chicago Press.

Hampshire, Katherine. 2006. "Flexibility in Domestic Organization and Seasonal Migration Among the Fulani of Northern Burkina Faso." *Africa* 76(3): 402–26.

Haraway, Donna Jeanne. 1991. *Simians, Cyborgs and Women: The Reinvention of Nature*. London: Free Association.

Harrell, Richard S. 2004. *A Short Reference Grammar of Moroccan Arabic*. Washington, DC: Georgetown University Press.

Harrell, Richard S., and Harvey Sobelman, eds. 2015. *A Dictionary of Moroccan Arabic*. Washington, DC: Georgetown University Press.

Hart, David M. 1981. *Dadda 'Atta and His Forty Grandsons: The Socio-Political Organisation of the Ait Atta of Southern Morocco*. Boulder: Middle East and North African Studies.

HCP (Haut-Commisariat Au Plan). 2014. "Recensement General de la Population et de l'Habitat 2014." Accessed August 7, 2020. http://Rgphentableaux.Hcp.Ma.

Heller, Charles, Lorenzo Pezzani, and SITU Research. 2014. "Left-to-Die Boat." In *Forensis: The Architecture of Public Truth*, edited by Forensic Architecture, 367–57. Oberhausen: Sternberg Press and Forensic Architecture.

Herzfeld, Michael. 1985. *The Poetics of Manhood: Contest and Identity in a Cretan Mountain Village*. Princeton: Princeton University Press.

———. 1987. "'As in Your Own House': Hospitality, Ethnography, and the Stereotype of Mediterranean Society." In *Honor and Shame and the Unity of the Mediterranean*, edited by David D. Gilmore, 75–89. Washington, DC: American Anthropological Association.

———. 1995. "It Takes One to Know One: Collective Resentment and Mutual Recognition among Greeks in Local and Global Contexts." In *Counterworks: Managing the Diversity of Knowledge*, edited by Richard Fardon, 124–42. London: Routledge.

———. 1997. *Cultural Intimacy: Social Poetics in the Nation-State*. New York: Routledge.

———. 2012. "Afterword: Reciprocating the Hospitality of These Pages." *Journal of the Royal Anthropological Institute* 18: S210–S217.

———. 2015. "Anthropology and the Inchoate Intimacies of Power." *American Ethnologist* 42(1): 18–32.

Hirsch, Jennifer S., and Holly Wardlow, eds. 2006. *Modern Loves: The Anthropology of Romantic Courtship and Companionate Marriage.* Ann Arbor: University of Michigan Press.

Hoffman, Katherine E. 2006. "Berber Language Ideologies, Maintenance, and Contraction: Gendered Variation in the Indigenous Margins of Morocco." *Language & Communication* 26(2): 144–67.

———. 2008. "Purity and Contamination: Language Ideologies in French Colonial Native Policy in Morocco." *Comparative Studies in Society and History* 50(3): 724–52.

Højer, Lars. 2009. "Absent Powers: Magic and Loss in Post-socialist Mongolia." *Journal of the Royal Anthropological Institute* 15(3): 575–91.

Holbraad, Martin. 2012. *Truth in Motion: The Recursive Anthropology of Cuban Divination.* Chicago: University of Chicago Press.

Hourani, George F. 1966. "Ibn Sīnā's 'Essay on the Secret of Destiny.'" *Bulletin of the School of Oriental and African Studies* 29(1): 25–48.

Humphrey, Caroline. 2008. "Reassembling Individual Subjects: Events and Decisions in Troubled Times." *Anthropological Theory* 8(4): 357–80.

———. 2014. "A Politico-Astral Cosmology in Contemporary Russia." In *Framing Cosmologies: The Anthropology of Worlds*, edited by Allan Abramson and Martin Holbraad, 223–43. Manchester: Manchester University Press.

Ilahiane, Hsain. 2003. "Making Histories on Location: International Migration and Social Change in Southern Morocco." *The Maghreb Review* 28(1): 27–40.

———. 2005. "Water Conflict and Berber (Amazigh) Perception of Time in the Upper Ziz Valley, Morocco." *Prologues: Revue Maghrébine du Livre* 32: 66–74.

Inhorn, Marcia C. 1996. *Infertility and Patriarchy: The Cultural Politics of Gender and Family Life in Egypt.* Philadelphia: University of Pennsylvania Press.

Inhorn, Marcia C., and Nefissa Naguib, eds. 2018. *Reconceiving Muslim Men: Love and Marriage, Family and Care in Precarious Times.* New York: Berghahn.

Ismail, Salwa. 2006. *Political Life in Cairo's New Quarters: Encountering the Everyday State.* Minneapolis: University of Minnesota Press.

ISTAT (Istituto Nazionale Di Statistica). 2019. "Cittadini Non Comunitari in Italia, Anni 2018–2019." Accessed January 12, 2020. https://www.istat.it/it/archivio/234457.

Jackson, Michael. 2013. *The Wherewithal of Life: Ethics, Migration, and the Question of Wellbeing.* Berkeley: California University Press.

Johnson-Hanks, Jennifer. 2002. "On the Limits of the Life Cycle in Ethnography: Toward a Theory of Vital Conjunctures." *American Anthropologist* 104(3): 865–80.

———. 2005. "When the Future Decides: Uncertainty and Intentional Action in Contemporary Cameroon." *Current Anthropology* 46(3): 363–85.

Jónsson, Gunvor. 2008. "Migration Aspirations and Immobility in a Malian Soninke Village." *International Migration Institute Working Paper* 10: 1–45.

Joseph, Suad. 1993. "Gender and Relationality among Arab Families in Lebanon." *Feminist Studies* 19(3): 465–86.

———, ed. 1999. *Intimate Selving in Arab Families: Gender, Self, and Identity.* Syracuse: Syracuse University Press.

Juntunen, Marko. 2002. "Between Morocco and Spain: Men, Migrant Smuggling and a Dispersed Migrant Community." PhD thesis, Institute for Asian and African Studies, University of Helsinki, Helsinki Printing House.

Kandel, William, and Douglas S. Massey. 2002. "The Culture of Mexican Migration: A Theoretical and Empirical Analysis." *Social Forces* 80(3): 981–1004.

Kapchan, Deborah. 1996. *Gender on the Market: Moroccan Women and the Revoicing of Tradition.* Philadelphia: University of Pennsylvania Press.

———. 2013. "Reflecting on Moroccan Encounters: Meditations on Home, Genre, and the Performance of Everyday Life." In *Encountering Morocco: Fieldwork and Cultural Understanding,* edited by David Crawford and Rachel Newcomb, 165–94. Bloomington: Indiana University Press.

Kelly, Tobias. 2007. *Law, Violence and Sovereignty among West Bank Palestinians.* Cambridge: Cambridge University Press.

Kenbib, Mohammed. 1994. *Juif et Musulmans au Maroc 1859–1948.* Rabat: Université Mohammed V.

Khachani, Mohamed. 2004. *Les Marocains d'Ailleurs: La Question Migratoire à l'Épreuve du Partenariat Euro-Marocain.* Rabat: Association Marocaine d'Etudes et de Recherches sur les Migrations.

Khalaf, Samir, and John Gagnon, eds. 2006. *Sexuality in the Arab World.* London: Saqi Books.

Khrouz, Nadia, and Nazarena Lanza, eds. 2015. *Migrants au Maroc: Cosmopolitisme, Présence d'Étrangers et Transformations Sociales.* Rabat: Centre Jacques-Berque.

King, Russell, Mirela Dalipaj, and Nicola Mai. 2006. "Gendering Migration and Remittances: Evidence from London and Northern Albania." *Population, Space and Place* 12: 409–34.

Laroui, Abdallah. 1970. *L' Histoire du Maghreb: Un Essai de Synthèse.* Paris: Éditions Maspero.

Lenoël, Audrey. 2017. "The 'Three Ages' of Left-Behind Moroccan Wives: Status, Decision-Making Power, and Access to Resources." *Population, Space and Place* 23: e2077. https://doi .org/10.1002/psp.2077.

Lévi-Strauss, Claude. (1950) 1987. *Introduction to the Work of Marcel Mauss.* Translated by Felicity Baker. London: Routledge and Kegan Paul.

Lewis, I. M. 1971. *Ecstatic Religion: An Anthropological Study of Spirit Possession and Shamanism.* Baltimore: Penguin Books.

Liebow, Elliott. (1967) 2003. *Tally's Corner.* Lanham: Rowman and Littlefield.

Lopez, Sarah Lynn. 2015. *The Remittance Landscape: Spaces of Migration in Rural Mexico and Urban USA.* Chicago: Chicago University Press.

Lucht, Hans. 2012. *Darkness before Daybreak: African Migrants Living on the Margins in Southern Italy Today.* Berkeley: University of California Press.

MacGaffey, Wyatt. 1968. Kongo and the King of the Americans. *The Journal of Modern African Studies* 6(2): 171–81.

———. 1972. The West in Congolese Experience. In *Africa and the West: Intellectual Responses to European Culture,* edited by Curtin D. Philip. Madison: University of Wisconsin Press.

Maghraoui, Driss. 1998. "The Moroccan Colonial Soldiers: Between Collective Memory and Selective Memory." *Arab Studies Quarterly* 20(2): 21–41.

———. 2004. "The 'Grande Guerre Sainte:' Moroccan Colonial Troops and Workers in the First World War." *The Journal of North African Studies* 9(1): 1–21.

Maher, Vanessa. 1974. *Women and Property in Morocco: Their Changing Relations to the Problem of Social Stratification in the Middle Atlas.* Cambridge: Cambridge University Press.

Mahmood, Saba. 2005. *Politics of Piety. The Islamic Revival and the Feminist Subject.* Princeton: Princeton University Press.

Malkki, Lisa. 1995. *Purity and Exile: Violence, Memory, and National Cosmology among Hutu Refugees in Tanzania.* Chicago: Chicago University Press.

Mandel, Ruth. 1990. "Shifting Centres and Emergent Identities: Turkey and Germany in the Lives of Turkish Gastarbeiter." In *Muslim Travellers: Pilgrimage, Migration, and the Religious Imagination*, edited by Dale Eickelman and James Piscatori, 153–71. London: Routledge.

Marsden, Magnus. 2007. "All-Male Sonic Gatherings, Islamic Reform, and Masculinity in Northern Pakistan." *American Ethnologist* 34(3): 473–90

Matory, Lorand J. 2009. "The Many Who Dance in Me: Afro-Atlantic Ontology and the Problem with 'Transnationalism.'" In *Transnational Transcendence: Essays on Religion and Globalisation*, edited by Thomas J. Csordas, 231–62. Berkeley: University of California Press.

Matz, Julia Anna, and Linguère Mously Mbaye. 2017. "Migration and the Autonomy of Women Left Behind." WIDER Working Paper 2017/64. Helsinki: UNU-WIDER.

Mauss, Marcel. (1925) 2002. *The Gift: The Form and Reason for Exchange in Archaic Societies.* London: Routledge.

McMurray, David A. 2001. *In and Out of Morocco: Smuggling and Migration in a Frontier Boomtown.* Minneapolis: University of Minnesota Press.

Menin, Laura. 2015. "The Impasse of Modernity: Personal Agency, Divine Destiny, and the Unpredictability of Intimate Relationships in Morocco." *Journal of the Royal Anthropological Institute* 21(4): 892–910.

———. 2016. "'Men Do Not Get Scared! (*rjjala mā tāy-khāfūsh*):' Luck, Destiny and the Gendered Vocabularies of Clandestine Migration in Central Morocco." *Archivio Antropologico Mediterraneo* XIX 18(1): 25–36.

Mernissi, Fatima. 1988. *Doing Daily Battle: Interviews with Moroccan Women.* London: The Women's Press.

———. 1994. *Dreams of Trespass: Tales of a Harem Childhood.* New York: Basic Books.

Meyer, Birgit, and Peter Pels. 2003. *Magic and Modernity: Interfaces of Revelation and Concealment.* Stanford: Stanford University Press.

Miller, Daniel. 2008. Migration, Material Culture and Tragedy. *Mobilities* 3: 397–413.

Miller, Susan Gilson. 2013. *A History of Modern Morocco.* Cambridge: Cambridge University Press

Mittermaier, Amira. 2011. *Dreams That Matter: Egyptian Landscapes of the Imagination.* Berkeley: University of California Press.

———. 2012. "Dreams from Elsewhere: Muslim Subjectivities beyond the Trope of Self-Cultivation." *Journal of the Royal Anthropological Institute* 18(2): 247–65.

———. 2013. "Trading with God: Islam, Calculation, Excess." In *A Companion to the Anthropology of Religion*, edited by Janice Boddy and Michael Lambek, 274–93. Chichester: Wiley.

Miyazaki, Hirokasu. 2004. *The Method of Hope: Anthropology, Philosophy and Fijian Knowledge.* Stanford: Stanford University Press.

Moktary, Mohammed. 2008. "L'Eldorado, la Barque et *l-Mmima*. L'Émigration dans la Chanson Italienne et Maghrébine." Paper presented at "Migration, Globalization and Cultural Dynamics" Round Table, Casablanca, December 25–27, 2008.

Mondain, Nathalie, Sara Randall, Alioune Diagne, and Alice Elliot. 2012. "Les Effets de l'Émigration Masculine dur les Femmes et leur Autonomie: Entre Maintien et Transformation des Rapports Sociaux de Sexe Traditionnels au Sénégal." *Autrepart* 61(2): 81–97.

Montgomery, Mary. 2019. *Hired Daughters: Domestic Workers among Ordinary Moroccans.* Bloomington: Indiana University Press.

Moore, Henrietta. (1986) 1996. *Space, Text, and Gender.* New York: Guilford Press.

Mumtaz, Zubia, and Sarah Salway. 2005. "'I Never Go Anywhere:' Extricating the Links Between Women's Mobility and Uptake of Reproductive Health Services in Pakistan." *Social Science and Medicine* 60: 1751–65.

Munn, Nancy. 1987. *The Fame of Gawa: A Symbolic Study of Value Transformation in a Massim (Papua New Guinea) Society*. Cambridge: Cambridge University Press.

Myntti, Cynthia. 1984. "Yemeni Workers Abroad." *Merip Reports* 124: 11–16.

Navaro-Yashin, Yael. 2007. "Make-Believe Papers, Legal Forms and the Counterfeit: Affective Interactions between Documents and People in Britain and Cyprus." *Anthropological Theory* 7(1): 79–98.

Neale Hurston, Zora. (1935) 2009. *Mules and Men*. New York: HarperCollins.

Newcomb, Rachel. 2009. *Women of Fez: Ambiguities of Urban Life in Morocco*. Philadelphia: University of Pennsylvania Press.

———. 2017. *Everyday Life in Global Morocco*. Bloomington: Indiana University Press.

Newell, Sasha. 2012. *The Modernity Bluff: Crime, Consumption, and Citizenship in Cote D'Ivoire*. Chicago: Chicago University Press.

Ngwa, Lydia, and Wilfred Ngwa, eds. 2006. *From Dust to Snow: Bush-Faller*. Princeton: Horeb Communications.

Nielsen, Morten. 2011. "Futures Within: Reversible Time and House-Building in Maputo, Mozambique." *Anthropological Theory* 11(4): 397–423.

Nyamnjoh, Francis B. 2011. "Cameroonian Bushfalling: Negotiation of Identity and Belonging in Fiction and Ethnography." *American Ethnologist* 38(4): 701–13.

Osella, Filippo, and Caroline Osella. 2000. "Migration, Money and Masculinity in Kerala." *Journal of the Royal Anthropological Institute* 6: 117–33.

Ossman, Susan. 1994. *Picturing Casablanca: Portraits of Power in a Modern City*. Berkeley: University of California Press.

———. 2002. *Three Faces of Beauty: Casablanca, Paris, Cairo*. Durham: Duke University Press.

Oxford Dictionaries. "Emigration." Accessed April 11, 2019. https://en.oxforddictionaries.com/definition/emigration.

Oxford Dictionaries. "Immigration." Accessed April 11, 2019. https://en.oxforddictionaries.com/definition/immigration.

Padilla, Mark B., Jennifer S. Hirsch, Miguel Muñoz-Laboy, Robert E. Sember, and Richard G. Parker, eds. 2007. *Love and Globalization: Transformations of Intimacy in the Contemporary World*. Nashville: Vanderbilt University Press.

Pandolfo, Stefania. 2007. "'The Burning:' Finitude and the Politico-theological Imagination of Illegal Migration." *Anthropological Theory* 7(3): 329–63.

———. 2018. *Knot of the Soul: Madness, Psychoanalysis, Islam*. Chicago: University of Chicago Press.

Pardy, Maree. 2009. "The Shame of Waiting." In *Waiting*, edited by Ghassan Hage, 195–209. Carlton: Melbourne University Press.

Parry, Jonathan, and Maurice Bloch, eds. 1989. *Money and the Morality of Exchange*. Cambridge: Cambridge University Press.

Pedersen, David. 2013. *American Value: Migrants, Money and Meaning in El Salvador and the United States*. Chicago: Chicago University Press.

Pedersen, Morten Axel. 2007. "Multiplicity without Myth: Theorising Darhad Perspectivism." *Inner Asia* 9(2): 311–28.

Peirce, Charles S. 1998. *The Essential Peirce: Selected Philosophical Writings*. Bloomington: Indiana University Press.

Persichetti, Alessandra. 2003. *Tra Italia e Marocco: Solidarietà Agnatica ed Emigrazione*. Rome: Cisu.

Peteet, Julie. 1994. "Male Gender and Rituals of Resistance in the Occupied Territories: A Cultural Politics of Violence." *American Ethnologist* 21(1): 31–49.

Piot, Charles. 1999. *Remotely Global: Village Modernity in West Africa*. Chicago: Chicago University Press.

Piot, Charles, with Kodjo Nicolas Batema. 2019. *The Fixer: Visa Lottery Chronicles*. Durham: Duke University Press.

Préfol, Pierre. 1986. *Prodiges de l'Irrigation au Maroc: Le Developpement Exemplaire du Tadla 1936–85*. Paris: Novelles Editions Latines.

Rabinow, Paul. 1975. *Symbolic Domination*. Chicago: Chicago University Press.

———. 1977. *Reflections on Fieldwork in Morocco*. Berkeley: University of California Press.

Rachik, Hassan. 2012. *Le proche et le Lointain. Un Siècle d´Anthropologie au Maroc*. Marseille: Éditions Parenthèse.

Rassam, Amal. 1980. "Women and Domestic Power in Morocco." *International Journal of Middle Eastern Studies* 12(2): 171–79.

Reed, Adam. 2011. "Hope on Remand." *Journal of the Royal Anthropological Institute* 17(3): 527–44.

Rignall, Karen. 2013. "Time, Children, and Getting Ethnography Done in Southern Morocco." In *Encountering Morocco: Fieldwork and Cultural Understanding*, edited by David Crawford and Rachel Newcomb, 40–55. Bloomington: Indiana University Press.

Robbins, Joel. 2004. *Becoming Sinners: Christianity and Moral Torment in a Papua New Guinea Society*. Berkeley: University of California Press.

———. 2009. "Is the Trans- in Transnational the Trans- in Transcendence? On Alterity and the Sacred in the Age of Globalization." In *Transnational Transcendence: Essays on Religion and Globalisation*, edited by Thomas J. Csordas, 55–72. Berkeley: University of California Press.

Roded, Ruth. 2006. "Alternate Images of the Prophet Mohammed's Virility." In *Islamic Masculinities*, edited by Lahoucine Ouzgane, 57–71. London: Zed Books.

Rosen, Lawrence. 2016. *Two Arabs, a Berber, and a Jew: Entangled Lives in Morocco*. Chicago: Chicago University Press.

Rustomji, Nerina. 2013. *The Garden and the Fire: Heaven and Hell in Islamic Culture*. New York: Columbia University Press.

Sa'ar, Amalia. 2001. "Lonely in Your Firm Grip: Women in Israeli-Palestinian Families." *Journal of the Royal Anthropological Institute* 7(4): 723–39.

Sadiqi, Fatima, and Moha Ennaji. 2004. "The Impact of Male Migration from Morocco to Europe on Women: A Gender Approach." *Finisterra XXXIX* 77: 59–76.

Sahlins, Marshall. 1985. *Islands of History*. London: Tavistock.

Salih, Ruba. 2003. *Gender in Transnationalism: Home, Longing and Belonging among Moroccan Migrant Women*. London: Routledge.

Saucier, P. Khalil, and Tyron P. Woods. 2014. "Ex Aqua: The Mediterranean Basin, Africans on the Move, and the Politics of Policing." *Theoria* 61(141): 55–75.

Sayad, Abdelmalek. 1984. "Tendances et Courants des Publications en Sciences Sociales sur l'Immigration en France Depuis 1960." *Current Sociology* 32(3): 219–304.

———. 1988. "La 'Faute' de l'Absence ou les Effets de l'Émigration." *Anthropologica Medica* 4: 5–69.

———. 1991. *L'Immigration ou les Paradoxes de l'Altérité*. Brussels: Editions Universitaires-De Boeck.

———. 1999. *La Double Absence: Des Illusions de l'Émigré aux Souffrances de l'Immigré*. Paris: Le Seuil.

———. 2000. "El Ghorba: From Original Sin to Collective Lie." *Ethnography* 1(2): 147–71.

———. 2004. *The Suffering of the Immigrant*. Cambridge: Polity.

Sayad, Abdelmalek, and Alain Gilette. 1976. *L'Immigration Algérienne en France*. Paris: Entente.

Schieffelin, Edward. 1996. "On Failure and Performance: Throwing the Medium Out of the Séance." In *The Performance of Healing*, edited by Carol Laderman and Marina Roseman, 59–91. New York: Routledge.

Schielke, Samuli. 2012. "Engaging the World on the Alexandria Waterfront." In *The Global Horizon: Expectations of Migration in Africa and the Middle East*, edited by Knut Graw and Samuli Schielke, 175–91. Leuven: Leuven University Press.

———. 2015. *Egypt in the Future Tense: Hope, Frustration and Ambivalence before and after 2011*. Bloomington: Indiana University Press.

———. 2020. *Migrant Dreams: Egyptian Workers in the Gulf States*. Cairo: The American University in Cairo Press.

Scott, Michael W. 2000. "Ignorance Is Cosmos, Knowledge Is Chaos: Articulating a Cosmological Polarity in the Solomon Islands." *Social Analysis* 44(2): 56–83.

Silverstein, Paul. 2004a. *Algeria in France: Transpolitics, Race, and Nation*. Bloomington: Indiana University Press.

———. 2004b. "Of Rooting and Uprooting: Kabyle Habitus, Domesticity, and Structural Nostalgia." *Ethnography* 5(4): 553–78.

———. 2015. "The Diaspora and the Cemetery: Emigration and Social Transformation in a Moroccan Oasis Community." *The Journal of North African Studies* 20(1): 92–108.

Simon, Gregory M. 2009. "The Soul Freed of Cares? Islamic Prayer, Subjectivity, and the Contradictions of Moral Selfhood in Minangkabau, Indonesia." *American Ethnologist* 36(2): 258–75.

Smid, Karen. 2010. "Resting at Creation and Afterlife: Distant Times in the Ordinary Strategies of Muslim Women in the Rural Fouta Djallon, Guinea." *American Ethnologist* 37(1): 36–52.

Smythe, SA. 2018. "The Black Mediterranean and the Politics of Imagination." *Middle East Report: Suffering and the Limits of Relief* 286: 3–9.

Sneath, David, Martin Holbraad, and Morten Axel Pedersen. 2009. "Technologies of the Imagination: An Introduction." *Ethnos* 74(1): 5–30.

Souiah, Farida, Monika Salzbrunn, and Simon Mastrangelo. 2018. "Hope and Disillusion: The Representations of Europe in Algerian and Tunisian Cultural Production about Undocumented Migration." In *North Africa and the Making of Europe: Governance, Institutions, and Culture*, edited by Muriam Davis and Thomas Serres. London: Bloomsbury.

Spadola, Emilio. 2014. *The Calls of Islam: Sufis, Islamists, and Mass Mediation in Urban Morocco*. Bloomington: Indiana University Press.

———. 2015. "Rites of Reception: Trance, Technology, and National Belonging in Morocco." In *Trance Mediums and New Media: Spirit Possession in the Age of Technical Reproduction*, edited by Heike Behrend, Martin Zillinger, and Anja Dreschke. New York: Fordham University Press.

Spivak, Gayatri Chakravorty. 1976. "Translator's Preface." In *Of Grammatology*, by Jacques Derrida, ix–lxxxix. Baltimore: Johns Hopkins University Press.

Stafford, Charles. 2000. "Chinese Patriliny and the Cycles of Yang and Laiwang." In *Cultures of Relatedness: New Approaches to the Study of Kinship*, edited by Janet Carsten, 35–54. Cambridge: Cambridge University Press.

Strathern, Marilyn. 1988. *The Gender of the Gift: Problems with Women and Problems with Society in Melanesia*. Berkeley: University of California Press.

———. (1991) 2004. *Partial Connections*. Updated Edition. Walnut Creek: AltaMira.

Strauss, Claudia. 2006. "The Imaginary." *Anthropological Theory* 6(3): 322–44.

Swancutt, Katherine. 2012. "The Captive Guest: Spider Webs of Hospitality among the Nuosu of Southwest China." *Journal of the Royal Anthropological Institute* 18: S103-S116.

Swearingen, Will D. 1988. *Moroccan Mirages: Agrarian Dreams and Deceptions, 1912–1986.* London: I.B. Tauris.

Taussig, Michael T. 1997. *The Magic of the State.* New York: Routledge.

Taylor, Charles. 2004. *Modern Social Imaginaries.* Durham: Duke University Press.

Taylor, Matthew J., Michelle J. Moran-Taylor, and Debra Rodman Ruiz. 2006. "Land, Ethnic, and Gender Change: Transnational Migration and its Effects on Guatemalan Lives and Landscapes." *Geoforum* 37: 41–61.

Tozy, Mohamed. 1999. *Monarchie et Islam Politique au Maroc.* Paris: Presses de Sciences Politiques.

Tsing, Anna Lowenhaupt. 2005. *Friction: An Ethnography of Global Connection.* Princeton: Princeton University Press.

Tuckett, Anna. 2018. *Rules, Papers, Status: Migrants and Precarious Bureaucracy in Italy.* Stanford: Stanford University Press.

Turner, Victor. 1967. *The Forest of Symbols: Aspects of Ndembu Ritual.* Ithaca: Cornell University Press.

Vacchiano, Francesco. 2007. "'Bruciare di Desiderio:' Realtá Sociale e Soggettivitá dei Giovani 'Harraga' Marocchini." PhD thesis, Dipartimento di Scienze Antropologiche, Archeologiche e Storico-territoriali, Universitá degli Studi di Torino.

———. 2018. "Desiring Mobility: Child Migration, Parental Distress and Constraints on the Future in North Africa." In *Research Handbook on Child Migration,* edited by Jacqueline Bhabha, Jyothi Kanics, and Daniel Senovilla Hernandez, 82–97. Cheltenham: Edward Elgar.

Verdery, Katherine. 1996. "The 'Etatization' of Time in Ceausescu's Romania." In Katherine Verdery, *What Was Socialism and What Comes Next?,* 39–57. Princeton: Princeton University Press.

Vigh, Henrik. 2009. "Wayward Migration: On Imagined Futures and Technological Voids." *Ethnos* 74(1): 91–109.

———. 2011. "Vigilance: On Conflict, Social Invisibility, and Negative Potentiality." *Social Analysis* 55(3): 93–114.

Viveiros de Castro, Eduardo. 2003. *(Anthropology) AND (Science).* After-dinner speech at "Anthropology and Science," Fifth Decennial Conference of the Association of Social Anthropologists of Great Britain and Commonwealth, July 14, 2003. *Manchester Papers in Social Anthropology 7.*

Vlahoutsikou, Christina. 1997. "Mothers-in-Law and Daughters-in-Law: Politicizing Confrontations." *Journal of Modern Greek Studies* 15(2): 283–302.

Vom Bruck, Gabriele. 1997a. "Elusive Bodies: The Politics of Aesthetics among Yemeni Elite Women." *Signs: Journal of Women in Culture and Society* 23(1): 175–214.

———. 1997b. "A House Turned Inside Out: Inhabiting Space in a Yemeni City." *Journal of Material Culture* 2(2): 139–72.

Wagner, Daniel A. 1993. *Literacy, Culture and Development: Becoming Literate in Morocco.* New York: Cambridge University Press.

Watt, William M. 1946. "Free Will and Predestination in Early Islam." *Muslim World* 36(2): 124–52.

Weber, Max. (1922) 1978. *Economy and Society: An Outline of Interpretative Sociology.* Berkeley: University of California Press.

———. (1920) 1993. *Sociology of Religion.* Translated by Ephraim Fischoff. Boston: Beacon.

————. (1905) 2010. *The Protestant Ethic and the Spirit of Capitalism*. Translated by Talcott Parsons. New York: Scribner's Sons.

Westermarck, Edward. 1914. *Marriage Ceremonies in Morocco*. London: MacMillan.

Xiang, Biao. 2014. "The Would-Be Migrant: Post-Socialist Primitive Accumulation, Potential Transnational Mobility, and the Displacement of the Present in Northeast China." *TRaNS: Trans-Regional and -National Studies of Southeast Asia* 2(2): 183–99.

Yurchak, Alexei. 2005. *Everything Was Forever Until It Was No More: The Last Soviet Generation*. Princeton: Princeton University Press.

INDEX

de Haas, Hein, 12, 42
de la Cadena, Marisol, 23, 110–11
deportation, 141–42
Derrida, Jacques, 76
destiny and divine predestination, 97–98, 107–21
double absence, 69, 141
drug dealing, 57
dyafa (hospitality), 15–19

education, 98–100
egalitarianism, 145n4
Eickelman, Dale, 29, 47, 122n9
emigration and emigrants: use of terms, 25n2. See also *l-brra* (the outside); Moroccan migration
Empson, Rebecca, 96n5
engagements and marriage arrangements, 27, 30–32, 59–62, 75, 81–82
English (language), 26n10
essentializing practices, 35, 87, 89

family nuclearization, 81–82
floating signifier, 152
Foucault, Michel, 151, 156
France: Algerian migration to, 21, 53–54, 69, 160; Moroccan migration to, 12–13, 14, 117
French (language), 26n10, 121n1
French colonialism, 11–12
fuqaha (Islamic scholars), 43–44
Fusha (Modern Standard Arabic), 16, 121n1

Gabaccia, Donna, 96n7
gales (sitting, m.), 123–24, 125–29, 131, 135–39
galsa (sitting, f.), 91–92, 127
Gardner, Katy, 57
gender performativity, 130
gender relations, 85–89. *See also* masculinities
Ghannam, Farha, 124, 125, 130
l-ghorba, 88–89
gifts and gift giving, 32–33
Glassé, Cyril, 113
Guyer, Jane, 29, 47

hammam, 36–37
l-harag (the burning; undocumented migration), 1–2, 19, 54, 146
Haraway, Donna, 70

hayat naqsa (lacking life), 78–80
Herzfeld, Michael, 10, 35, 129, 130, 158
heterotopia, 151, 156
l-hijra (migration): use of term, 8, 19. See also *l-brra* (the outside); Moroccan migration
Højer, Lars, 111
Holbraad, Martin, 163
hospitality (*dyafa*), 15–19
household spaces and activities, 38–41, 137–38
house-making, 130–35
Hugh-Jones, Stephen, 132–33
Humphrey, Caroline, 34

Ibn Battuta, 11
imaginary elsewhere (*zagranitsa*), 7, 150
imagination, 8, 69–71, 149–51
immigration and immigrants: use of terms, 25n2. See also *l-brra* (the outside); Moroccan migration
initiation rites, 62–63
intimate distance, 73–74, 94–96
Islamic scholars (*fuqaha*), 43–44
Israel, 25n5
Italy: deportation policies in, 141; disillusionment with, 164–68; Moroccan migration to, 2–3, 13–14, 55–56, 58, 116–17; "white widows" in, 96n7

jnun (spirits, sing. *jenn*), 65–66
Johnson-Hanks, Jennifer, 34–35
Joseph, Suad, 76–77

"The Kabyle House" (Bourdieu), 125–27
Kapchan, Deborah, 82, 126–27, 128
l-kharij (outside, abroad, overseas), 7. See also *l-brra* (the outside)
kinship, 32–36, 80–84

lebsa dyal brra (clothes of/for [the] outside), 3, 7, 40
Lévi-Strauss, Claude, 32–33, 152
Lewis, I. M., 66
life stages model, 34–35
love, 101–4

MacGaffey, Wyatt, 149, 153, 156
Maher, Vanessa, 54, 81

marriage: absent husbands and, 74–80, 87–89; arrangements for, 59–62, 75, 81–82; destiny and, 97–98, 107–21; impact of *l-brra*'s temporality on, 30–32; intimate distance and, 73–74, 94–96; kinship relations and, 80–84; migrant men as potential husbands and, 97–98, 100–106, 120–21; migration's impact on gender relations and, 85–89; premarital relationships and, 117–20; sexuality and, 37–39, 66–67; waiting and, 89–94; wedding ceremonies and, 27, 30–32, 48

Marsden, Magnus, 130

masculinities: circulation of damaging information on migrant men and, 140–42; gendered expectations and, 123–25; house-making and, 130–35; "movement" and, 129–34; repetitive materialization of, 142–44; sitting and, 123–24, 125–29, 131, 135–39

materialization of masculinity, 124, 130, 142–44

Matory, J. Lorand, 43–44

Mauss, Marcel, 32–33

McMurray, David, 71n1

Menin, Laura, 104

Mernissi, Fatima, 126–27

migrant men: as absent husbands, 74–80, 87–89; *l-azma* (the crisis) and, 134–37; circulation of damaging information on, 57–59, 140–42; as *hayawanat* (animals), 49, 57–58, 61, 67–69; as potential husbands, 97–98, 100–6. *See also* destiny and divine predestination; sitting and, 123–24, 125–29, 131, 135–39; as "technologies of the imagination," 69–71. *See also* masculinities

migration and migrants: use of terms, 25n2. See also *l-brra* (the outside); migrant men

migration studies, 4–7, 160–63

miroir inversé (reversed mirror), 150

Mittermaier, Amira, 114

Modern Standard Arabic (*Fusha*), 16, 121n1

money, 39–44

Montgomery, Mary, 54

Moroccan Arabic (Darija), 16

Moroccan authoritarianism, 145n4

Moroccan egalitarianism, 145n4

Moroccan migration: to Algeria, 11, 12; anthropological scholarship on, 10–11;

evolution and characteristics of, 11–15; to France, 12–13, 14, 117; to Italy, 2–3, 13–14, 55–56, 58, 116–17; sending communities and, 1–2; to Spain, 2, 13, 14, 55–56, 116; women and, 21, 74–75, 105–6. See also *l-brra* (the outside); Tadla

Morocco: Jewish population in, 25n5; official and foreign languages in, 26n10, 121n1; women and education in, 98–101

mothers-in-law, 80–81

Navaro-Yashin, Yael, 32

Ndembu circumcision ceremonies, 63, 69

Netherlands, 12–13

Newell, Sasha, 153

Norway, 116

Nyamnjoh, Francis, 68, 153

Osella, Caroline, 140

Osella, Filippo, 140

Ouled Meskin, 13–14

the outside. See *l-brra* (the outside)

Pandolfo, Stefania, 155

patriarchal connectivity, 76–77

Pedersen, Morten, 144

Peirce, Charles S., 58–59

Persichetti, Alessandra, 77

personal care, 36–37. *See also* beauty

The Poetics of Manhood (Herzfeld), 158

Portugal, 96n7

positionality, 21–23

premarital relationships, 118–20

proportional sociality, 96n4

Protestantism, 111–13

punctuated time, 29, 47

qualisigns, 58–59

remittances, 39–44

research participants, 20–21

reversed mirror (*miroir inversé*), 150

revolutionary upheavals (Arab Spring), 166

Robbins, Joel, 153–54, 156

romance, 101–4

Sa'ar, Amalia, 83–84

Salih, Ruba, 74–75

ALICE ELLIOT IS LECTURER IN ANTHROPOLOGY AT GOLDSMITHS, UNIVERSITY OF LONDON.